THE PRINCIPAL AS THE LEARNING LEADER

A GUIDE TO INSTRUCTIONAL SUCCESS FOR PRINICIPAL CANDIDATES AND ENTRY-LEVEL PRINCIPALS

Timothy M. Powers, Ed.D.

Copyright © 2020 by Timothy M. Powers

All rights reserved. Except for usage, no part of this book may be reproduced or utilized in any form or by any means, electronic or mechanical, including photocopying, recording, or by any information storage and retrieval system, without permission in writing from the author.

For additional information, contact the author at timpowerswf@gmail.com

Cover Art provided by Brian Joseph
Used by permission
bydeeartgallery@gmail.com

WHAT OTHERS ARE SAYING ABOUT THE BOOK

In *The Principal as the Learning Leader,* Dr. Powers has bridged the world of aspiring principal candidates and entry-level principals with a how " to be" and a how " to do" guide that reflects his own deep knowledge of the artful practice of campus leadership combined with the meaningful application of research-informed concepts relevant to the challenging work of school leaders.

Vivid, rich descriptions of exemplar practice will equip aspiring candidates, entry-level principals, and experienced principals with clarity about the knowledge, skills, and mindsets so vital to ensuring the best outcomes for Texas schoolchildren. Readers, whether in urban, suburban, or rural schools, will find meaning and support in this timely book. Truly, this is a gift to new campus leaders and those who aspire to be.

Dawson R. Orr, *Ph.D.*
Program Director, K-12 Ed.D. in Educational Leadership
Southern Methodist University and for former Texas superintendent of 25 years in Pampa, Wichita Falls, and Highland Park (Dallas).

Dr. Tim Powers is a well-respected school leader across the state of Texas. His experience at the school district and university levels allows practitioners and aspiring leaders to learn from his expertise as an experienced school leader. Dr. Powers' desire to place relevant and informative resources in the hands of principal candidates comes to fruition to this book that will not only guide the candidate during preparation, but also while performing the job in real time on a daily basis.

Mr. Keith Bryant
Superintendent, Lubbock-Cooper ISD
2020 Texas Superintendent of the Year

"I first met Tim Powers when I was working as a journalist covering education. Later, I got to know him better when training as a classroom teacher. He's a man who passionately wants both educators and students to succeed. This book is a valuable resource in carrying out that mission."

Bear Mills
Podcaster and former
Texas Teacher of the Year

ACKNOWLEDGEMENTS

The first Person I would like to acknowledge is my Lord and Savior, Jesus Christ. Practicing many years as an administrator, I cannot imagine going through the day-to-day challenges of being a campus principal without being able to rely on the wisdom of Christ. Those instances when I sought His guidance and direction did not always mean the road was easy, but it certainly was better than trusting in my own judgement. I give Him all the glory for this work accomplished through me. I pray I was a vessel unto honor to Him.

My wife, Janice, has been a tremendous support during this entire time of writing, editing, re-editing, and helping me review the manuscript for typos and additional corrections. Without her constant support and encouragement, I seriously doubt that this textbook would have ever made it to print.

A huge thank you goes out to Dr. Dawson Orr. He has served as my mentor and friend for more than two decades. He graciously committed to reviewing my manuscript, suggesting some additional meaningful comments to this work.

Bear Mills was instrumental in helping to review and edit this manuscript. He edited the manuscript out of the kindness of his heart. He is that type of person. Bear is formerly a Teacher of the Year for the state of Texas. Now, he devotes his time as a writer, speaker, and as host of his own podcast wrapped around the theme of hope.

Many thanks to all the teachers, staff and other administrators I worked with throughout the years that helped to mold me during my professional educational journey. Your input was invaluable in helping me to grow as an instructional leader.

I would like to thank the Wayland Baptist University family. We ARE a family grounded in the faith of Jesus Christ. They are a supportive group of people who nurture and encourage each other.

I also want to thank my children. As I watched my children, Zane and Janelle, grow into adulthood, I always wanted the best for them in school. Zane Powers is now a successful Education and Student minister. Janelle Styne is a successful instructional coach in public education. Their learning started in our home, but their public education served as an extension. Thanks to all those in education who touched their lives.

TABLE OF CONTENTS

ACKNOWLEDGEMENTS 3

TABLE OF CONTENTS 4

ABOUT THE AUTHOR 7

INTRODUCTION 8

PREFACE 12

COMMENTS ON THE STATE EXAM AND BEING A LEARNING LEADER 14

PART I - BREAKING DOWN THE DOMAINS, COMPETENCIES, AND INDICATORS 16

    DOMAIN I 18

        SCHOOL CULTURE (School and Community Leadership) 18

            CHAPTER 1 20

            DOMAIN 1, COMPETENCY 001 20

            CHAPTER 2 40

        DOMAIN I, COMPETENCY 002 40

    DOMAIN II – LEADING LEARNING (Instructional Leadership/Teaching and Learning) 53

        CHAPTER 3 55

        DOMAIN II, COMPETENCY 003 55

        CHAPTER 4 67

        DOMAIN II, COMPETENCY 004 67

    DOMAIN III – HUMAN CAPITAL (Human Resource Management) 80

        CHAPTER 5 82

        DOMAIN III, COMPETENCY 005 82

        CHAPTER 6 106

        DOMAIN III, COMPETENCY 006 106

    DOMAIN IV – EXECUTIVE LEADERSHIP (Communication and Organizational Management) 121

        CHAPTER 7 122

- DOMAIN IV, COMPETENCY 007 122
  - CHAPTER 8 138
  - DOMAIN IV, COMPETENCY 008 138
- DOMAIN V – STRATEGIC OPERATIONS (Alignment and Resource Allocation) 155
  - CHAPTER 9 156
  - DOMAIN V, COMPETENCY 009 156
  - CHAPTER 10 167
  - DOMAN V, COMPETENCY 010 167
- DOMAIN VI – ETHICS, EQUITY, AND DIVERSITY 184
  - CHAPTER 11 185
  - DOMAIN VI, COMPETENCY 011 185
- PART II – THE KNOWLEDGE, SKILLS, AND MINDSETS FOR THE PRINCIPAL 196
  - CHAPTER 12 198
  - KNOWLEDGE: CANDIDATES DEMONSTRATE AN UNDERSTANDING OF BASIC KNOWLEDGE 198
  - CHAPTER 13 219
  - SKILLS: CANDIDATES DEMONSTRATE AN ABILITY TO… 219
  - CHAPTER 14 245
  - MINDSETS: CANDIDATES DEMONSTRATE THE BELIEF THAT… 245
- PART III – CONSTRUCTED RESPONSES – DESCRIPTION 255
  - CHAPTER 15 258
  - BREAKING DOWN THE CONSTRUCTED RESPONSE INTO MANAGEABLE STEPS 258
- DIAGNOSE 258
- PRIORITIZE AND SET GOALS 260
- PLAN 261
- IMPLEMENT/MONITOR AND ADJUST 262

PART IV - PERFORMANCE ASSESSMENT FOR SCHOOL LEADERS 263

    CHAPTER 16 265

    CLOSING COMMENTS 265

ANSWERS TO SAMPLE CHAPTER QUESTIONS 268

APPENDIX A 275

PRINCIPAL DOMAINS 275

APPENDIX B 281

EDUCATOR'S CODE OF ETHICS 281

REFERENCES AND RESOURCES 284

INDEX 287

ABOUT THE AUTHOR

Dr. Timothy M. Powers received his Bachelor of Arts degree from Wayland Baptist University with an elementary certification and secondary certification in English and history. He began his public education career as a junior high classroom teacher, teaching English and history. He was a girls' athletics coach. When Dr. Powers received his Master's degree in Educational Leadership from Texas Tech University, he began his administrative career serving as a Vice Principal of a high school, an elementary principal, a junior high principal and Assistant Superintendent in charge of food services and transportation. He received his Doctorate in Educational Leadership at Texas Tech University. He finished his 37-year career as the Assistant Superintendent in charge of curriculum and instruction in a district of 14,000 students.

Dr. Powers is currently serving as the coordinator of the Master's degree program in Educational Administration for Wayland Baptist University. He instructs teachers who are working on their principal's certification and administrators who are seeking their superintendent's certification.

Dr. Powers has been married to Janice for 42 years and has two children, Zane who is serving in the ministry and Janelle Styne who is an instructional coach in a public school district.

INTRODUCTION

I am excited to bring you this new textbook designed to help you achieve success on mastering the new 268 TExES Principal Exam and the Performance Assessment for School Leaders (PASL) tasks *and most especially, for entry-level principals*. I created this textbook with the direct intention to help you to step into the administrator's role as an entry-level administrator, ready to add to and promote the success of students on your campus. I recognize most of you will not step immediately into the role of a campus principal. It would not be wise of you or a district to put that expectation upon someone who has not had a chance to experience administration from an assistant principal's role. This does not mean you cannot be an effective instructional leader in an assistant's role. In fact, this option would provide you with a great opportunity to utilize your knowledge, skills and mindsets developed through your university preparation coursework.

My experience of assisting many principal candidates through the courses the university offers in preparing them is that many principal candidates do not process the material and are not intentional about their learning. What do I mean by that? Well, the principal candidate is excited about wanting to be a principal because they have usually been encouraged by someone else who told them they could do the job without any thought about what it takes to become an entry-level principal in today's educational world.

Therefore, many principal candidates enroll in a university preparation program called an Educator Preparation Program (EPP) without really considering the knowledge, skills and mindsets necessary to be successful on the state exams and more importantly, as an entry-level principal. Many principal candidates are in a *check off* mode when it comes to the course material requirements. They fail to stop and seriously consider the material from a knowledge based perspective, a personal application perspective and most importantly, from a personal values perspective. That is the *intentional* part of learning; being a life-long learner with a focus on reflective learning that will eventually translate into real life success you, the teachers, and the students.

This textbook references on several occasions two people who I consider the premier researchers in the education field. Lee Bolman and Terrance Deal have greatly added to the advancement of improving instruction using their Frames of Cognition as a basis for effective decision-making. I would like to acknowledge their body of work in this area as I reference them on many occasions throughout the textbook.

Their work evolves around the campus principal being able to frame an issue or concern and then use that particular frame to make decisions that are more appropriate. Leaders who are able to reframe, develop a liberating sense of choice and power both for themselves and for their organizations. Bolman and Deal (1997) also stated that, "The ability to reframe situations is one of the most powerful capacities of great artists." It can be equally powerful for administrative leaders who are able to redefine situations, meeting the organizational challenges, based on the appropriate frame (Bolman & Deal, 1997).

Structural Frame

The structural frame focuses on designing a pattern of roles and relationships that will accomplish collective goals and accommodate individual differences (Bolman & Deal, 1997). The core assumptions of the structural frame are:

1. Organizations exist to achieve established goals and objectives.
2. Organizations work best when rationality prevails over personal preferences and external pressures.
3. Structures are designed to fit an organization's circumstances (including its goals, technology, and environment).
4. Organizations increase efficiency and enhance performance through specialization and division of labor.
5. Appropriate forms of coordination and control are essential to ensuring that individuals and units work together in the service of organizational goals, and
6. Problems and performance gaps arise from structural deficiencies. They are remedied through restructuring.

Human Resource Frame

The human resource frame (Bolman & Deal, 1997) relies on the organizations recognizing the employee as an individual who has needs with the organization being sensitive to understanding those needs. The core assumptions of the human resource frame are:

1. Organizations exist to serve human needs rather than the reverse.
2. People and organizations need each other: organizations need ideas, energy, and talent; people need careers, salaries, and opportunities.
3. When the fit between individual and system is poor, one or both suffer. Individuals will be exploited or will exploit the organization or both will become victims.
4. A good fit benefits both: individuals find meaningful and satisfying work, and organizations get the talent and energy they need to succeed.

Political Frame

The political frame (Bolman & Deal, 1997) views organizations as alive with political arenas that have a web of individual and group interests. The core assumptions of the political frame are:

1. Organizations are coalitions of various individuals and interest groups.
2. There are enduring differences among coalition members in values, beliefs, information, interests, and perceptions of reality.
3. Most important decisions involve the allocation of scarce resources, who gets what.
4. Scarce resources and enduring differences give conflict a central role in organizational dynamics and make power the most important resource.
5. Goals and decisions emerge from bargaining, negotiation, and jockeying for position among different stakeholders.

Symbolic Frame

The symbolic frame (Bolman & Deal, 1997) develops the conceptual umbrella that fosters meaning, belief, and faith within the framework of the organization. The six core area concepts that support the frame are:

1. What is most important about any event is not what happened but what it means.
2. Activity and meaning are loosely coupled: events have multiple meanings because people interpret experience differently.
3. Most of life is ambiguous or uncertain, what happened, why it happened, or what will happen next are all puzzles.
4. High levels of ambiguity and uncertainty undercut rational analysis, problem solving, and decision-making.
5. In the face of uncertainty and ambiguity, people create symbols to resolve confusion, increase predictability, provide direction, and anchor hope and faith.

6. Many events and processes are more important for what is expressed than what is produced. They form a cultural tapestry of secular myths, rituals, ceremonies, and stories that help people find meaning, purpose, and passions.

I would encourage all who are reading this to take a deeper dive into the Frames of Cognition by reading the research of Lee Bolman and Terrance Deal. Implementing their process of decision-making through adequately reframing issues may save the reader time and frustration in the long run.

This textbook is more than about providing you with sample questions to help you develop the frame of mind for passing the 268 TExES Principal Exam and mastering the Performance Assessment for School leaders. It is an in-depth dive into the domains, competencies and indicators, to give the entry-level principal a thorough understanding of the responsibilities as the campus instructional leader.

I believe this textbook provides you with the tools to be successful **beyond the mastery of the state assessments**. To the principal candidate and entry-level principals who achieve success on the state exam, I wish you even greater success in your aspirations to become leaders of learning.

PREFACE

This textbook has been prepared as a deep dive study into the various aspects of school leadership for primarily two purposes. The first is to help principal candidates successfully navigate through the 268 TExES Principal Exam and the three Performance Assessments for School Leaders (PASL) tasks. I have provided an in-depth look at every aspect of the principal as an instructional leader, a communicator, a developer of teachers as leaders, an evaluator, a manger of human capital and resources, an energizer of high-quality instruction, a plant manager and a modeler of appropriate ethics and values.

Additionally, this textbook is directed toward the entry-level principals and other interested principals who seek to improve their instructional problem solving skills. The entry-level principal must be ready to navigate through the many challenges that are waiting for you when you start your position at the helm of this great and noble responsibility. **When you read a reference to entry-level principal from this point forward in this textbook, it means both the principal candidate and the entry-level principal.**

Many graduate students who are engaged in preparation to receive certification as a principal, do not complete many deep dives into how the domains, competencies and indicators actually apply to real-life settings for improving school achievement. This textbook is an attempt to give you a much richer look at who entry-level principals must be and what they must do when presented the opportunity to lead a campus.

Part I of this textbook consists of eleven chapters that focus on the domains, competencies and indicators of an effective campus principal. Each chapter will present the specific competency, dissect the meaning, and show you what it looks like in an exemplar. These chapter presentations will also include an explanation of the indicators in an action-oriented manner. Each of these chapters will end with some practice questions for those studying to master the 268 TExES Principal Practice Exam.

Part II of this textbook consists of a lengthy in-depth presentation of the knowledge, skills, and mindsets that an entry-level principal needs to assimilate and internalize in a way they can demonstrate those attributes when leading for change.

These knowledge, skills, and mindset are learned traits. It takes a commitment to perseverance to utilize these assets for the greater good of the students and the campus.

Part III targets how to address the constructed responses for the exam portion of the state assessment. The constructed response is a new expectation in the assessment process. It provides the entry-level principal with additional tools needed to be successful from day one as a campus leader. This part includes an explanation on how to read the prompts for the exam and successfully navigate through the important steps needed to address the constructed responses.

Part IV of this textbook addresses the three different Performance Assessments for School Leaders, otherwise known as the PASL tasks. This section attempts to explain in more detail the steps required in producing an effective product based on the rubric used in evaluating the principal candidate's mindset. It is my desire that this in-depth look will provide you with the foundation you will need to lead your campus of instructional learners to academic success.

Part V are some closing comments where I attempt to bring this information together into some useful thoughts for the entry-level principal to move forward toward success on the campus.

COMMENTS ON THE STATE EXAM AND BEING A LEARNING LEADER

State educators, parents, students, and the community want principals who are willing to prepare themselves as learning leaders for the campus. There should be high expectations for everyone, but most especially the campus principal. As the principal goes, so goes the campus. It is not just a job, it is a responsibility entrusted to you. Make the best of it to be the catalyst for improving instruction.

That is why the Texas Education Agency collaborated with state leaders to realign the expectations for entry-level principals and for Educational Preparation Programs. This type of leadership requires one who keeps the main thing, the main thing, even in the face of adversity. The whole process of the coursework designed by EPPs is not just about preparing principal candidates to pass the state exam. That is just a small part of the process. It IS about sending prepared, responsible administrators onto Texas campuses with the leadership courage to do the right thing in all situations, making a positive difference with student academics.

One of the last expectations of the entry-level principal is to demonstrate mastery on the 268 Texas Principal Exam as well as the Performance Assessment of School Leaders. Both of these are required prior to awarding a principal certification. If you have done your homework, assimilated, and internalized the information presented by your EPP, then you will be ready to prepare yourself for these last two challenges.

The selected response portion of the state exam is currently 70 questions. It will count approximately 60% of the exam. It is expected to take approximately two and a half hours to complete. The questions will be in A, B, C, and D format with multiple choice selections meaning there may be more than one answer. These types of multiple selections are more advantageous to the test-taker because he/she can generally rule out one or more of the responses and come up with a higher percentage of answering the question correctly.

The constructed response portion of the new state exam is currently four questions. That portion will count for the other 40% of the exam and will take another two and a half hours. The test is five hours in length. It is expected you will need all of that time to complete it. In fact, you are encouraged to take all of the allotted time to complete the exam.

Wilmore (2019) provides some great insight on focusing on key words for each of the competencies. She provides the test-taker with exceptional test-taking strategies to help the entry-level principal to pass the test. I would highly recommend you invest in her textbook for more specific test-taking strategies.

However, this textbook is designed to give you an in depth look at the domains, competencies, and indicators so that when you pass the exam and the PASL tasks, you will have developed several skills that will be available in your administrative toolbox. In addition, you can walk confidently onto your campus as the learning leader, ready to influence student achievement from day one.

PART I - BREAKING DOWN THE DOMAINS, COMPETENCIES, AND INDICATORS

Why should we even have domains and competencies for administrators? If you were to talk to a practicing administrator right now, it is doubtful that any of them could refer to these competencies as their core beliefs or practices. In fact, most of them would tell you their real training ground was their first year of being an administrator. Their university Education Preparation Programs provided a knowledge base, but did little to prepare them for the real world leading for change on a campus. Principals have been on both sides of the fence of that pasture and understand the feelings of the campus principal who is stretched thin at best when it comes to handling the daily challenges of being a successful administrator.

The truth is, if you were to sit down with a campus principal and asked him/her if he/she addressed any of these indicators found under the competencies, most of them would agree they address those from time-to-time, as needed. The entry-level principal must be willing to move students and staff from an "as needed" situation, to proactive success for all students. You must be *intentional* about the process of improving student achievement and serving as the instructional leader of the campus. Student learning must be moved from an "as needed" basis to a priority with the campus principal intentionally being the lead learner.

There are no more learning curves for campus administrators. That is why these domains and competencies are so important for the entry-level principal to learn, internalize, and assimilate into their professional value system. View these domains and competencies (and indicators) as the critical attributes for a successful principal. The more you use these competencies and indicators in a proactive situation, the better your chances will be for advancing student academic success. This is your recipe for success.

No one can guarantee to another person that he/she will have complete success. However, if you use the material provided in this textbook throughout your course preparation process, as you enter into the administrative leadership role, your chances of being successful on the 268 TExES Principal Exam (Texas Examinations of Educator

Standards), the PASL (Performance Assessment for School Administrators) and a beginning principal, will be greatly enhanced.

As you begin your walk through these domains, competencies and indicators, think of yourself as an *educational physician*. You are a leading *educational* doctor. You have committed yourself to helping as many patients (students) as possible. From what are you helping them? You are helping them out of the illness of ignorance, into a healthy life of productive, responsible citizens. Just like with doctors who are practicing medicine, it is a process of isolating the illness, so you can target the remedy. This is true in education. You are constantly searching for the right cure (strategy) to help your teachers eradicate ignorance.

You need to become the best educational physician you can be so your students can enjoy the amenities of what our society has to offer for individuals who have successfully completed their education. That is why it is important to carry an understanding of these domains and competencies beyond your formal learning. Put them into practice when you begin your leadership role as a campus principal.

Good luck on your instructional leadership adventure.

DOMAIN I
SCHOOL CULTURE (School and Community Leadership)

Experienced educators and administrators will tell you that within just a few minutes of walking into a public school building, they can describe the "climate" of the building. However, it may take a little longer to command a good grip on the "culture" of the building. These two terms are not exactly interchangeable. The day-to-day issues and challenges that may be occurring within the school may affect the emotional IQ of the students and staff. It is important for the principal to keep a high emotional IQ during these times.

For instance, a well-known student of the campus may be seriously ill or injured and the students and staff are aware of the situation. They are all genuinely concerned about the welfare of the student and this may establish a temporary mood or climate in the building. This climate may improve or deteriorate based on the situation with the improvement or decline of the student's health. This is just one of many examples that attack the school's climate on a daily basis. It could actually BE the weather, a ballgame or the threats of a particular group of students upon another group of students. The possibilities are limitless. It is up to the campus leadership to control those daily interrupters of the environment as much as possible.

However, the culture of the campus is a little different challenge. It takes some observations and discussions with students, staff, and constituents, to get a good idea of the school's culture. Rodriguez (2008) defined school culture as "what schools *do* and how they do [it]." Whenever possible it is best to simplify terminology into its core critical attributes where you can do so. In this case, it is important for the entry-level principal to have a mastery understanding of what school culture means. After all, you will be responsible for ensuring the quality and integrity of that culture from day one as the <u>leader</u> of the <u>ship</u>.

Think of yourself as the captain of your ship (campus). You are trying to guide your students and staff to academic success. A single rudder that is relatively small in comparison to the rest of the ship guides that huge ship. Your rudder is your school culture. You do not necessarily SEE it, but just by the way you turn the ship's wheel while you are at the helm of this ship, others can get a sense of the school's mission, vision, and focus. Do not take the school's culture lightly.

That is why we will be talking in depth about Domain 1 – School Culture, because it really is the rudder of your ship. When you master the competencies and indicators in relationship to the school's culture as an entry-level principal, you will be well on your way to guiding your ship in the right direction.

After all, approximately 22-23% of the 268 TExES Principal Exam will focus on school culture alone. If you do not have a good mastery of this concept, then you will struggle from the beginning, not just on the exam, but more importantly, as a campus instructional leader.

Okay, so let us begin our deep dives into learning this portion of the principal domains and competencies.

CHAPTER 1
DOMAIN 1, COMPETENCY 001

WHAT DOES IT SAY?

Competency 001: The entry-level principal knows how to establish and implement a shared vision and culture of high expectations for all stakeholders (students, staff, parents, and community).

WHAT DOES IT MEAN?

When you think of the words *vision* and *mission*, sometimes the water can get a little muddy. It is hard to separate the two from one another because they appear together in most phrases and conversations related to schools. To help you understand with a little more clarity what these two concepts mean, consider vision as an aspect of what you SEE that you want to accomplish. Mission is the action or what you will DO to fulfill your vision (See Figure 1.1). You have heard people say, "He's on a mission." That typically means that person is focused on accomplishing or doing something. Your vision becomes (or eventually translates into) your campus' concrete measurable goals, *the seeing part of the process*, and your mission becomes your strategies, *the doing part of the process*.

Your thinking process about this vision and mission process is probably one of the most vital components OF the process. It is a process of reflective and systemic thinking. Reflective thinking is a personal routine that you need to go through on any significant decision-making process. This is a system of process thinking that will take you through what you "believe," and how you will "act" and "react" to certain situations. This is what a vision and mission statement should be. If your value and belief system does not match up with what a vision and mission statement should be and do, then some serious personal soul searching should take place.

Systemic thinking is a progression by which you complete deep analysis of the process of creating a vision and mission statement that includes and anticipates the steps involved with the possible roadblocks and any issues and concerns that may arise. Your ability to systematically think through these issues and prepare for possible concerns will help you minimize the possibility of the distractors in the process.

When you complete reflection and systemic thinking activities, these procedures are not limited to creating a vision and mission statement. You begin to develop certain mindsets needed to be successful. Having a mindset does not mean your mind is set. It means your mind is prepared with the right frame of mind to address the challenge of creating a meaningful, productive vision and mission statement.

Here are some examples of what a *vision* statement might look like:

- We will dedicate all our resources to ensure learning for all.
- Student success is our number one priority.
- We will devote our time and effort into developing responsible and productive citizens.
- Leaning for all is our number one priority.
- Learning is not an option. It is an opportunity. No exceptions.

Here are some examples of what a *mission* statement might look like. The mission statement will be a little more detailed because it is the doing or action part of the process.

- At [Your School], we will dedicate our human capital, resources, and time to commit ourselves to learning for all. Every person has value and worth. They have permission to learn at their highest potential.
- No child will be left behind at [Your School]. Every person will commit to support learning for all. Every student will achieve a level of academic success that will provide him or her with the learning tools to be successful beyond graduation.
- Our mission at [Your School] is to empower all students with the skills and tools necessary to achieve success in the classroom. These tools and skills will allow every student to be responsible, productive citizens of our community, ready to contribute in a positive manner.

You begin to establish the culture of that campus when you put these two together. Your campus makes a concerted effort to fulfill the agreed upon vision and mission statements. Your culture will grow out of the seeing and doing part of this process. That is why it is so important for the campus administrator to keep a close eye on monitoring the members of this leader "ship." It is important to ensure everyone is seeing the mission through.

Continuing to break down this competency a little further, look at the "high expectations for all stakeholders" section. It is a simple process for a campus principal to go in and establish a set of criteria or goals for the campus to achieve. It is another thing for teachers, staff, students, parents, and constituents to embrace those goals. Therefore, to master this competency by the entry-level principal, it is going to take some time to understand the attitudes and behaviors of others.

The statement that principals cannot control what goes on in the classroom is a myth. On the contrary, the school culture begins and ends with establishing a set of professional values and belief systems in which the conversation is open and honest about what teachers, staff and students are capable of achieving in meeting instructional expectations.

The conversation must eventually begin to focus on what the entry-level principal desires to have as a laser-like focus on, for student achievement. Lezotte (2011) stated, "Leaders must help transform their schools, as cultural organizations, from teacher-centered institutions to learner-centered organizations in which teachers have high expectations of themselves as professionals, and have access to appropriate resources to help them ensure that every child learns." This statement goes back to the attitudes and behaviors mentioned. Again, we can say we want an expected outcome, but unless the teachers and staff members believe that outcome is possible, it more than likely will not be achieved. So now, we must distinguish between attitudes and behaviors.

Attitudes are those sets of beliefs and values a person has formulated about a particular topic or societal expectation. Behaviors are the ways a person reacts to those beliefs. Here is where the entry-level principal does have some say in how staff reacts to the campus vision and mission, the indicators of a campus culture. Attitudes do not usually change until the behavior changes. Yes, that was stated correctly. It is not backwards. You start with an expected behavior of the teachers and staff. Then, you provide them with the support and resources necessary to reinforce those behaviors.

The expectation of the entry-level principal is that all staff will behave in a manner that creates a culture of success for all students.

The teachers and staff members do not necessarily have to support the agreed upon professional values and beliefs…yet. Those beliefs are personal. They are embedded in an individual's psyche. They are not easily changed. How are they changed? The teacher or staff member behaving in an expected manner and experiencing success changes them. Then, they share about it with other members of the campus organization. It is a process of reverse dynamics; the individual demonstrates the actions of the organization's expected behaviors. Once success is achieved over time, the professional attitudes and values begin to be reshaped. It is amazing to watch what a little success and encouragement can to do a person's belief system.

Now we get into the more challenging aspect of this competency. That is how the entry-level principal will establish and implement a shared vision and mission of a culture of high expectations for all stakeholders. An established set of requisite knowledge, skills, and mindsets necessary to actually establish and implement the vision and mission. It is not an easy task or for the faint of heart, because this is where the real work of the entry-level principal takes place.

To establish means to set up something intended to continue or be permanent. This process of setting up has to be intentional by the entry-level principal. You must be aware of the steps needed to take place to go from no vision or a misunderstood vision and mission, to something that is embraced by the campus and constituents. By constituents, this means the broader community. In today's world of immediate news via all types of social venues, it is even more important the school campus to not be viewed as an isolated learning center. This is your opportunity to open up the concrete barriers of brick and mortar. Invite the public to be a part of the learning process. In doing so, you begin to slowly create advocates for learning.

Creating a vision (see) and a mission (do) statement takes a system of steps and planning that must include all stakeholders (students, staff, parents, and community.) It is not something you whip up in your office and then present to your constituents. This is about a process that communicates a message to your stakeholders that they are all a part of the success for students. Remember, we are still in Domain I, Competency 001.

Vision What You See + **Mission What You Do** = **Results What You Get**

Figure 1.1: Results are what a campus works toward using the vision of what you see, and the mission of what you do.

WHAT DOES IT LOOK LIKE? (EXEMPLAR)

Why do we want to create a sense of collaboration on developing and implementing a shared vision of culture and high expectations rather than just putting one out there? Booher-Jennings (2005) found that forcing change without a *shared* (italics by the author) vision and sense of mission created a climate of competition that undermined collegiality, making it almost impossible for staff to work together. The entry-level principal must have the support of as many constituents as possible to establish a successful vision and mission. By the way, putting it on paper and plastering it on the walls of the classroom does not make it a vision and mission. Implementing it by processing through every conceivable decision regarding students and staff creates a culture based on the vision and mission.

To be clear, there is no one right way to get to a finished product that elaborates the vision and mission of your constituents. The key in this domain and competency is to be inclusive. There is a helpful website called Community Tool Box that can provide you with a number of inclusive suggestions for engaging your stakeholders. So, let us just elaborate on some basic steps you could execute that would get you to a point where you have mastered the expectations of Competency 001.

Step 1: *Figure out where you are with your current campus vision and mission and determine if it is geared toward setting high expectations for all.* You are not trying to reinvent the wheel here. However, you cannot get to a place that establishes a vision and mission with high expectations for all stakeholders until you have a feel for the current campus culture. Bambrick-Santoyo (2012) states, "Great cultures do not come from irreplaceable charisma; they come from the careful development of habits that build a strong staff community. Discover what the current habits are in the school by listening to the teachers, staff, students, parents and community talk about learning. Write those phrases down. Use them as a beginning point to establish the kind of culture that should be in place.

Step 2: *Find out who the movers and shakers are in your school community.* Keep in mind, there are leaders who operate in the forefront (everyone knows who they are). However, there may be quiet passive leaders who do their job every day and people go to them for advice and direction. You want to get them on board as well. Bring them in individually, or on a small group basis, to discuss the current culture. Encourage them to think about what the culture should be like. This is where you begin to develop a nucleus of leaders who will begin to get on board with what you are trying to do. Do not worry if everyone is not where you would hope they would be. People need time to hear what you are saying. They need time to reflect and internalize a possible shift in the school's culture. Give them some space and time to let that happen, but be ready to move forward when the time comes. Some will join willingly. Some will get on board cautiously. Others will come screaming and hollering until they see success.

You will want to be inclusive of all stakeholders by modeling the appropriate development of all your constituents. It does not matter what the reading level of your stakeholders are; they can *always read you!* Leave your biases at the door. Better yet, do some personal soul searching at this point. Determine that every stakeholder has worth, not only in this process, but also in the process of educating all students. When your level of expectation goes up, so does the level of those who choose to follow your example.

Step 3: *Plan meetings with your various constituents with an understanding that not all parents and community members will be there or are willing to participate.* That is okay as long as you provide multiple opportunities for them to participate. This is where you will need to show some genuine leadership because you want to demonstrate this process is not just a check-off-the-requirements sort of meeting. You should genuinely be seeking input while directing and establishing a sense of expectation that includes high performance from students, staff, parents, and the community.

However, before you dive in too deeply, one of the first steps that should occur at every meeting is to effectively communicate some basic procedures for all participants to follow. These procedures do not have to be very elaborate, but they do need to be clearly defined. You should include communication that all input is considered and valued. Every participant has worth and is needed for the process to be successful. The rules for these meetings should also include an emphasis on being courteous to the one speaking and offering input.

It will be in these meetings that you and the participants in the process will begin to develop a sense of vision and mission for your campus. That vision and mission is not created from thin air. You will lead these meetings using longitudinal data on your students that show concrete evidence of where your students and campus have been. You will also display the anonymous comments you received from teachers, staff, students, parents, and the community to give the participants a perception of where you are at that point. You will use emerging issues of the campus, and recent research that would be appropriate for establishing your vision and mission. Any other types of data such as student learning and campus demographics are necessary to collaboratively develop a shared campus vision and a plan for implementing the vision. The process contains a frontload of time-consuming actions and activities. However, in all actuality, it will save you time because you and your staff will have developed your destination point. That will keep you focused during challenging sessions.

You will also want to use your students' demographics to display information that will be helpful in developing a picture of the student population. Why do you want to do this? Because you are the instructional leader, you understand not all students learn the same way. This is the beginning point for identifying instructional strategies later on that will address your student population needs.

Step 4: *Develop your vision and mission statement in collaboration with your constituents.* This should be a positive process that allows for open and honest dialogue among the participants. One of the more important aspects in developing and creating a vision and mission is ownership. People should feel <u>a *part*</u> <u>OF</u> the process, not <u>*apart*</u> <u>FROM</u> the process. This may take some time. However, the investment in building strong professional relationships culminating in a collaborative vision and mission with high expectations will pay dividends.

YOU are the lead facilitator in this process. There is a difference between facilitator and dictator. You should be the former rather than the latter. Being the facilitator and campus principal does not mean you must know everything. In fact, when people see your focus is on academic success for all students and you are genuine and vulnerable, the participants will be more likely to embrace your leadership style. They will want to be a part of building a successful campus culture based on high expectations. Furthermore, your primary responsibility as a leader is to help everyone else around you become better at what they do. This process can add deposits to your emotional and psychological bank account that you may need later when the challenges of being the instructional leader may be tested.

Step 5: *Implement and monitor your vision and mission statement.* There is so much to cover here. Let us start with a key theme in this whole process. You may have glanced down the page of the book and thought this is the last step. In one sense, it is, but there is really no endpoint in this process. It is really just the beginning. It involves two major actions that keep it in motion. First, it is a continuous process. Note in the italicized portion of this step the word, monitor. Monitor is an action verb. It means you will observe the process closely. Use your dashboard, vision and mission to make minor adjustments to the process of improving student achievement. Then your students, staff and constituents, understand that high expectations for all stakeholders is not just a mantra posted on the wall; it is an actionable process that is non-negotiable.

The second major aspect of this step is that it is cyclic. You must maintain your vision and mission by periodically revisiting the above steps to ensure you are retaining a focus that others will follow. This maintenance period of the vision and mission statement affirms your trust and belief in others. In turn, they will return that same trust. It is a values-based process that will be embedded in others that you are focused on establishing a culture of high expectations for all.

What does this look like when you *implement* the vision and mission? Yes, you have a printed vision and mission. You probably have a copy of it posted in high traffic areas of your campus, as well. However, the true vision and mission begins to become ingrained in the very fibers of the school's many decision-making processes. Your budget begins to get a major overhaul because you realize there are many misdirected expenses that do not address your vision and mission. Every single professional learning community meeting or data dig meeting begins with a review of your vision and mission statement. Your faculty and department meetings focus entirely on how you and your staff can meet your vision and mission.

These types of actions help the vision and mission to become ingrained into the fabric of the learning community, but it cannot stop there. Think about ALL of your constituents. Consider their emotions, opinions, and what is at stake. When you begin to communicate your new vision and mission, you will more than likely have what Peterson, et. al. (2012) refers to as crucial conversations. People's emotions may run high and they may have their own opinions about learning. You can move the discussion forward by being prepared, determined, resolute, courteous and patient with your constituents. When change occurs that raises the level of expectations for all learners, there will be a certain amount of resistance because people are typically comfortable in their learning lane because they are used to it.

Once you have a workable vision and mission statement, you begin to look at ALL your staff and determine if every staff member is in the best high-leverage position to make the greatest impact in fulfilling that vision and mission statement. These types of decisions do not come lightly. They require a solid emotional IQ and a staff that understands student achievement is the highest priority. It requires leadership courage.

You are an entry-level principal. If you wait until those fires of discontent begin to smolder before you have reflectively counted the cost of what it means to be an instructional leader, you will automatically default to your personal path of least resistance. Instructional leadership takes true grit, determination, and a realization that it takes a commitment to a strong culture of high expectations. You can do it!

Once you have staff in the correct positions to get the most out of your highest leverage opportunities, the question is, "How do I monitor and adjust?" This is where you will want to create, with the collaboration of your staff, an instructional dashboard that contains concrete indicators of how you will measure your campus' effectiveness of meeting your vision and mission that will be embedded in your instructional goals. Your dashboard will need to be aligned with the specific three or four instructional goals your campus has identified. It would also include the resources you are using, the budgeted amount, a checklist of what instructional coaches are looking for as they relate to the specified goals, student attendance, staff attendance, and a number of other indicators.

You must create an atmosphere of trust and safety for all participants in the process from the beginning to the end. This safe and orderly environment does not stop with the physical safety, but must also include the social and emotional safety for all. Teachers must be provided a venue that allows them to become instructional risk-takers. You have raised the bar for learning and it does not happen in a vacuum. They need the freedom to know they can try the plethora of research-based ideas that are available to them, to enable them to help their students become a culture of successful learners.

Students learning is not an option. You and your staff will provide as many resources as possible to help them to become successful learners. Too many students have developed a mental picture of themselves that they cannot learn at a higher rate of success and have developed a mental capacity of learning avoidance. Their thoughts are, "If I do not try, then I will not expose my limited skills in my learning toolbox." You are the entry-level principal. You must help to create a platform where students are allowed to master the material no matter how many attempts it takes, with a system of structured interventions in place to help them to achieve.

A final thought about getting in and *doing* this process. Do not exclude an important component of this process. Those are the people outside the walls of the campus who may have participated somewhat or not at all in the process. Public educators are notorious about ignoring an untapped resource here. That resource is parents, community members and business partners. There are a lot of volunteer tutors, substitutes and supporters who are willing to help, if only asked. It is your job to communicate your need for them to be active participants in the development and implementation of the process, and in the fulfillment of the vision and mission statement.

By including as many constituents as you can to help with fulfilling the vision and mission statement, you have created a cadre of support that serve as an undercurrent to keep the ship headed in the right direction. They are also voters. The more they know about what schools are about, the more likely they will support the school system when it is time to go to the polls. They will vote in favor of additional finances needed to help students achieve success.

A LOOK AT THE INDICATORS FOR COMPETENCY 001

If you take a moment to peruse all of the ten indicators for competency one, you will discover that every one of them begins with some sort of action verb. There is a reason for that. The Texas Education Agency, acting principals, and teachers will tell you that the responsibility of a principal is to serve in this leadership position. To do that, there must be a set of observable and measurable actions the entry-level principal places in their instructional and administrative toolbox. You do this to achieve the high expectations demanded for this position. There is little or no learning curve for the entry-level principal. You are not only expected, but also required to meet the demands of this competency. To help you do so, these critical actions have been identified for you to DO in the process of obtaining success in this competency. Let us look at these indicators a little more closely. Keeping in mind, they focus on establishing and implementing a shared vision and culture of high expectations for all stakeholders. Here are a few ideas of what each of these indicators look like when *doing* them.

A. Creates a positive, collaborative, and collegial campus culture that sets high expectations and facilitates the implementation and achievement of campus initiatives and goals
   - You focus on the activities that create a supportive climate.
   - You establish professional learning communities that have specifically agreed upon expectations and agendas that focus on meeting the vision and mission statement, using the goals that have been identified.
   - You encourage open and honest dialogue among staff members with the focus on improving student achievement.

- You design questions for staff to respond to on how the campus can move from the current student performance level to meeting the standards set by the campus.
- You encourage individuals to share stories of success at every professional learning community meeting and staff gathering.

B. Uses emerging issues, recent research, knowledge of systems (e.g., school improvement process, strategic planning, etc.), and various types of data (e.g., demographic, perceptive, student learning, and processes) to collaboratively develop a shared campus vision and a plan for implementing the vision
- You provide data from the most recent state and local assessments to evaluate student performance.
- You provide attendance rate data to help with generating ideas on how student and teacher attendance rates can be improved.
- You provide teacher attrition rates to help analyze and determine next steps for reducing teacher attrition and retaining teachers of excellence. Use these data points to identify areas of incentives that will retain quality teachers in the classroom. Some ideas might include negotiating better insurance coverage, developing creative stipends for encouraging action research among the teachers and extra wage-earning opportunities.
- You provide targeted research-based instructional strategy studies on how to improve the specific areas of achievement based on your identified goals.
- You ensure your instructional goals are aligned with your vision and mission statement and those goals are measurable and attainable.
- You establish a systematic approach to effectively implementing, monitoring and evaluating the vision and mission of your campus that includes participation by all constituents.

C. Facilitates the collaborative development of a plan that clearly articulates objectives and strategies for implementing a campus vision

- You plan and facilitate various meetings focused on generating a concrete vision and mission statement that targets achieving academic excellence for all students.
- You facilitate the refining of your vision and mission statement so that it is clear, concise, and easy to interpret.
- You clearly define what a collaborative process looks likes.
- You ensure that collaboration is an emphasis in the process and that all constituents are a part of the process.
- You ensure your plan is measurable using standards established during the collaboration processes.

D. Aligns financial, human, and material resources to support implementation of a campus vision and mission
- You advocate for the necessary support and resources for your campus to achieve the goals outlined in your vision and mission.
- You evaluate the experience of your current staff and reposition your staff to the highest leverage positions to give you the greatest return for your human resources.
- You collaborate with your staff on the current resources you have to determine the best use of those resources.
- You eliminate resources that do not add value to meeting your vision and mission statement.
- You realign your budget to meet the vision and mission statement.

E. Establishes procedures to assess and modify implementation plans to promote achievement of the campus vision
- You facilitate the collaboration of team members, using all constituents, to establish specific measurable checkpoints for monitoring and adjusting the goals, vision and mission.
- You create a timeline for implementation of the monitoring and assessing of the vision and mission.

- You provide time for staff and community feedback on how well the vision and mission are being met.
- You promote the vision and mission by reiterating it whenever you are at meetings inside and outside of the building.
- You set specific dates in your timeline for an overall review of your current vision, mission, and goals, to make any adjustments or changes as necessary, and to keep the focus on high expectations for all students.

F. Models and promotes the continuous and appropriate development of all stakeholders in the school community, to shape the campus culture
- You keep the vision and the mission statement in the forefront by communicating the importance of it to all constituents, including students, parents, community members, and business partners.
- You lead out in identifying and facilitating discussions of improving student achievement through analysis of data, book studies, teacher conferences and presentations to the public.
- You facilitate the development of your teachers into better teachers through coaching and using instructional coaches.
- You verbally challenge your staff to envision what the vision and mission statement looks like and ask them to identify what "we" need to do differently to achieve that culture.
- You are visible on your campus, in the classrooms, serving as a part of the solution.

G. Establishes and communicates consistent expectations for all stakeholders, providing supportive feedback to promote a positive campus environment
- You communicate the vision and mission statement to all stakeholders using electronic media and personal meetings with students, parents, businesses, and community members.
- You enlist the help and support of all constituents.

- You identify with your staff through a process of facilitating meetings to show exemplars of what success looks like based on your vision and mission statement.
- You encourage and solicit feedback from all parties regarding the progress of meeting the goals of the vision and mission.
- You use the feedback to make adjustments as necessary to fulfilling the agreed upon vision and mission.

H. Implements effective strategies to systematically gather input from all campus stakeholders, supporting innovative thinking with an inclusive culture
- You promote instructional strategy risk-taking with your teachers by encouraging them to use research-based strategies to perform their action research.
- You encourage your teachers to share successes and failures of teaching strategies within the professional learning community meetings.
- You encourage your teachers and staff to continue the use of research-based teaching strategies when previous strategies have not worked.
- You create an online anonymous evaluation tool to allow input from constituents, regarding the progress of meeting your vision and mission.
- You summarize and share those comments in your ongoing process of monitoring and adjusting your vision and mission statement.

I. Creates an atmosphere of safety that encourages the social, emotional, and physical well-being of staff and students
- You facilitate the development and promotion of clearly defined rules and consequences to establish order for the classroom and campus.
- You facilitate the teaching of these expectations and the consistency of application of the rules of order for all staff and students.
- You follow through with the approved consequences on a consistent basis.
- You communicate the expectations to all constituents.

- You ensure that diversity of culture; ethnicity, religion, gender, and gender preference are protected while students are under the care of staff.

J. Facilitates the implementation of research-based theories and techniques to promote a campus environment and culture that is conducive to effective teaching and learning and supports organizational health and morale
- You investigate research-based theories that would affect the attainment of your instructional goals as they relate to meeting the vision and mission of your campus.
- You facilitate the use of these research-based strategies to engage in a positive outcome for student achievement.
- You utilize best practices of leadership theories to promote a campus environment that is conducive to learning and academic success.
- You explore possible techniques of instructional delivery to help determine what practices would work best for all types of student learners.
- You advocate and provide for the resources necessary to implement research-based theories and procedures to promote a campus environment and culture that is conducive to effective teaching and learning.

This is a limited selection of ideas provided for you to begin developing your own mindset of what you can do as an entry-level principal to move toward the successful establishment and implementation of a shared vision and culture of high expectations for all stakeholders. However, as you reflect on these suggestions, you will begin to create your own version of your "dos" for your unique campus. To ignore this competency and these indicators would be tantamount to setting sail on a ship without a rudder, allowing your campus to be controlled by the winds of daily distractors. In the end, this competency will serve as your instructional compass you will use in times of rough waters and it will keep you and your staff focused on the main thing; improving student achievement for all students.

SAMPLE 268 TExES QUESTIONS FOR COMPETENCY 001

This is an opportunity to stretch your thinking process, now that you have a foundational base of knowledge regarding, "The entry-level principal knows how to establish and implement a shared vision and culture of high expectations for all stakeholders." The 268 TExES Principal Exam will consist of approximately seventy selected responses of which approximately 10%-12% may come from Competency 001. The questions are created to help prepare you for success on the exam and to reinforce the information in this chapter. You will get the full experience of these practice text questions by completing a thorough study of this chapter prior to answering these sample questions.

Take the time to answer all of the questions without looking back at the chapter information and without looking forward to the answers, which are found under the "ANSWERS TO SAMPLE CHAPTER QUESTIONS" in Part IV of the textbook. That section will list the question number, the correct answer, and the rationale for the correct answer.

1. Mr. Rogers is the principal of an established high school. He was named as the principal toward the end of the school year. In his introductory individual and small group meetings with teachers, staff, parents, and community members, he realized there was little or no recollection of a clear vision and mission statement. What would most likely be the first step in addressing the need for a vision and mission statement?
    a. Contact the superintendent and express his concerns for a need to create a mission and vision statement.
    b. Complete a process of personal reflection and systemic thinking on what steps, data, resources, and procedures need to be considered to begin this task.
    c. Assign your assistant principals the responsibility of identifying the most supportive members of the stakeholders.

d. Call a meeting of the core faculty members to announce you will be developing a vision and mission statement and you need their support to implement it.

2. Mrs. Florence has just finished developing a vision and mission statement with the collaboration from her staff and other stakeholders. As a new entry-level principal, she has also collaborated with the staff and stakeholders on clearly defined measurable goals that are directly targeted to the campus' vision and mission statement. At this point, what would most likely be her next step to move the implementation process forward?
    a. Ask the staff to evaluate the vision and mission process to see if any additional changes need to be made.
    b. Share with other campus principals, to see if the vision and mission statements seem appropriate and consider their input.
    c. Investigate research-based theories that would affect the attainment of the instructional goals as they relate to meeting the vision and mission of her campus.
    d. Instruct her campus secretary to have the vision and mission statement placed on all formal stationery used by the campus administration.

3. Several of Mrs. Hatt's more tenured teachers have been mildly resistant to the process of developing and implementing a new vision statement since she mentioned the need for one when she was introduced to the faculty as their new principal. The previous principal was more of a "hands off" principal and left the faculty and staff to their own devices. Mrs. Hatt is concerned that if they are not brought more into the process, they will begin demonstrating more of a passive aggressive attitude about the vision and mission statement. To encourage them to participate more in the process, she decides to talk with them individually for the following reason.
    a. She explains her need for their help in thinking creatively for ways to change the culture of the campus since they have been there longer than

others have. She needs their help to generate ideas on how to create an interest and excitement in the process.

   b. She explains to each one that she wants their participation in the process, but plans on moving forward with or without their support

   c. She assigns each one of them the responsibility of bringing at least one outside stakeholder from the business or community to attend the first meeting to collaborate on the development of a vision and mission statement.

   d. She politely informs them against undermining the process and explains to them in a professional manner that there will repercussions if they do not participate in the process in a manner that would be considered as team players.

4. Mr. Frankton's process of working with the staff and other stakeholders to develop and implement a vision and mission statement has gone well, but he realizes there is a sense of confusion at what teachers will do with it and how they will apply it to the classroom. After some careful consideration, Mr. Frankton decides to:

   a. Suggest that all faculty and staff memorize the vision and mission statement so they can recite it to other stakeholders.

   b. Set up meetings using the professional learning communities to engage the staff to describe what success would like in their classrooms based on the vision and mission statement.

   c. Open the floor for discussion about any questions or concerns, to see if the teachers will be open and honest with their apparent concerns.

   d. Visit each one of the teachers individually in his office and find out their feelings about the vision and mission statement.

5. The implementation of the vision and mission statement is in full swing. However, Mr. Glover notices at the professional learning community meetings he

is attending, there seems to be some frustration about improving student achievement. He decides at the next full faculty meeting to:
   a. Remind them they are doing a good job and to keep up the good work.
   b. Ask them why the professional learning community meetings seem to appear difficult for them. Provide wait time for staff to respond.
   c. Raise their level of expectation by reiterating what he expects them to do in the professional learning communities. Let them know he will continue to visit their meetings.
   d. Encourage as many staff members who are willing, to stand up and share any student academic success stories. Follow up by praising the staff member publicly in the meeting for his/her efforts.

CHAPTER 2
DOMAIN I, COMPETENCY 002

WHAT DOES IT SAY?

Competency 002: The entry-level principal knows how to work with stakeholders as key partners to support student learning.

WHAT DOES IT MEAN?

This has been a universal challenge for previously and currently practicing principals. The emphasis on including stakeholders as a partner in the leaning process for students has risen consistently in the past thirty years. Years ago, the principal was considered more of a building manager who ran the business of the campus and left the teaching to the teachers. The principal protected the classroom experience except for the customary open house for parents and the occasional parent conferences that needed to occur when students were at risk of failing. Times have changed.

Today, with the advent of social technology, if the principal does not include the stakeholders, they could be portrayed in a negative light with stakeholders using the social media to vent their frustration. Stakeholders include anyone who would remotely touch the campus in any way. To *touch* the campus means they would have a stake because they have a child attending, a grandchild attending, or live within the campus attendance lines. They may operate a business within the campus attendance zone or contribute to the campus through district personnel visiting to assist in meeting student needs such as district administrators, counselors, diagnosticians or other district personnel. This group would certainly consist of the students, staff or workers who attend the campus on a daily basis.

In breaking down this competency, it is important to consider the stakeholders from the critical perspective of student learning. Think of this as a sphere of influence (See Figure 2.1) on the learning process. Picture this sphere of influence as a dartboard with the bull's eye being the students engaged in learning. The students must be considered the key stakeholder in the process of improving student achievement and attaining academic excellence. The next concentric circle on the stakeholder bull's eye would be the teachers and staff, including the principal. The next concentric circle would consist of the parents or guardians of the students, including grandparents, followed by concentric circles for central office staff and for business and community members.

Your responsibility as the campus principal is to include these influences on student learning in a positive and productive manner, allowing for true input from interested stakeholders and genuine responsiveness from you and your staff as members of the learning community.

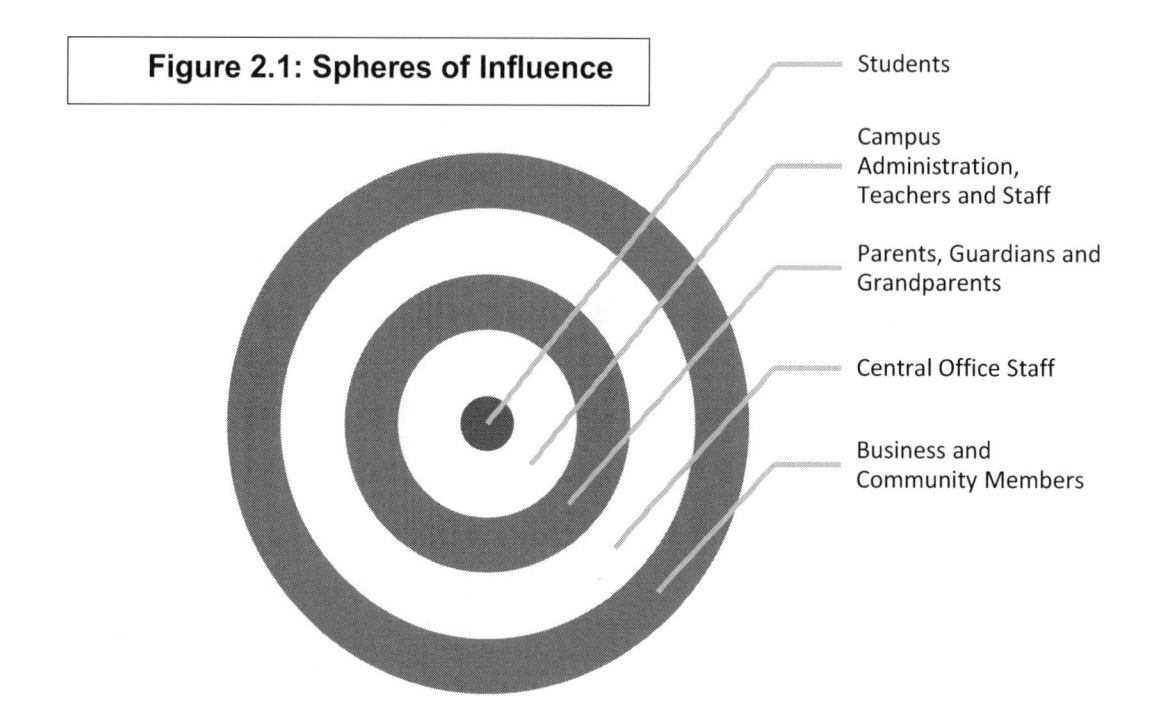

Figure 2.1: Spheres of Influence

- Students
- Campus Administration, Teachers and Staff
- Parents, Guardians and Grandparents
- Central Office Staff
- Business and Community Members

Keep in mind this competency is located within the domain of the school culture but, the eleven competencies are inter-connected with one another. Repeating a quote from John Dunne, "We are all a part of the continent, a piece of the main." The more inclusive environment you can have, the greater the opportunity that you will hit the bull's eye and engage all students in mastery learning. What an exciting thought!

WHAT DOES IT LOOK LIKE? (EXEMPLAR)

This competency (002) is under the domain of school and community culture. It is a sister to competency 001. This competency is related to the development of the vision and mission statement. However, the responsibility of the principal to include stakeholders moves far beyond the boundaries of solely including them in the vision and mission development and implementation process. Keep that in mind as you read this exemplar.

Let us look back at the competency statement: *The entry-level principal knows how to work with stakeholders as key partners to support student learning.* The key parts of this competency are "work with" and "partners" in this process. Our students' success is far too important for the campus principal not to use these critical stakeholders in the process of creating a vision and mission statement.

Early on, it is critical for the entry-level principal to engage with the stakeholders, to create a healthy professional relationship with them that allows the stakeholders to get to know you on a professional level. This takes time, but it will be an investment for you to take that time up front to create within the community of stakeholders that you are serious about success for all students. You will have to work at this by taking notes about individuals in each of the concentric circles starting with the students and working your way out.

Your campus students need to know early on that you are investing in them as learners. You will not excuse anyone from the learning process. Your intention for students is to create a learning environment that produces an atmosphere of success. You do this by including them in creating a vision and mission statement that targets success for all students. This is an important step because what you SAY and what you DO has to match up. Truly, this is where your actions will speak much louder than your words.

Start by meeting with students in small groups and asking them to describe the campus as it is right now with respect to learning and expectations for all students. You do not have to meet with every student on the campus, but be sure you do meet with a good representation of your student body. Be prepared for students who have grown comfortable with you to give you some harsh realities about how students are viewed by the campus administration, teachers and staff. Do not question the comments, but do clarify what they may be saying so you can have an understanding about what the students perceive. Some of it may come as a surprise to you, but you must keep them engaged in the conversation. Take good notes.

Next, you ask the students to explain to you what they *want* the campus to look like with respect to a learning community. You still need to take good notes because you are going to have some run over from the first conversation. Here, you are going to get an idea from the students about what kind of help your students need. An excellent divergent question would be, "How can we help you be a successful student learner?" As you compile your notes from the various meetings with the students, you will begin to get a clear picture of the school's current culture and climate. When students feel comfortable talking with you, they will be brutally honest with their perceptions of student learning.

A word of caution here for the entry-level principal is not to allow the conversation to deteriorate into identifying specific teachers or groups of staff who the students feel may not be contributing to the academic success of students. You want to keep the focus on creating a systemic learning process that eventually creates a vision and mission statement focused on all students achieving mastery.

How many student meetings should you conduct as an entry-level principal for this purpose? There is not a set answer, but there should be enough meetings with the students for you to be able to begin to understand the big picture. In doing so, you begin to have consensus among the different meetings about what the student perception looks like and what students want the learning process to be like. That may be as few as 3-5 meetings or as many as 8-10 meetings. You will know when the conversation begins to sound familiar; you have your consensus among your students.

The next step is to meet in small enough groups with your teachers and staff to create an atmosphere conducive to them submitting to the same scenario of questions about what the current situation is with student learning and what they want the perception to look like. Do not be surprised by their answers, either. Some staff members may mention the amount of apathy in the students towards learning and even try to mention student names. Again, keep the conversation professional and general in nature while moving from the current perception to targeting the ideal situation from the teachers. You want the teachers and staff to be honest and collaborate in creating a vision and mission statement where all students are achieving at a high level of mastery. To get there, you may need to allow some baggage to be cut loose before you can move forward in this process.

As before, you will need to take good notes because all of these notes will come in handy when you go through the steps outlined in chapter one. These notes will also serve you well because you will want to reinforce the thinking process of the teachers and staff on one-on-one conversations where personal clarity is needed without putting the teacher or staff member in an uncomfortable situation. A great fringe benefit will be that many of the teachers will begin to take more ownership in ensuring student success.

The next step is to move to the concentric circle that includes the parents and anyone who would claim guardianship of the students. This is such an important group people who are critical to the process of creating a vision and mission statement. They will appear to be reluctant participants, most likely because some of the parents have been given a narrow path to the school entrance as far as participating in the learning process. Many parents will be reluctant to participate based on their own personal experience with learning when they were in school. It is up to the entry-level principal to create more of an inviting atmosphere for parents.

The campus is the most obvious place for these meetings to take place, but do not limit your options with parents. You may have a community of diverse cultures. It is okay for you to venture out beyond the walls of your campus and meet parents in the community. Churches and community centers are great places to meet. It provides for a more comfortable setting for parents to open up about their current perceptions of the campus learning process.

If your community is diverse, you may need to take a translator with you who can help overcome the language barrier. It is generally a good idea if you can take someone to translate who has a good knowledge of your campus, but it is not a requirement.

Parents should be afforded the same questions and opportunity as the students, teachers, and staff members in working through the issues of the campus with you taking your notes and facilitating the conversation from what *is* to what *is desired*. Parents will be appreciative of your willingness to include them in the conversation.

This will also provide you with a base of support among your parents as long as you walk the talk you had with them. You will do what you say you will do. Once you get to the point where you are meeting with mixed groups of students, staff, parents, central office, and business and community members, your parents will become a significant asset in the process. Remember, it is not just about including your stakeholders in the process, but *doing the process with the stakeholders.*

Central office staff are critical stakeholders as well. You can meet with them to get the same perceptions as you would the other groups. Think about including your Chief Financial Officer in the process, too. You are creating relationships that may pay dividends for you when you get to the part of the process where your budget needs an overhaul. If your CFO is at least familiar with your process, then you have a fighting chance to influence additional funding to help with improving student learning based on your instructional goals.

This central office group should include counselors, diagnosticians, instructional coaches and any other central office staff member that may be visiting your campus in one capacity or another. When they realize you are serious about placing a priority on student achievement, they make mental notes about what you will need when you get to the point of making instructional decisions related to the vision and mission statement and setting concrete, measurable goals.

Do not leave out business and community members. They help pay the expenses for public education. They want to see their dollars at work, but it is much more than just providing them a seat at the table. They can become solid participants and supporters of what you and your campus are trying to accomplish by creating a culture that focuses on high expectations for all students. Give them the same courtesy as you have the other stakeholders. Let them know their input is meaningful and adds to the conversation related to creating a vision and mission statement.

At some point in the process, a portion of all of these stakeholders need to come together to hear the same information as they begin to assist in tweaking the constructing of a meaningful vision and mission statement. Be sure to express your interest in the importance of all the stakeholders and most importantly, communicate that the process does not have a terminal meeting; the process of a developing, implementing, adjusting, and evaluating still demands the participation and support of all stakeholders for effective continuous process improvement to occur.

Finally, this is not a process for one with a timorous attitude about bringing in stakeholders from outside the walls of the campus. If you allow your fear to control your decision-making process about including stakeholders to help craft and implement a vision and mission statement, you will miss the mark. You will also miss an opportunity to build a significant base of support tor your campus. This is not just about creating a vision and mission statement; it is about creating a wave of support for your students that culminates in developing a culture of success.

You must be on the ground and in the lead with this process. You do not view it from a dirigible perspective at 30,000 feet, but more as a fulcrum perspective. You want to move as close to the issues that are being generated out of this process so you can be the point of reference and use the solutions as high leverage points to move those problems out of the way.

It is a messy process and not everyone will be on board with what you are doing. There may be some who will use social media to attempt to discredit or derail your attempts to create a culture focused on student success. However, if your stakeholders see you as genuine and willing to take risks for students, your support will overwhelm the negative talk that may be out there. Be a courageous leader!

A LOOK AT THE INDICATORS FOR COMPETENCY 002

We are going to take an in-depth look at the indicators for competency 002 – The entry-level principal knows how to <u>work **with** stakeholders</u> as <u>key partners</u> to <u>support student learning</u>. There are some definite actions a principal can take to be more than just inclusive, but participatory with stakeholders. Notice in this competency, the entry-level principal needs to work *with* stakeholders in a way that will build trust. The decision to use the word "key" in this competency was by design. As you know, a key is an important instrument to help you unlock a treasure-trove of resources in building partnerships. The entry-level principal understands stakeholders can unlock the full potential of the student learning process. It is a group effort if the goal of achieving mastery for all students is to be achieved.

All of this dialogue points to supporting student learning and achieving high academic excellence for all students. The entry-level principal cannot do this alone. If you play the role of the Lone Ranger, you will soon become the Lone *Stranger* because the stakeholders will soon leave you to your own demise if you do not keep the focus on students. Allow them to become real partners in growing student success.

Here are some examples of how an entry-level principal can stimulate a more inclusive environment for stakeholders:

A. Acknowledges, recognizes, and celebrates the contributions of all stakeholders toward the realization of the campus vision
   - Gives positive feedback to the participants who offer solutions and ideas for creating a vision, mission and student success.
   - Responds in writing to thank the people who were willing to go out on a limb and offer ideas and suggestions.
   - Recognizes people by name publicly for their contributions in the process.
   - Identifies significant submissions and celebrates those by describing how they will add to the creation of a culture that places a high priority on student success for all.
   - You publicly thank members of each of the stakeholder groups for their efforts in helping to identify themes and expectations for creating a culture of success for all students.

B. Implements strategies to ensure the development of collegial relationships and effective collaboration
   - Builds a sense of trust and respect with the staff.
   - Provides a well-designed agenda that outlines the process for questions and input.
   - Understands the unique stages of creating group dialogue and can react to the stages of forming, norming, storming and conforming as they appear in the group dynamics.
   - Commits to generating comments from all stakeholders.

- Allows for opposing views on topics of discussion while giving positive feedback to participants.
- Engages in crucial conversations while helping the person or group to feel comfortable with differing opinions.
- Establishes a process of small group interaction within the group meetings to stimulate more than one conversation at a time.

C. Uses consensus-building, conflict-management, communication, and information-gathering strategies to involve various stakeholders in planning processes that enable the collaborative development of a shared campus vision and mission focused on teaching and learning
- Understand that consensus is a process of building trust, agreement, and takes time. It cannot be done in one meeting. There will be differences based on unclear messages, different sets of values, personalities and even history tied to the topic.
- Begin with the frame of mind that conflict is not negative when managed correctly. Conflict management contains strategies related to effective communication, working openly to resolve disagreements, and becoming a mediator between opposing points of view. It is being able to lead the group to an acceptable compromise that meets the intended goals of developing a vision and mission statement addressing success for all students.
- Communicates using written formats to get your message out to your stakeholders. This could include mail, email, or mass texts.
- Articulates and communicates your message clearly and concisely through oral presentations in front of large, small, and individual meetings with your stakeholders.
- Gathers the correct data such as prior student performance, attendance, teacher attrition rate, teacher attendance rates, student discipline reports, student mobility rates, and any other pertinent data that would allow you to formulate a vision and mission statement to address these areas while focusing on improving student achievement.

D. Ensures that parents and other members of the community are an integral part of the campus culture
- Invites parents to come to the campus to observe the teaching-learning process going on in their child's classroom.
- Moves beyond the customary parent conferences to include them in more meetings and activities.
- Encourages staff to write personal positive notes to students and parents when students are performing well or have mastered a challenging skill.
- Establishes a parent-learning center for parents to come and view the textbooks used in the classrooms and other literature that would benefit them and help their children improve academically. Be sure to have someone explain the resources to them when parents visit the parent-learning center.
- Provides meaningful parent development seminars to allow parents and guardians to grow as learners and as parents.

SAMPLE 268 TExES QUESTIONS FOR COMPETENCY 002

It is time to test your comprehension of this chapter's information. These few questions are only a beginning check for understanding in your knowledge and comprehension process. The real learning takes place when you internalizes the information based on what you are required to do as an entry-level principal.

1. Mr. Riley has just completed an in-depth process of including his students, staff and constituents in creating a vision and mission statement. His campus has collaboratively agreed to kick off the new vision and mission statement announcement with a parent meeting in the evening. Mr. Riley gives his cursory greeting to the group of students, parents, staff, and several business and community members. What should be his next comments?
    a. He makes sure everyone knows where the restrooms are located and reminds everyone refreshments will be served immediately following the meeting.

b. He announces the vision and mission statement and asks for comments.
   c. He explains how many hours he invested into the process and tells the group the campus has arrived at a vision and mission statement.
   d. He publicly thanks members of each of the stakeholder groups for their efforts in helping to identify themes and expectations for creating a culture of success for all students.

2. Mrs. Williams, the new principal of Valley Grove Elementary is about to meet with a group of parents to begin the collaboration process for a vision and mission statement. Her well prepared agenda is ready to go but she realizes that after the initial introductions, before getting started on generating information and ideas regarding a vision and mission statement, she should:
   a. Present information to the group on the unique stages of creating group dialogue and how groups react to the stages of forming, norming, storming and conforming, as they appear in general group dynamics.
   b. Warns the parents not to bring personal problems or issues about their students with teachers to the collaboration process.
   c. Gives an opportunity for each parent to voice their concerns about problems at the school.
   d. Presents her credentials so the groups know about her pedagogy, to establish herself as the group leader.

3. Mrs. Styne is in the third meeting with a group of teachers attempting to come to a consensus on a draft vision and mission statement, knowing that other groups are working on their versions as well. Five of the seven teachers have come to an agreement on a draft of a vision and mission statement, but two teachers are adamantly opposed to the draft statement and will not agree with the group. Mrs. Styne decides to:
   a. Explain the meaning of consensus to the group. Share that not everyone has to be on board with the draft statement. Announce the statement will be proposed to the other groups since a majority of the group agrees.

b. Call a ten-minute break to allow for some think time for the group. This will allow her to privately approach the two individuals to seek their input about what concerns they have regarding the proposed draft. This also allows each to give feedback in order to clear up any perceived misunderstandings.
c. Thank the committee for their work and explain the difficulties of trying to reach consensus with such a difficult topic. Let them know she will move forward with their recommendation.
d. Tell the two opposing teachers in the group meeting that she plans to move forward with the draft and that she expects the two will continue to be supportive of the process.

4. Mr. Chavez, the new principal of Lamar Elementary has noticed a significant lack of parent participation and presence on his campus since taking over as the campus principal. He is concerned because the parents of this high socio-economic campus appear to be reluctant to become engaged in their children's learning process. After consulting with several parents in the community, Mr. Chavez' first step is to:
   a. Personally invite parents at the next parent meeting to come and observe in the classes.
   b. Send a note home with the children inviting their parents to come to school
   c. Convert an extra classroom as a safe haven for parents to come and view the books used in the classrooms and other literature that would benefit them in helping their children be successful.
   d. Contact the central office for help on how to get parents engaged in the campus culture.

5. Mr. Johns has just completed a lengthy but thorough process of creating a succinct vision and mission statement where all of the constituents appear in agreement. Prior to publically announcing the new campus guiding statement, what might Mr. Johns do next?
   a. Print up the new vision and mission statement on large placards. Place in all classrooms and businesses willing to post them in their establishment.

b. Call the superintendent and explain that the campus has a new guiding vision and mission statement.
c. Bring in all of the campus instructional coaches and require them to identify instructional strategies that would directly address the new mission and vision statement.
d. Respond in a handwritten thank you note to the individual participants who were willing to offer ideas and suggestions that helped move the process to its guiding vision and mission statement.

DOMAIN II – LEADING LEARNING (Instructional Leadership/Teaching and Learning)

This is one of the most critical of all of the domains for the campus instructional leader. This domain requires the entry-level principal to demonstrate courageous leadership in many facets of the teaching and learning process. The principal is expected to facilitate collaboratively to develop high-quality instruction that meets the needs of the students for academic success. The principal is the campus instructional leader who holds himself/herself accountable for the success of all students. Therefore, he/she has the right and the responsibility to hold others accountable as well.

Student performance is not left to a default system of principal expectations, but the principal must be an active, participating member of the development of high-quality instruction and the monitoring and assessment of student academic improvement. This means the principal is a visible and participatory member of student engagement in the learning process. The principal observes student and teacher dialogue and discourse with an eye toward improving teaching strategies and processes. The principal engages in professional learning community dialogue on a regular basis to make himself/herself as a resource for solutions to barriers in student learning.

The principal keeps everyone focused on the vision and mission statement to use as a guide to high-quality instruction for all students. The principal demonstrates the level of expectation and commitment to all stakeholders for high academic student achievement.

The entry-level principal knows how to monitor and assess classroom instruction to promote teacher effectiveness. Marshall (2013) states, *"Research has shown that the quality of instruction is the single most important factor in student achievement,"* but principals, especially entry-level principals typically spend the minimum amount of time in the classroom based on the current evaluation instrument and process. A deeper and richer analysis of teaching and learning requires a more systematic approach of short-term walk-through observations with immediate feedback to teachers.

This domain will account for approximately 41%-45% of the 268 TExES Principal Exam. It will focus on the principal's ability to facilitate high-quality instruction while monitoring and assessing classroom instruction. If you do not have a good mastery of these skillsets, then you will have a challenge with the selected response portion of the 268 Exam. It is imperative you learn these skills to help your students and staff to master the challenging curriculum used to assess student mastery at the state level.

Now it is time to begin our deep dives into learning this portion of the principal domains and competencies.

CHAPTER 3
DOMAIN II, COMPETENCY 003

WHAT DOES IT SAY?

Competency 003: The entry-level principal knows how to collaboratively develop and implement high-quality instruction.

WHAT DOES IT MEAN?

It is important for the principal to be invested in the success of students. The process of *doing instructional leadership* is dirty and messy. The principal must be the leader in the process or the culture of the campus will adopt the path of least resistance. This will result in the campus reverting into the routine of complacency if the principal does not assume the instructional leadership role.

The courageous principal will not leave student success to chance with random pockets of instructional classroom excellence. The demands of the structural frame of campus leadership will attempt to push the need for the principal as the instructional leader off the table. The principal, who understands the role, will refuse to allow the day-to-day needs distract him/her from the central goals of improving student success.

The principal as the instructional leader is one who understands that the entire campus including the personnel, the resources, the budget and the staff work together. They do this to achieve student growth through a process of continuous questioning of strategies and assessments. You do this to achieve maximum academic success (See Figure 3.1). This is no small task because this process is fluid with changing students, personnel and budgets. A constant vigilance over the process is necessary to keep headed in the right direction. Just like the captain of a large ship, there will always be course corrections, because the current of prevailing issues are constantly trying to pull the ship off the course it needs to take.

How do we achieve a high-quality instructional process? It is done through a consistent and fluid process of collaboration. Green (2017) stated, "Leadership is a process used by leaders to give purpose to the collective efforts of members of the organization while influencing them to work *collaboratively* (emphasis by this author) in an environment of mutual respect and trust." This definition is a great clarifier for this leadership competency.

How does one recognize high-quality instruction? High-quality instruction is the process of teaching and learning whereby the teacher has significant engagement of the students in the learning process. Rivkin, Hanushek, and Kane's (2000) research highlighted that students who have an above-average teacher for three years in a row outperform students who have a below-average teacher for three years by an entire grade level. The high-quality teacher is in a continuous monitoring process, adjusting strategies as needed. Students are able to model the learning objectives at a high level of mastery.

You cannot *be* an instructional leader unless you *do* the instructional leadership skills and mindsets. It is putting knowledge, skills and concepts into *action* and getting yourself dirty with the work of improving student achievement. Not all of the ideas and strategies will work. Keep trying because that is what you do. If you walk away from this part of your responsibility as a principal, your student achievement scores will wander aimlessly at the mercy of whoever chooses to take the rudder of the ship. The result will be a gamble and most likely, declining scores.

The key words of this *doing* process are **collaboratively develop**. No one person is smarter than the whole group. Start by building a high level of trust and respect in your staff. They want to know you will be there for them and they cannot know that unless they see you as actively participating in the process. You are not an overseer but a participant invested in the process.

Your first thought is you are not an expert. You are right. It is best to admit your shortcomings because the staff already knows them. Join in with them in working to find viable high-quality instructional strategies that raise the bar for all students. You will find that the staff's perception of you will increase with you participation and honesty.

Figure 3.1: Collaboration is the process of submitting ideas to challenges to arrive at the best possible solution.

WHAT DOES IT LOOK LIKE? (EXEMPLAR)

Competency 003 comes under the umbrella of the LEADING LEARNING domain, not the WATCHING LEARNING domain. You are the campus instructional leader. Before you begin to meet with your staff, you want to make sure your data resources are ready to go for the staff to review and analyze. Do not limit your resources to the state assessment results. You need to include teacher assessments, discipline data, teacher and student attendance, teacher attrition rates and any other information that may influence student performance. You would best serve your campus if you could provide the data from at least the past three years. This will give you a better look at repetitive concerns on which you and your campus can focus.

Using your professional learning groups, ask your staff to **collaborate** and describe what high-quality instruction looks likes for your campus. It is important to have a mental picture of what student success looks like. Give the staff time to invest in what they believe needs to happen to achieve high-quality instruction. This task is important to do prior to investing time in analyzing the data. This will help teachers have a sense of what resources they will need to achieve success and close the gap between what is, and what is desired.

You will monitor each of the groups as they begin to formulate their perceptions of high-quality instruction, especially what it looks like in the classroom. Be careful here to participate but not dominate. Your participation demonstrates your investment in the staff and students.

Once the professional learning communities have had the time to create a sense of high-quality learning, you will bring them together to share their perceptions. You will encourage them to **collaborate** in creating one or two descriptive paragraphs of what high-quality instruction looks like for your campus. Marshall (2013) states that, "Research has shown that the quality of instruction is the single most important factor in student achievement." Your responsibility is to ensure the group **collaboratively** reaches a consensus on what high-quality instruction looks like based on some measure of your understanding of collaboration. It is important to use guiding questions to keep the focus on your goal.

Now, it is time to distribute the data to the staff and begin to identify the crucial areas of concern in student achievement. However, do not stop there. Every result has a root cause. This is where the additional information from the data may come in handy. Inform the staff this part may get messy. Remind them to keep the focus on the processes and not people. Everyone can get better when we remove the barriers of failure. Complete this process in your professional learning communities as well. The smaller groups promote more participation since they are used to being together. You will monitor and participate in these groups, encouraging **collaboration** as they work through the data. This will take some time. Just know the groups will come back with differing opinions about what they believe are the areas of concern.

It is important not to overwhelm yourself and the staff with too many critical issues generated through this process. This part of the process is where your leadership abilities will come into play. Not all of the issues generated are going to be resolved in one calendar year. In the large group, give each of the smaller groups plenty of time to share their issues. Be careful not to eliminate or be overly concerned about what is communicated at this point. The large group dynamics through **collaboration** and your monitoring will lead to identifying the two or three critical issues to address for the year. Be sure to allow all the groups to participate. Give them time for discussion, **collaboration**, and consensus.

You become essential at this stage of the process. It is necessary to convert the two or three critical issues into well-defined, measurable goals. Not only that, but it is necessary for the staff to see the connection between the goals and their perception of high-quality instruction.

This part of the process becomes more meaningful and impactful. Ask the PLC groups to describe what these learning goals look like in the classroom using their definition of high-quality instruction. You can begin to see this in not a half day staff development and then, go on your way process. This is about asking staff to identify who they are and what they do to improve student success.

All of the research based instructional strategies and teaching processes identified are useless unless they connect to the curriculum that is aligned with the state standards. In addition, both of these must be connected to the assessment piece as well.

Moreover, how about campus and district-based assessments? Are your curriculum, teaching and learning, and assessments aligned? This responsibility is not passed off to some district coordinator. Anytime you relinquish your responsibility of the campus instructional leader to another, you open the opportunity for gaps in student learning.

Staff needs to understand and be cognizant of the critical alignment of these three components. The process of critically evaluating and analyzing the compatibility of these three components is called triangulation. If staff do not see the connection between the three components of curriculum, instruction in the classroom and assessments, then you will continue to have gaps in learning. This will impede student academic success.

The PLC groups are where this constant review of the connective parts are kept intact. The PLC members meet on a weekly basis to review the progress of students based on the identified goals of the campus by using the research strategies and practices to keep the focus on student improvement. You monitor and participate in the PLC groups on a regular basis.

It is important to have a strong framework for how an effective PLC works. Eaker, DuFour, and DuFour (2002) have developed one of the stronger frameworks for establishing effective PLCs. PLCs begin by asking the right questions and the questions they propose are:

1. What do we want students to learn?
2. How will we know what students are learning?
3. How can we assist and support students in their learning?
4. What can we do to improve student learning? And,
5. How can we recognize and celebrate improvements in student learning?

When the campus professional learning communities begin with these essential questions, the PLC develops the framework for improving individual student achievement. This gradual improvement of the process begins to show successes, and teacher attitudes shift to a higher expectation level.

You share with the staff on a continuous basis the resources available. You serve as an advocate for your campus with district personnel and the community. This means you will do battle for any available resources at the district level that will help your staff achieve the identified instructional goals.

Your job as the campus instructional leader is never finished. Student achievement always remains a fluid process. Your response to the changing needs to improve student success will determine your effectiveness as an instructional leader who is consistent about student achievement.

A LOOK AT THE INDICATORS FOR COMPETENCY 003

The principal has to be a good communicator to collaboratively develop and implement high-quality instruction. All the competencies and indicators for this domain are meaningless unless you are willing and able to participate with your staff individually and collectively through effective communication. Any conversation that may have an effect on you or the other person is considered crucial. Patterson, Grenny, and others (2012) state that crucial conversations are, "A discussion between two or more people where (1) stakes are high, (2) opinions vary, and (3) emotions run strong."

These indicators assist the principal in achieving improved student success through a campus who is collaborating and working together. This process requires constant communication while improving the quality of instruction the students receive. Collaboration for high-quality instruction means you will implement these indicators. Be cognizant these indicators are not distinctly separate and apart from each other. In fact, most of them are integrated. Some of the suggestions for principals are used in multiple indicators.

1. Prioritizes instruction and student achievement by understanding, sharing, and promoting a clear definition of high-quality instruction based on best practices from recent research
    - Invest in the process of how to communicate effectively with others on an individual and group basis.
    - Develop a personal understanding of what high-quality instruction looks like in the classroom.
    - Create a media process that allows you to effectively share the campus instructional strategies.
    - Promote the high-quality instructional strategies and support the teachers and staff as they implement them to improve instruction.
    - Participate in PLC groups regularly to support campus staff in effective teaching practices.
    - Become a researcher for teachers; helping them to identify high-quality instruction practices.

2. Facilitates the use of sound, research-based practices in the development, implementation, coordination, and evaluation of campus curricular, co-curricular, and extracurricular programs to fulfill academic, development, social, and cultural needs
    - Assists in providing outlets for researching resources that allow teachers to research and compare research-based strategies with measurable curriculum indicators.

- Helps with the development of a framework to plug in the strategies with the measurable student outcomes.
- Provides a platform to show teachers what the research-based strategies look like when staff presents them in the classroom.
- Ensures the PLC groups have a time to discuss those strategies during their collaboration, to determine the effectiveness of those strategies.
- Provides opportunities for open discussion on the strategies as they relate to cultural norms and differences.
- Develops a generic evaluative instrument that assesses the usefulness and success of the strategies implemented.

3. Facilitates campus participation in collaborative district planning, implementation, monitoring, and revision of the curriculum to ensure appropriate scope, sequence, content, and alignment
    - Encourages campus leadership teams to participate in collaborative planning with the development, implementation and monitoring of curriculum at the district level.
    - Provides a defined process for use in evaluating the process of planning, implementing and monitoring the curriculum at the campus and classroom level.
    - Provides written frameworks for each step of the delivery and assessment of the curriculum to allow for immediate course corrections at the classroom level.
    - Provides opportunity for individual face-to-face feedback on the curriculum and processes used, both informally and formally.
    - Participates in all aspects of the curriculum implementation process on a daily basis.

4. Implements a rigorous curriculum that is aligned with state standards, including college and career-readiness standards

- Promotes education beyond the high school level. This begins when students begin school.
- Evaluates the current curriculum with the next level curriculum, to ensure alignment and success at the next level.
- Provides strategies that challenge students' learning mindset, to improve their capacity for learning and supporting them in mastering the more rigorous curriculum.
- Creates personal expectations for staff and students that encourage continuous and life-long learning.
- Models life-long learning by continuing personal learning. Shares with staff, new insights.

5. Facilitates the use and integration of technology, telecommunications, and information systems to enhance learning
   - Becomes familiar with the latest technology available for staff and students.
   - Encourages the use of appropriate technology within the scope and sequence of the curriculum.
   - Provides funding sources for technology hardware and programs used to promote student academic success.
   - Promotes ongoing training of current and new staff on how to use the technology programs more effectively.
   - Promotes communication that is more open with parents using current technology programs available.

SAMPLE 268 TExES QUESTIONS FOR COMPETENCY 003

1. Mr. Pepper has successfully served as the disciplinarian of a junior high campus. He was promoted to principal of another junior high in the district that is struggling with meeting the minimum standards on the state assessments. If the campus does not show significant academic improvement the next year, the campus will be placed on "Improvement Required" status. Although Mr. Pepper demonstrated his

capabilities as a disciplinarian, he has participated very little on the academic side of school leadership. The first thing Mr. Pepper should most likely do is to:
   a. Begin reading the top two or three books on instructional leadership. Be prepared to respond to staff questions.
   b. Start accumulating all data on students and staff that affects student learning from at least the past three years. Familiarize himself to what the data is beginning to tell him.
   c. Hire an instructional improvement firm to come in and complete a staff development day on improving student scores.
   d. Phone a friend in the education business and ask this person to develop a school improvement plan for him to introduce to his staff on the first day they return.

2. Ms. Wright has just completed a rigorous morning with her staff developing a perception of what high-quality instruction looks like through a process of collaboration and consensus. The teachers participated in some small and large group discussions. Three well-respected staff members finally agreed upon the consensus after some lengthy discussions. She and the staff are excited, but exhausted after a full morning. However, she does not want to let this learning opportunity to pass by with the group going to lunch, so she decides to encourage the staff to go to lunch together in small groups to think about the next step in the process. The next thing she most likely will ask them to think about is:
   a. How will each staff member demonstrate high-quality instruction in the classroom?
   b. What kind of data do they need to help them identify the two or three measurable instructional goals for the next school year?
   c. Should PLC meetings be required of all teachers?
   d. How should they promote their new vision of high-quality instruction to their students, parents, and the community?

3. Mrs. Johns has been facilitating a meeting with her staff in small groups wrestling with how to convert critical learning issues with students in math and reading for the past hour. Several of the groups have been confused on how to write measurable goals for these two areas. One of the issues is many of the staff members do not assist in these two areas and believe they should not participate in creating those goals. Other members are not sure what Ms. John means by measurable goals, so the initial language in their drafts appear ambiguous. Discovering this after completing her participation in most of the small groups, she decides to:
   a. Call the groups together and provide some training on how to write measurable goals by giving some clear examples and touching on the important aspects of goal writing.
   b. Invite the groups to take a 20-minute break. Afterwards, come back and try to tackle the task.
   c. Bring the small groups back together and explain that since they are struggling with this part of the process, she will draft some instructional goals for their approval.
   d. Leave the staff in small groups, but address them as a whole and encourage them to continue working until they have strong instructional goals to present to the whole group.

4. Mr. Powell is pleased with the collaborative sessions he had with his staff and they are excited about the direction they are taking with the three new measurable instructional goals for the year. Mr. Powell's next step should most likely be to:
   a. Ask the staff to keep these goals posted somewhere in the classroom, to review them weekly with the students.
   b. Ask the staff to identify what research-based instructional strategies related to the goals would best serve their students in achieving success.
   c. Create committees to communicate the new direction the school is going in with the new strategies.
   d. Write personal notes of gratitude to the team leaders for their facilitation of the meetings.

5. Mr. Grant completed his third round of attending the PLC meetings for his campus. He is excited about the new instructional goals and the fact teachers are participating in the PLC process. However, Mr. Grant is concerned about the lack of discussion regarding the new learning goals and how they are taught in the classroom. Mr. Grant's decides to:
    a. Send a letter out to his staff reminding them PLC meetings need to focus on teaching strategies related to the learning goals.
    b. Pull in the PLC group leaders and inform them they are not performing their duties as group coordinators. Give them verbal instructions on how to talk about strategies in the classroom.
    c. Allow for more time for the PLC groups to formalize their norming processes before becoming too concerned.
    d. Formulate a plan to ask some guided questions to the groups at their next PLC meetings that would stimulate conversations about using instructional strategies in the classroom.

CHAPTER 4
DOMAIN II, COMPETENCY 004

WHAT DOES IT SAY?

Competency 004: The entry-level principal knows how to monitor and assess classroom instruction to promote teacher effectiveness and student achievement.

WHAT DOES IT MEAN?

This competency also falls under Domain II: Leading Learning. The principal's major responsibility is student academic success. The principal cannot walk into the classroom without some background and knowledge of the connection between the three main components of assessment and student achievement. These include an identified curriculum, classroom instructional strategies that directly correlate to the curriculum, and assessment instruments. These are used to evaluate what teachers want the students to know, understand, and apply from the curriculum. As indicated earlier, these three areas provide a triangulation of processes and information to increase the chances of success for students.

First, we need to break down what curriculum means. There is not a well-defined description upon which scholars agree, but the principal needs to have a working concept as a foundation for understanding to move forward with helping teachers teach from a curriculum perspective. Curriculum is a set of knowledge, values, beliefs, ideas and critical information divided into various academic disciplines; the staff wants students to learn and apply to be successful, responsible citizens of a collective society.

This is a broad spectrum from which to create a specified curriculum, but all curriculum evolves from these general building blocks. Curriculum development advances from the question, "What do we want students to know and learn?" The state develops, with teacher input, much of the curriculum for the local districts. Interestingly, the curriculum development may not be the first step in the process. There are two pervasive views on the process of curriculum development. One process is called frontloading. The other is termed back loading.

From the perspective of frontloading, educators determine what they want all students to learn at specific grade levels and disciplines. Then, they create a curriculum they will use to identify a scope and sequence of instructional strategies to prepare students to take assessments related to the curriculum. Hence, the term frontloading the curriculum, since the process begins with what information students need to know at each level.

The other process of back loading a curriculum begins with creating a series of assessments by which to evaluate student performance. Once these assessments are established, educators develop curriculum to address the assessments. Then, the teaching strategies are created to connect the assessments with the curriculum.

Most states and school districts have moved to the process of frontloading the curriculum. These become the basic learning expectations to build the other two processes. It is a continuously evolving process because curriculum changes as our knowledge and understanding of the world around us changes, especially in the areas of career and technology courses.

The second focal point is the identification and implementation of research-based teaching strategies. The strategies connect to the curriculum developed and those strategies help teachers present the curriculum in a way that allows students to master the standards. The more the instructional strategies can engage students, the greater the possibility of success for students to participate in the learning and demonstrate proficiency of the intended curriculum. These strategies help teachers visually connect the critical attributes of the curriculum to the student learning.

Teachers and administrators are educational physicians. As with any person who is ill and needs an attending physician, what works for one person may not work for the next. Medicine is a process of individualized testing, diagnosis and prescription.

The teaching process is not too different from that of the medical field. Teaching strategies that work on some students may not work on other students. Teaching using research-based strategies is a process of elimination. There are many reasons for this phenomenon. Students come from varying backgrounds and cultures. Societal issues and concerns contribute to dysfunctional student learning. Therefore, teachers must be prepared to use a plethora of teaching tools in their skillset to reach and teach students. In many cases, the teachers must address the individual needs of the student prior to any effective learning taking place.

The successful administrator is one who encourages teachers to be instructional risk-takers, based on the research of good instructional practices others are using to overcome the challenges students face. This type of "action research" creates opportunities for sharing the results with other members of the professional learning community. The effective principal will encourage teachers to become active researchers because students will benefit from this process. It is important for principals to support teachers when the action research may not achieve its intended results. Continuous action research promotes high-quality teaching and student growth.

Finally, the third part of the triangulation process is the assessment piece. There are two major forms of student assessments, formative and summative. Teachers use the formative assessments as an evaluation **for** learning to determine the amount the amount of knowledge and degree of mastery the students have achieved at a particular point in the learning process. Effective teachers use the formative process of learning on an ongoing daily basis with quick learning checks and brief large-group evaluations. Teachers use these formative assessments to make course corrections in their teaching process to reteach and to gain maximum learning from their students.

The summative assessment is the assessment **of** learning, usually presented at the end of the objective cycle. It gives teachers and administrators a summary of student mastery for the curriculum taught during that cycle. Final exams and state assessments are good examples of summative assessments.

Principals should be keenly aware of the connection between the assessment tools and the teaching strategies. Education has moved beyond the stage of mystery testing. There is too much information students are required to learn to make the process of assessment more difficult than it has to be for them. Do not hide information nor make the path to learning an ambiguous road. It is the responsibility of principals and teachers to provide seamless learning for all students.

So, what does all of this mean? The principal is the learning leader. He/She serves as an instructional support to assist teachers in locating and using the most effective instructional strategies for the identified curriculum. The principal is an advocate for connecting instructional strategies to the identified curriculum. They ensure teachers are providing appropriate checks of student learning, to make continuous and ongoing adjustments during the learning process.

Figure 4.1 gives a pictorial example of the connection of these three components and student achievement. The more closely connected these three components become, the greater the opportunities for mastery of the intended curriculum.

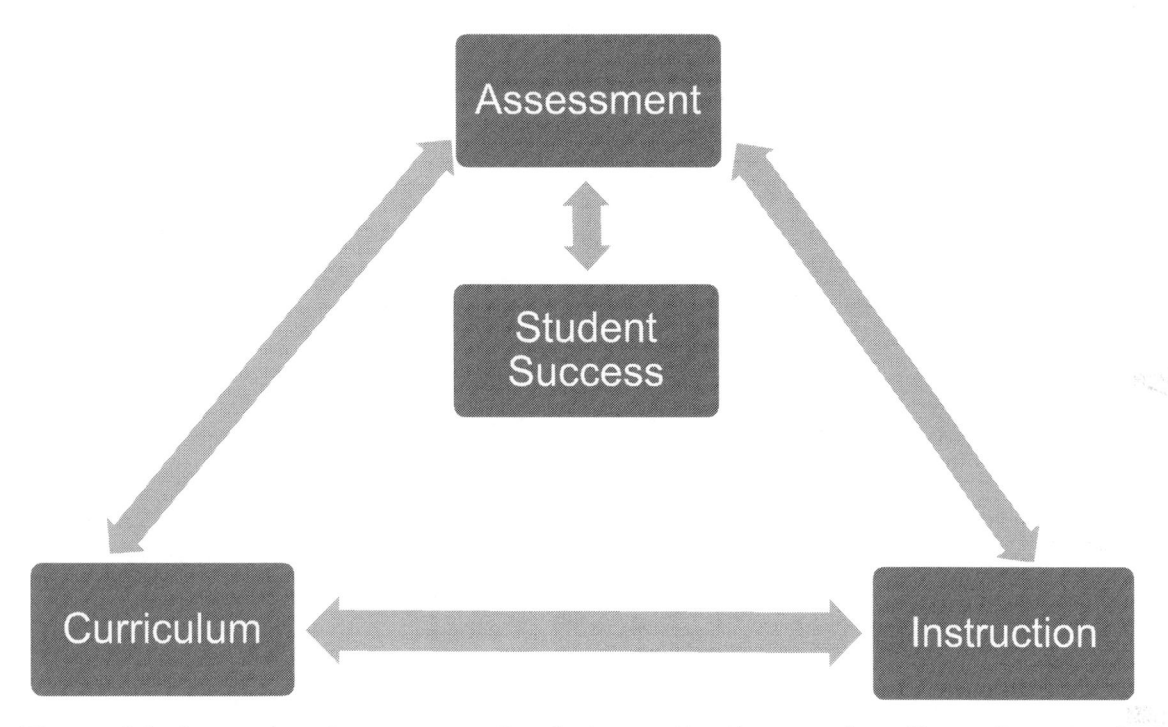

Figure 4.1 shows the close connection between the three major pillars of academic achievement that are curriculum design, instructional delivery and student assessment.

Figure 4.2 gives another view of the relationship to the three pillars of student achievement with the use of the pyramid. It begins with a strong foundation of a well-designed curriculum. At the local level, teachers work closely with district curriculum staff to take the curriculum and create a scope and sequence by dividing the curriculum into learning chunks. They develop a timeline to present the information to students in an organized sequential order. Here is where the instructional strategies need to be content specific to the identified curriculum.

Assessments are ongoing and focused on effectiveness of the strategies as they relate to the curriculum. Teachers provide daily checks for understanding. Campus teachers generate their own formative assessments for students during the process.

Districts regularly provide learning checks through campus-based assessments, to evaluate student progress toward mastery.

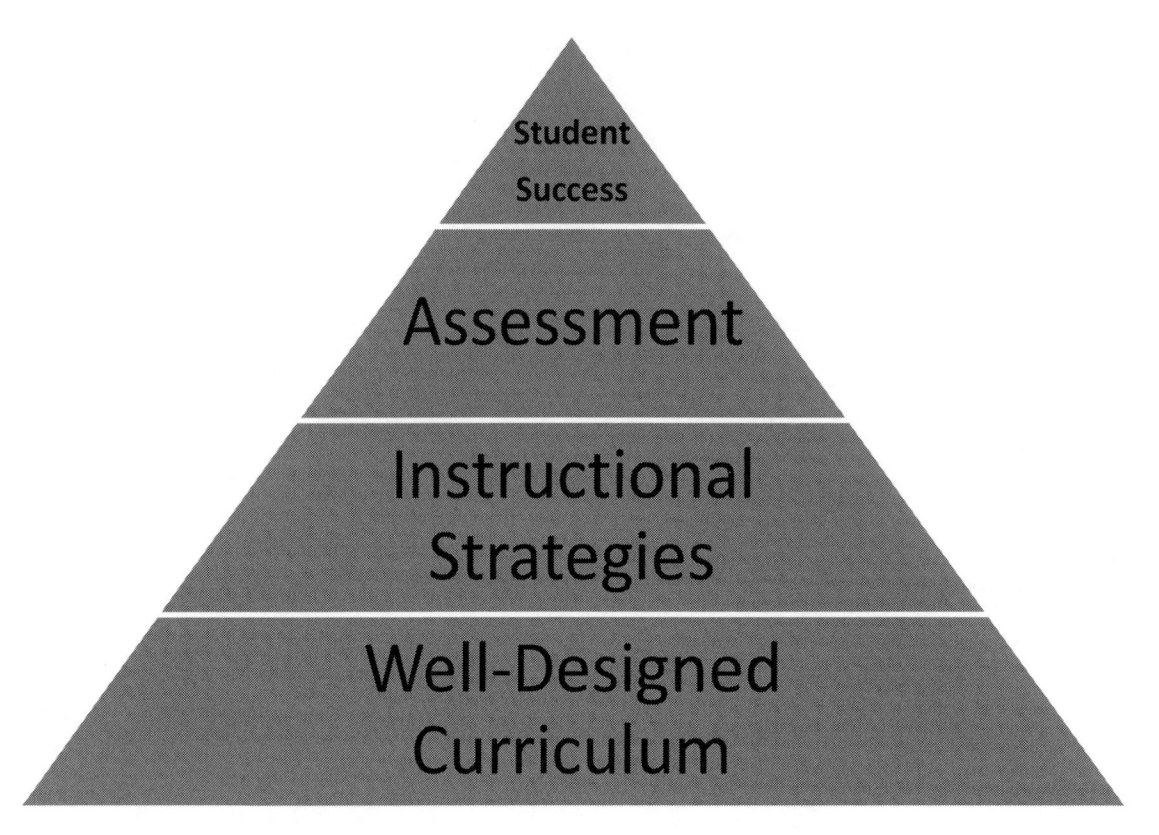

Figure 4.2 shows the building blocks for student success: A well-designed curriculum, instructional strategies, and assessments that all produce student academic success.

WHAT DOES IT LOOK LIKE? (EXEMPLAR)

Competency 004 comes under the umbrella of the LEADING LEARNER domain, not the WATCHING LEARNING domain. You demonstrate your effectiveness as a learning leader by monitoring and assessing classroom instruction in order to promote teacher effectiveness and student achievement.

The principal monitors teacher instruction on a routine basis. To do this, you will create a walk-through calendar that focuses on visiting teachers a minimum of once every three weeks. Your walk-through observations will focus on the interaction between the instructional strategies presented, student engagement and comprehension. You will meet briefly with the teacher in her classroom during the teacher's conference at the earliest possible time to give the teacher positive feedback and to ask guided questions when you have a concern or need clarity. You will complete this part of the process by adding a note to the observation file for end-of-year evaluation and provide a copy of the note to the teacher.

The principal attends professional learning community meetings on a regular basis to provide support and encouragement to the PLC members. You participate when you see a need by asking guided questions when you are unclear of the direction the PLC meeting is taking. When the meeting is over, you take notes to add to your personal file to keep your memory fresh on what was discussed. You do this so you can follow-up on any needs the PLC group may have expressed and give them feedback on their concerns.

You are the gatekeeper for the identified curriculum so you periodically monitor the connection between the curriculum with the scope and sequence. You observe the presentation of the curriculum using the agreed upon instructional strategies. In short, are you doing in the classroom what you said you would do in your PLC meetings?

The principal helps teachers find research-based strategies that directly address the scope and sequence of the presented curriculum, when teachers and PLC groups struggle with identifying those strategies. You monitor the discussion of the effectiveness of those strategies in the PLC meetings. You help individual teachers whose students may not be achieving success on the same scale as other teachers who are presenting those strategies. You provide constructive and positive feedback when teachers make the necessary corrections to improving instruction. You use those improvement models as examples, strengthening the teaching process for all students, to build a community of learners.

You collaborate with teachers to find new strategies when you or the teachers discover a gap or disconnection between the curriculum and current teaching strategies or the curriculum and assessment. You work closely with teachers to find new strategies and to rewrite assessments to meet the demands of the curriculum. You evaluate the scope and sequence to determine the effectiveness of the alignment to the curriculum.

The principal assists teachers when there is a challenge between the teaching and learning process and social and/or cultural concerns or behavioral conflict. You provide resources for teachers to overcome the social, cultural, and behavioral barriers.

You are responsible for helping teachers to use data responsibly so they can analyze it to improve student mastery. Assist the teachers in peeling away the layers of data to help them formulate next-step actions for improving student achievement.

The principal meets with teachers in their PLC groups to identify the gaps in student learning and participates in formulating plans of action to close those gaps with effective teaching strategies. You assist in helping teachers to locate and implement research-based strategies that will close those gaps.

The principal dedicates time for teachers to review and analyze teacher-made formative and summative assessments to determine the effectiveness of the teaching and learning process. You collaborate in helping to determine the validity of the assessment questions as they relate to the teaching process and the curriculum.

In summary, this domain is one of the most important domains for the principal as the instructional leader. You are the one who is ultimately responsible for student learning. Unless you play a major role in leading the learning, the campus will struggle with student achievement. Lead from the front!

A LOOK AT THE INDICATORS FOR COMPETENCY 004

This domain and especially this competency is excellent rationale for principal candidates to have experience in helping campuses to overcome the challenges of instructional delivery and student mastery. The main purpose of having assistant principal roles is to provide a training ground for eventual principal roles. This would include allowing assistant principals the opportunity to lead instructional groups while still serving in the assistant principal role. There are many skills to learn. It is unfair and unwise to ask an inexperienced person to step into the leadership role of the principal without practicing these indicators in the field.

Principal candidates need to become familiar with the suggested practices to go with each of the indicators to demonstrate mastery. As with learning how to perform any function, the entry-level principal demonstrates mastery at a high level of acuity over time through practice. No baseball player ever batted a thousand and no basketball player hit every free throw. Neither will you hit the mark every time you try implementing these indicators. Do not quit applying them and give yourself grace as you attempt to master these indicators.

A. Monitors instruction routinely by visiting classrooms, observing instruction, and attending grade-level, department, or team meetings to provide evidence-based feedback to improve instruction
   - Creates an observation checklist of instructional strategies and behaviors to observe in the classroom.
   - Provides appropriate and timely feedback to teachers in a non-threatening manner.
   - Participates in professional learning community meetings on a regular basis as a member of the group.
   - Uses guided questions to help PLC groups to stay on task by focusing on student learning and mastery.
   - Serves as a resource for PLC groups when they do not have options for locating research-based instructional strategies.
   - Locates examples of good instructional strategies from various research-based sources.

B. Analyzes the curriculum collaboratively to guide teachers in aligning content across grades and ensures that curricular scopes and sequences meet the particular needs of their diverse student populations (considering sociological, linguistic, cultural, and other factors)
   - Collaborates with teachers and staff on breaking down the data into its simplest components for evaluation.
   - Assists staff in understanding what the data means in terms of student performance.
   - Provide a number of data points to assist teachers in identifying criteria that influence student success.

- Generates data resources such as commercial programs that help to disaggregate the data into manageable information.
- Assists the teachers in evaluating the alignment of the curriculum with the scope and sequence as well as from grade level to grade level.
- Provides opportunities for staff to fill the learning gaps found in the curriculum with research-based strategies.
- Assists the staff in overcoming cultural and societal barriers of learning by seeking out learning tools and programs that bridge these gaps.

C. Monitors and ensures staff use of multiple forms of student data to inform instruction and intervention decisions that maximizes instructional effectiveness and student achievement
- Demonstrates to staff how different forms of longitudinal data can help identify gaps in student learning.
- Provides instructional programs to assist staff in ways they can intervene with students who may be learning at a slower pace.
- Assists in helping staff to understand how cultural and social differences may be inhibiting student learning and how to overcome personal bias by staff.
- Communicates often about expectations of student mastery for all students.
- Models how teacher-made assessments are used to evaluate teacher effectiveness and making changes in the delivery of instruction.

D. Promotes instruction that supports the growth of individual students and student groups, supports equity, and works to reduce the achievement gap
- Creates additional learning time in the day to assist students who are struggling with academic mastery.
- Provides before and after-school learning opportunities for all students who need or want additional help with mastering the curriculum standards.
- Assists in locating and implementing technology that would provide additional support for student learning.
- Trains teachers in recognizing cultural learning gaps using research-based books and resources to close the learning gaps.

- Participates in identifying learning gaps in students using campus professional learning communities.

E. Supports staff in developing the capacity and time to collaboratively and individually use classroom formative and summative assessment data to inform effective instructional practices and interventions
   - Creates time within the professional learning community meetings to develop teacher capacity to evaluate formative student responses.
   - Models identifying student performance gaps with the PLC groups while searching for research-based instructional strategies to implement to close those gaps.
   - Creates a fault-free zone in the PLC meetings to allow for open dialogue and solution-finding activities to close the achievement gap.
   - Develops processes to assess the results of formative and summative student performance. Analyzes the effectiveness of instructional teaching strategies connected to the stated curriculum.
   - Encourages and supports individual active research by teachers to promote improvement of the teaching and learning process.

SAMPLE 268 TExES QUESTIONS FOR COMPETENCY 004

1. Mr. Williams, the campus principal, has been participating in the fifth grade professional learning community meeting. The teachers are struggling with teaching a specific instructional strategy. There are five teachers and two aides in the group. Nearly every one of the members have a different perception of what the critical attribute of the learning statement means. The result has been differing student performance on the formative assessments. To help the teachers to formulate a common understanding of the skill to be taught and learned, he decides to:
   a. Bring in an instructional specialist from the district to tell them what the critical attribute of the learning objective means.

b. Allow them to work it out themselves knowing they will eventually figure it out in a few meetings.
c. Ask them to submit their perceptions in written form to him for review. He will get back to them for an answer on how they should teach the information.
d. Guide them to review what the formative assessment is evaluating on this particular learning objective. Encourage them to work backwards to determine the best strategies to allow for student success on the assessment using their current student performance data.

2. Mrs. Penn, the campus principal, has observed the same instructional presentation in several classes. She noticed the teaching strategies covering the objective are entirely different from class to class. Mrs. Penn asked each of the teachers why they are not using the agreed-upon strategy. The response from each teacher was basically, "We decided to select our own strategy because we were not comfortable with the one selected." After pondering over the teacher responses, at the next professional learning community meeting, she decides to:
   a. Present the agreed upon strategy in writing and instruct the teachers to reteach the lesson using the agreed upon strategy.
   b. Do nothing. As long as they are teaching the skill, it is fine.
   c. Use guided questions to lead the teachers to the understanding they are to present the material using the agreed upon research-based instructional strategies.
   d. Pull in an instructional specialist from the district to reteach the professional learning community on the importance of using the agreed upon strategy.

3. Mrs. Vincon, the campus principal, comes in to a professional learning community meeting a little late due to meeting with a parent. When she arrives at the PLC meeting, she observes a deafening silence in the room. When Mrs. Vincon inquires about what is going on, the members in the meeting express their frustration with how to go about identifying instructional strategies that accurately teach to

curriculum objectives. They are all looking to her for answers. Mrs. Vincon decides the best way to support them is to begin by:
   a. Asking them to open their district-provided laptop computers, as she opens hers, and encouraging each of them to search the internet by entering how to teach the objective identified. When the teachers come up with ideas, guide them in discussing the best strategies to use for the learning objective.
   b. Telling them to skip the issue for now. Ask them to go on to the next item on their agenda. Explain she will get back to them with some kind of answer.
   c. Directing them to keep searching because she knows they will figure it out eventually.
   d. Asking each person to write their name on the paper and give a brief description of how they might teach the learning objective. Have each person fold the paper and place it in a small box. Draw a name out of the box and use their idea for teaching the objective this time around.

4. Mr. Martinez has served as the building assistant principal for a number of years. The campus was excited to learn of his promotion to building principal following the retirement of previous principal. He was grateful for the mentorship of the previous principal, but did not agree with her on how to monitor the pulse on what was going on in the classroom and the professional learning community meetings. The previous principal used a firm hand with autocratic decision-making when it came to student performance and the teaching/learning process. As a result, the teachers were unwilling to go outside of the boundaries of the accepted delivery process. The student performance scores were acceptable, but not great. There are students not being adequately served. There are many gaps in the learning. To help improve the chances for all students to learn and to begin closing the identified gaps, the principal decides to:
   a. Take a laissez faire position toward this issue the first year or two until he can get his feet on the ground as the principal.

b. Encourage the teachers to continue to meet in their PLC groups. However, inform them they have free-reign on how to teach the learning objectives so they can improve student achievement.

c. Train his teachers on how to use action research to improve student achievement. Encourage his teachers to be instructional risk-takers while communicating the results to the professional learning communities and making improvements to the instructional strategies.

d. Do not do anything with the student achievement scores since they are okay, until he has had a chance to visit with the campus leadership. Let them decide whatever they want to do and let them run with it while he works on mentoring new teachers.

5. Mr. Snodgrass has been working closely with his campus professional learning communities. He has been pleased with the progress they are making, focusing on student achievement rather than other nonessential topics unrelated to student mastery. However, his past two visits with the sixth grade team indicated no discussion related to the formative assessments that have been given over the past couple of weeks. After reflecting on the situation, Mr. Snodgrass decides to:

    a. Create time within the professional learning community meetings to develop teacher capacity to evaluate formative student performance.

    b. Allow them more time to figure out the process on their own for a few more meetings before intervening.

    c. Pull in the PLC group leader to direct the leader to adhere to the specifically approved agenda.

    d. Collaborate with other building principals on the best way to handle the situation and then, address the problem.

DOMAIN III – HUMAN CAPITAL (Human Resource Management)

The *Human Capital* Domain is the domain that challenges the entry-level principal to utilize his/her personnel to achieve maximum student performance. The use of *Human Capital* is the ability to know individual skillsets, understand people's talents and direct them to the areas that will achieve the most effective results.

One of the frames of cognition Bowman and Deal (2017) promote for educational leaders is that of the Human Resource Frame. The entry-level principal must utilize all areas of this frame to help teachers and staff achieve academic success.

Bowman and Deal (2017) promote two main dimensions within the Human Resource frame. The first is the *supportive* dimension and the successful entry-level principal will demonstrate the following characteristics: Shows support and concern for others.

1. Shows genuine interest in others.
2. Is responsive to others.
3. Is approachable to others, and
4. Gives recognition to others for a job well done.

The other aspect within the Human Resource Frame is the *participative* dimension. The characteristics of this part of the Human Resource dimension is are:

1. Fosters collaboration and participates involvement in decisions.
2. Listens well and attuned to what the speaker is saying.
3. Is open to new ideas, and
4. Is highly participative in the learning process.

In brief, the entry-level principal, as a new campus leader, participates in the learning and growth process of the teachers and students, creating an environment of life-long learners. These are action verbs and the entry-level principal is expected to be a working cog in this machine called improving student achievement. The entry-level principal is a participant in the learning process. Maximizing *Human Capital* means changing mindsets to understand learning is a continuous process because knowledge about how to best teach learners never stops changing.

It is recognizing your *Human Capital* that is continuously changing. The entry-level principal must have guidelines and processes in place to train new staff and students on learning expectations and procedures. This calls for effective new teacher orientation programs that have built-in performance measures, which allow the new staff to demonstrate understanding and proficiency prior to stepping into the classroom. Most districts have some form of new teacher orientation, but most of those focus on policy and procedures rather than high-quality teaching. Your responsibility is to ensure your new staff understands their expectations for student learning and growth for students and staff.

CHAPTER 5
DOMAIN III, COMPETENCY 005

WHAT DOES IT SAY?

Competency 005: The entry-level principal knows how to provide feedback, coaching, and professional development to staff through evaluation and supervision, knows how to reflect on his/her own practice, and strives to grow professionally.

WHAT DOES IT MEAN?

The principal remains the campus instructional leader throughout all of the domains and competencies. Within this particular competency, the principal leads the staff by providing formal and informal feedback, coaching the teachers on instructional delivery strategies, participating in and leading professional staff development by reflecting on his/her own growth and decision-making processes in these areas of leadership. To understand these characteristics, we need to take a deeper dive in what all of this means.

The principal is able to provide appropriate feedback. This comes through the process of formal and informal communication. Emphasis on communication is important in building and maintaining relationships on your campus to improve instruction. This is especially important when providing feedback. Let us investigate a few informal methods of feedback. Bear in mind, they can occur at any time and place within the physical school campus and outside the building. When you become a campus principal, you are the principal of that staff 24/7. The constituents believe they can approach you at any time with a question or concern.

Informal feedback is ongoing and when talking to the staff throughout the day. This feedback provides clear information and direction into a topic or issue. Much of the time, these opportunities for informal feedback do not require any form of written documentation unless it involves working with a low performing teacher. It comes in many forms. Here a just a few examples;

- Daily encouragement. Staff need to feel supported when the expectations are high. They feel most supported when the principal is encouraging them.
- Staff development training results. Staff want to know your thoughts on all staff development training and that you are a full participant. These are great opportunities to provide informal discussions on the usefulness of the training.
- Comments from parents or other staff members. Share comments from parents or other staff members in a non-threatening manner to achieve change and improvement. You measure informal comments to others are against the expectations of learning for staff and students.
- Recognition from administration. Genuine informal praise in public stimulates personal support for the staff member and encourages positive results. While the negative comments tend to get our attention, it is important to be intentional in sharing positive feedback.
- Approval from co-workers and supervisors. Staff need to know it is okay to proceed with classroom decisions regarding student achievement.
- Exceeding set performance targets. Giving credit to staff when they meet and exceed performance standards.
- Mentoring advice for new staff. Give advice, tips, suggestions, and guidance for new teachers and staff to improve student performance in the classroom.
- Clarification of learning directives or expectations. This is a two-way communication between the principal and the staff member. The objective is to ensure teachers meet appropriate learning expectations in the classroom.
- Explanation of campus routines or policies. Use informal feedback to correct misunderstandings of current policies or procedures.

The list of examples can be never ending. The important part for the principal is to utilize these opportunities as informal opportunities for growth with the staff. This requires the principal to be fully engaged in the daily routine of student learning. That expectation translates into visibility of the entry-level principal. Staff and students need to see you as a participant of student learning. You are, after all, the campus instructional leader.

Formal feedback is exactly what it says. Formal feedback takes places in a more formal setting with fewer or no other people around except for the person receiving the information. This type of feedback requires a written copy of information to be saved in either an electronic file or a hard copy (or both) for providing a summative evaluation of the person at some time in the near future. This information could be positive or negative. What determines whether it is formal or informal feedback is the nature of the facts as it relates to student performance and safety.

Formal feedback should always have a set of clear expectations with an opportunity for the staff member to improve or correct the behavior. This means there should be a clear timeline as to when the corrective action is completed with an open conversation between the principal and the staff member during the process.

Here are just a few examples of formal feedback:

- Comments from scheduled walk-through observations.
- Addressing validated refusal to follow school policies by the staff member.
- High performance that requires documentation for evaluation.
- Low performance activities that require immediate corrective action.
- Mentoring new staff on how to provide evidence of performance.
- Responding to parent or community concerns.

Feedback by the principal is very important. It provides course correction and information to help everyone clearly understand the vision and mission of the campus. It provides the principal with the opportunity to lead by example. No one will follow unless the principal is willing to lead. That takes time and commitment on the part of the principal to provide continuous, constructive formal and informal feedback.

Coaching is another important aspect of Competency 005. Many current principals are either unwilling or unprepared to step into the coaching responsibility because of other pressing demands of the principal. The process of coaching is just what it implies. The principal takes the time to review a teaching action of a classroom teacher, then explains and models the expected behavior in the classroom. Coaches do this all the time in their different sports fields. They show their athletes how to perform a specific task. Then, they ask the athlete to demonstrate it back repeatedly until there is mastery. The classroom is no different. The principal is the campus instructional coach. The more you demonstrate your ability to lead in classroom instruction and have healthy dialogue, the more classroom instruction will improve.

Classroom coaching is not a drive-by procedure. It is a process of continuous observations, guided questioning, and modeling. You are demonstrating, practicing, and improving the teaching performance. Yes, this takes time, but when principals have teachers improve, then they do not need to spend as much time with higher performing teachers. Principals can spend more time with newer and struggling teachers. Successful principals do this on a continuous basis. It matters to the staff and students when the principal is engaged in improving the capacity of existing human resources. The principal is not expected to know everything, but he/she is expected to be an active participant.

When plants are not fed or cared for properly, they wither and die from lack of sunlight and nourishment. When plants receive the appropriate amount of water, nutrients and sunlight, they flourish. That is not a great revelation to most of you, but this same principle also applies your campus staff.

Successful principals provide the appropriate amount of professional development to allow staff (and self) to grow into productive educators. What is the appropriate professional development? Professional development is appropriate when it assists the staff in reaching the identified campus instructional goals. The professional development clearly addresses the issues that close the gaps in student learning and mastery. Professional development includes training in technology targeting the specific learning objectives of the campus. This takes time and resources by the principal to plan, design, and implement staff development that addresses those needs.

Professional development assists in helping teachers (and self) grow in the areas of learning for them to keep apprised of what types of research-based strategies are out there to help students master learning. It is providing the training and the opportunity to implement the newfound knowledge in a classroom setting. Professional development is also providing the coaching, supervision and the implementation of the professional development strategies and programs.

This professional development is ongoing, continuous, evaluative, and cyclic. It is ongoing because the expectation is the training promotes improved student achievement. It is continuous because it builds upon previous professional development and training to come. It is evaluated formally and informally to improve upon the strategies and programs from professional development. This is done to make campus decisions whether to continue a specific professional development if it is successful or to discontinue because it did not address the campus goals.

The next area of managing *Human Capital* is evaluation and supervision. The principal can see the connectivity of all of the previous topics under this competency. Feedback, coaching, and professional development all support the process of evaluation and supervision. Most of the school districts in Texas have adopted the state tool, Texas Teacher Evaluation and Support System, otherwise known as T-TESS™. This system, as well as locally developed and adopted systems, provide a framework for assisting and supporting teachers in improving their teaching skills. The T-TESS™ evaluation and support system contains four domains: planning, instruction, learning environment and professional practices and responsibilities.

The principal uses this framework or a locally developed and adopted framework in managing *Human Capital* to improve the teaching process so students will achieve mastery of the stated curriculum. It all works together to focus on helping students succeed. Teachers have to be successful for students to be successful. Moreover, the principal is the leader in personal growth.

This process requires leadership courage by the principal to successfully navigate and make decisions about staff and continued employment. The focus is on student achievement and the principal has applied the principles of sound judgement through coaching, feedback, professional development and evaluation. Finally, the principal must have the courage to counsel low performing staff away from teaching if they are unwilling or unable to improve.

Evaluation comes by a series of observations throughout the year. These observations provide opportunities for feedback, coaching, and supervision with open dialogue. Most teachers and aides who are poor performing, and continue to struggle without improving are not surprised when you begin to counsel them into resigning their current position. This part of the process is never easy or enjoyable, but necessary if the principal is going to improve instruction and advance student achievement.

The visual below in figure 5.1 summarizes the impact these indicators have on managing human resources and improving the teaching process. They are all important in achieving the goal, which is student mastery.

To help keep all of these *Human Capital* characteristics moving in a positive direction, it is important for the principal to develop a process of personal reflection as part of his/her own personal growth. This process is an investment by the principal that takes some time in the beginning, but actually saves time over the long run. It is a process of formally guiding yourself through a set of questions to determine whether past decision-making processes were appropriate, accurate and if improvement in those decisions can be made.

Consider it a method of reverse systemic thinking in order to help the principal to grow into a more effective systemic thinker. The principal is able to consider several steps ahead and reflect on what the repercussions are for each of those steps in the decision-making process.

What are the steps the principal takes as a reflective thinker? First, principals informally think reflectively throughout the day by performing simple mental analyses of decisions they make in the course of their routine. Unfortunately, many practicing principals stop there. The growing principal completes a more formal process of his/her decisions toward the end of the workday. In addition, they take the time to record those decisions as to what they could do to improve on them. When the principal writes those improvement possibilities, then he/she makes incremental growth.

Here are some examples of guiding questions a principal can ask himself/herself at the end of the day when wanting to engage in a reflective activity:

- What were my major decisions of the day?
- What were my perceptions of how people or individuals reacted to those decisions?
- What are some other ways I could have handled those decisions?
- What are the expected consequences of my decisions, both good and bad?
- If I had the decisions to do over again, would I change any decisions?

- If I have decided that one or more of the decisions can be improved upon, is there a corrective action I can take now to remedy the situation?

The end of the day becomes hectic with parents coming on campus, students leaving, buses loading and many other activities. The principal needs to visible and available to parents and staff during this transition. However, it is vital for professional growth to carve out some time at the end of each day to complete this reflection process. Your day may be a little longer; however, your future success will be greater.

Of course, the principal can ask himself/herself many more questions when reflecting on the decisions of the day. The important aspect of the process is that you do it. The other very important part of the routine is you record your thoughts. Transferring the information from your brain to paper (or computer) reinforces your thought process. It releases you from having to remember every detail.

Finally, review your written reflective thoughts at the end of the week. This is a slow growth process, but you will begin to see how much you improve in your decision-making and you will minimize your mistakes. Call it the beginning of wisdom.

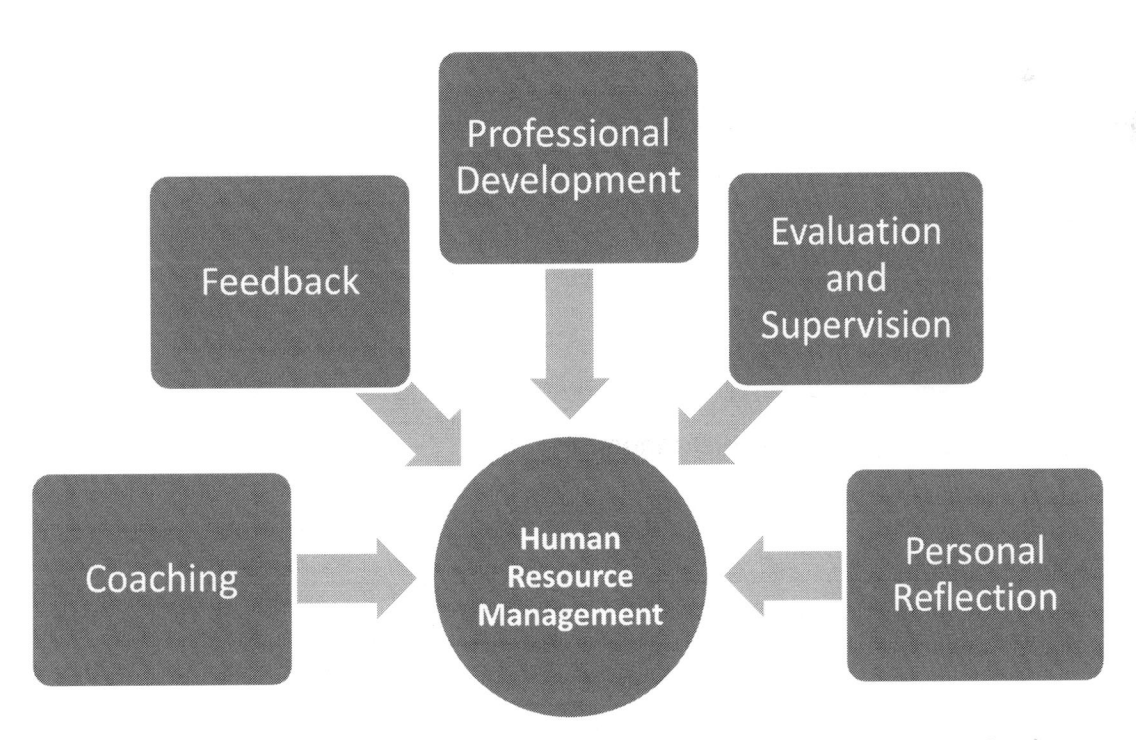

Figure 5.1 shows the connection between the characteristics of Competency 005 with Human Resource Management.

WHAT DOES IT LOOK LIKE? (EXEMPLAR)

There are an unlimited number of ways to create an exemplar for Competency 005. The objective of including an exemplar here is for you to obtain a clearer understanding that this competency is very real. It is applicable on a daily and continuous basis. The intent of the entry-level principal for reading this section is to get a visual of how important this competency is and to be intentional about applying it.

1. You arrive on your campus an hour before the students and staff because you will utilize this time to take care of the structural frame issues and the paperwork, before the arrival of most of the rest of the staff.

2. During this time, you take care of any priority emails not addressed before you left school on the previous workday.

3. You also review the summary of disciplinary issues and attendance concerns compiled by your two assistant principals before they left their work on the previous day.

4. You jot down a few notes to discuss with them at your morning meeting.

5. You go over your inbox and make a decision about what to do with the information. You do your best not to keep any existing work in your inbox for a later time.

6. Your two assistant principals arrive to meet with you for your fifteen minute regularly scheduled meeting. You listen to them give brief reports in their areas of responsibility. You ask questions related to your review of their previous day's reports and allow them the opportunity to clear up any issues or concerns.

7. You strive to finish the meeting within at least fifteen minutes so you can greet students prior to the start of school. You target students who require your attention to reinforce good behavior and study skills.

8. During this time, you also ask students relevant curriculum questions based on the instructional discipline and the student grade level.

9. You are aware of these general curricula because of your investment and continuous focus on your vision and mission statement as well as your schedule of daily walk-through observations and feedback.

10. When the passing bell rings to begin the school day, you continue to greet students as you make your way to the office.

11. In the office, you pick up a copy of your walk-throughs and observation schedule for the day.

12. Before leaving the office, you check with the secretary to ensure she has a copy of your observation schedule and is able to contact you only in cases of emergency.

This will be a typical instructional emphasis day for you because you will be doing 3-4 walk-though observations and a full 45 minute observation. You are looking forward to this day, because your pre-observation conference the previous day went very well with the 7th grade pre-algebra teacher. She was able to give you a clear outline of the teaching objectives and strategies using the elements of instruction to plan her lesson. To facilitate the pre-observation conference, you utilized the Bambrick-Santoyo (2012) blueprints for leverage leadership. You understand that the purpose of instructional leadership is not to evaluate teachers, but to develop them based on Bambrick-Santoyo (2012) strategies. Accordingly, you help the teacher finalize her presentation. In doing so, you focus in on two leverage points that should help the teacher get the most out of the teaching strategy. This is where you will direct most of your attention.

During this pre-observation conference, you ask questions that allow the teacher to think about her goals and how she is going to present them to the class. You also talked about the presentation of the new information including the steps she would take to model the performance of mastering the new information. You inquire about how the students will practice modeling mastery of the information. You also inquire about what type of scaffolding, if any, would be used to assist the students in learning the new material. You both were able to agree that the leverage points will focus on student independent mastery. You agree upon, through a series of questions and responses, the best research-based strategies for independent mastery. You explain exactly what you would be looking for and how you would be evaluating the student performance. Although there was some disagreement on what constituted student mastery, you were able to work through the disagreements and move to an acceptable conclusion to the conference.

You finish the pre-observation conference by thanking the teacher for her dedication to excellence and willingness to improve. She thanks you for the input as you leave her classroom to go back and summarize your notes. You add the specific notes to your daily observation schedule for this teacher and you send her a summary of the pre-observation conference. In the summary, you ask her to correct you if there is any information not communicated correctly.

When you leave your office, you survey the halls of the campus, to ensure all students are in the classrooms and preparing for the day. The two assistant principals are completing the same task. This gives you a chance to engage with them while helping to get school started with students in class. It also allows teachers the opportunity to speak informally to you about school-related topics. You patiently listen, respond to those concerns, and take note of the issues that need more direct attention.

After teachers have had time to provide time-on-task and warm-up activities to get students engaged in the learning process, you begin one of your walk-through observations. This particular teacher struggled on a previous walk-though with distinguishing between an essential knowledge and skills and a purpose for a learning objective. In a previous walk-through, the teacher had simply posted the essential skill on the board, which in itself was not a bad idea, but the teacher fell short in explaining to the students the reason students needed to be able to master the specific skill.

Your most recent one-on-one and written communication with this particular teacher helped the teacher understand the difference between the two. You both agreed that this would be the leverage point for your next walk-through observation. You communicated in both verbal and written form, that you would look to see if the teacher used the suggestions and ideas generated from the previous meeting to generate an appropriate objective or reason for learning the material in the day's lesson.

In your fifteen-minute observation, you sit in the back of the room until the teacher presents the essential skill and explains the objective for needing to learn the skill. You give positive visual cues to the teacher to affirm the appropriateness of this portion of the presentation while you are viewing and listening to student responses to the explanation. The teacher moves directly in to the presentation of the skill. There is not a moment for you to speak with the teacher, but you give the teacher a thumb's up as you leave.

After leaving the classroom, you make some informal notes on your pad as to what you observed and how the teacher used the previous meeting's information to improve on creating a more meaningful objective for student learning. You are pleased with the teacher's response to growing professionally and make a note on your notepad to that effect.

You have approximately 15-20 minutes before the next period begins, so you walk through the campus. You use your schedule to note who has a conference during this period. You use this time to make informal visits to those teachers and check in with them about any support and resources they may need. This process serves as a benefit to the principal and the teacher. For the principal, this is a good opportunity to serve as an encourager and support for the quality teachers. It also serves as an opportunity to help lower performing teachers seek out additional support and resources. You have learned to always take good notes and to respond to any issues or concerns in a timely manner.

Just prior to the end of the period, you check in with the main office, to make sure there are no immediate needs or concerns. You have trained the office staff to defer as many issues and concerns as possible to the assistant principals. However, they also understand to refer any issues that need your attention, to you.

While classes are transitioning to the next period, you are in the halls, engaging with students and staff. Students know to be prepared to answer knowledge and skill questions. You can call most students by their first name because you help monitor students in the cafeteria and the student-learning center when they are at lunch.

The next period begins. This happens to be the day on your schedule when you sit in on the professional learning community for English Language Arts. Part of mentoring your two assistant principals is for them to sit in once a week on the learning discipline they agreed to monitor and provide assistance as needed. You take the remaining disciplines.

When you enter the teacher's room who is holding the PLC, they have already begun and you immediately sense a culture of professionalism with a focus on student learning and success. The teachers possess an agenda that highlights student learning and mastery successes as well as teacher instructional concerns. The teachers have been sharing student successes and the lead teacher is complimenting everyone for the input received. A teacher is writing a summary of the meeting and will send it to the principal's office by the end of the day.

Teachers quickly move to the agenda items listed with one of the items being a formative campus-based assessment. They discuss the results of student performance. One of the four teachers is excited because the students were able to grasp a challenging learning objective, while the others did not get as favorable a response from their students. The discussion turns to the teacher whose students' showed more progress. The teacher begins to dissect her instructional delivery. They find out she used a scaffolding procedure that really supported the students' mastery of the essential learning skill. The teacher proceeds to share how she utilized the scaffolding technique and then slowly took away the steps in an order that allowed the students to remain successful.

The other teachers determined to reteach the essential learning skill using the teacher's scaffolding technique, but wanted the teacher to demonstrate the technique before they retaught the skill. The group agreed to meet later in the week during their common conference period to observe how the teacher presented the learning skill.

The teachers move on to the additional agenda items, all of which focused on student learning. One of the upcoming lessons require a search of the internet and mobile lab. Unfortunately, the science department has reserved the lab for the three days that the ELA department needs the lab. The teachers turn to the principal for direction. After a few questions, you approve the use of student personal technology for that specific part of the lesson, only. The teachers agree they will closely monitor the student use of the technology.

After the second period, you return to the classroom of the teacher you observed during the first period and you quickly go over your notes from the walk-through observation. You congratulate the teacher on the improvement of the lesson objective explanation and inform the teacher you will put the comments in written form. The comments will be placed in the teacher's campus mailbox. You finish the conversation by thanking the teacher for applying the comments of the previous observation to the daily presentations.

You do not have time to check into the office in between classes because the next period you are completing a full observation of the pre-algebra teacher. You are able to enter the class just as the students are beginning their warm-up activities, which consist of reviewing concepts previously learned. You observe the teacher walking around the classroom at this time, assisting students who raise their hand for additional help. After about five minutes, the teacher signals the students to focus their attention at the front of the classroom to begin a summary of the warm-up review and to begin the day's lesson.

During this time, you are taking brief notes of what is taking place, including the appearance of student engagement in the process. You continue to take copious notes throughout the class period noting the essential teaching elements modeled, how the scaffolding was used, and the types of instructional strategies used to help students grasp the new learning concept.

When the teacher moves to the concluding part of the lesson, you focus your attention on the leverage points discussed in the pre-observation conference. You give attention to how the teacher assigns and presents the skill for students to practice independently. Your knowledge of independent practice is grounded in your study of Archer and Hughes' (2011) work noting independent practice allowing students the opportunity to demonstrate the skill with a high degree of accuracy. You note that the teacher utilizes the leverage point agreed upon by directly tying the independent practice to the skill that was introduced, modeled, and demonstrated during the lesson. The teacher uses a quick check for understanding technique during the independent practice and verifies a high percentage of the students are mastering the critical skill introduced. You observe the teacher providing additional support to a few students who were struggling with mastery of the critical skill. You get out of your seat to get close enough to hear the conversation between the teacher and the students. It is apparent the students have been redirected. There is evidence the students are more at ease with completing the independent practice.

Just prior to the end of the class period, the teacher brings all of the students' attention to focus on him. He begins a brief summary of the learning that took place during the class session. He includes a review of the critical skill, the purpose for learning the skill, how the skill was demonstrated, and a summary of the guided and independent practice. Students are reminded unfinished independent practice is due at the beginning of the period the following day. The passing bell rings.

While the students leave, you approach the teacher and give him a high-five for the lesson he just presented. You can tell the teacher is exhausted, but pleased. You give him a 60-second summary of the observation and provide praise for his dedication to students. Before leaving his room, you remind him to come by your office approximately 20 minutes after the end of the school day.

You are the principal and this is how your days will look ONLY if you consider yourself the "principal as the learning leader" for your campus. All of your subjective decisions about instruction may not be completely accurate, but as you practice and experience the daily routine (which is routine), you will become better at what you do.

You continue your day by being visible in the cafeteria and talking to students. You ask about their school day while you talk about learning objectives. No, it is not an easy process for you to be fully engaged with your students during lunch, especially when they are reluctant learners, but it is your responsibility when students express negativity.

During the remaining school day, you complete the additional walk-throughs. You continually check in with the office and take care of any priority responsibilities you can while still keeping the focus on the vision and the mission. This also includes checking in with your two assistant principals to get feedback from them on how their day is going.

During one of the afternoon periods, you go to your office to review your walk-through and observation notes. You provide a summary write-up for the walk-through observations and you place those in the teachers' boxes. You have already talked to them after the walk-throughs, so you just provide a written documentation for their records. You place the same notes into their file for use in making an exit report on their summative evaluation.

You summarize the observation notes from the full observation. As you are looking at your notes, you create 3-4 divergent questions for the teacher, to allow the teacher to respond. These non-invasive questions should open up a good dialogue about the lesson and may prove to be a leverage point for improving the already great presentation.

You finish your school day by checking with the main office to see if there are any critical issues you need to address. Since there are none, you glance in on your two assistant principals and get a thumbs up from each of them.

You continue to walk the halls and visit with teachers during their conferences. You are able to gather information you need to address with a couple of aides who are at odds with each other. You check your schedule. You do not have an observation or a walk-through scheduled for the first period the next day, so you will notify them to visit with you during that period. You will visit with the two in the morning to help them to resolve their differences and shoot a note of thanks to the teacher who brought it to your attention.

By now, the school day is ending. The students are exiting the building to their waiting parents and busses or to walk home. You make it a point to be visible to as many parents as possible. You visit with as many as you can and intentionally compliment the student in front of the parent whenever possible. This action helps to develop a sense of safety and support in the minds of the parents. It lets them know you have a relationship (know) with their child.

When you get back to the office, the teacher you observed is waiting for you, and you apologize for being a few minutes late. You direct the teacher to the conference room used for conferences such as these. It is equipped with a whiteboard and other resources that allow you and the teacher to replicate parts of the lesson as needed.

You begin the post-conference by congratulating the teacher on a well-presented lesson. You thank him again for his good preparation. At this point, you allow the teacher to respond in any manner the teacher wishes until the teacher has exhausted his response. It is your turn to focus more specifically on the presentation and results.

You use your diverse questions you developed based on the lesson to allow the teacher to respond and think more critically from a self-evaluation perspective. From your questions and the teacher's responses, you are able to generate some plusses you had not observed, but recognized occurred. The teacher also raised some instructional issues that may have been handled differently and could have added to the success of the lesson. You both jot those ideas down. The teacher makes a note to use the information in a way that will improve the delivery of the lesson the next time he presents the critical attribute. You note the teacher made a self-assessment to improve on an already good presentation.

During the course of the conversation, you cover all of the domains of the evaluation process. The teacher is pleased with your overall review of his performance. You inform him that a copy of the evaluation will be put in a sealed envelope and placed in his campus mailbox for him to pick up in the morning. You remind him to sign and return the necessary forms to your office in another envelope you will provide for him.

When the teacher leaves, you look at your watch and realize the post-conference lasted longer than the actual observation, but it was a productive conference. You exit the conference room and make one last check with the secretary to see if there are any messages or issues you need to address before she leaves. She gives you a few phone messages you will need to return before leaving.

Before leaving, you go to your office and finish the write-up for the observation you made earlier. You include the additional information from the post-conference as appropriate. You complete the evaluation by complimenting the teacher's presentation and the success on the leverage points on which you both agreed to focus. You note the areas of improvement in the lesson that can be made based on the teacher's self-assessment. You sign, date the report, and make a copy of it for the teacher to keep for his records and you place the information in the sealed envelope with the instructions for signing and returning the document to you.

It is about an hour and 40 minutes since the students have left school, but you are not quite done. Before completing your self-refection of the day, you take a quick survey of the campus, to see who is still in the building. This will provide you with another opportunity to visit with any teachers still available. You visit briefly with those who are there and thank them for their preparation for the next day's lessons.

Back in your office, you review your written messages given to you by your secretary. You address those through phone calls and emails. Most of the messages are handled quickly, but a few take some time for you to think about before responding. You read and re-read the emails prior to sending them out, to check for spelling errors, tone and whether the message is communicated clearly. You understand the email message can be shared with many other people, so you want to be sure of your communication before sending the message.

Now, it is time for you to complete your personal reflection. You go through a list of questions you created to help you complete a self-assessment of the day's decisions and actions. A *few* of the questions you ask yourself are:

- Did I listen with my ears and my body language when people were talking to me?
- Did I respond to all of my constituents in a professional manner?
- Did I treat each person with the same degree of respect and attention with which I would want to be treated?
- Did I do what I said I would do with pending action items?
- What decisions did I make that had positive outcomes?
- What decision did I make that had negative or unintended outcomes?
- Did I miss an opportunity to support learning through a kind word or note?
- Do I need to apologize to anyone for my responses, lack of responses, tone of responses, or body language?
- What will I do differently to become a better person and learning leader?

You summarize your self-reflective activity in your personal notes and review them one last time before you close the file. The summary includes actions you will complete on the next day, to improve your personal and leadership skills. It is now two and a half hours past the time the students left school. You turn the lights out in your office. It is good to head home. This is an exceptionally good and rare day because you have no extracurricular activities you need to attend.

A LOOK AT THE INDICATORS FOR COMPETENCY 005

Performing these indicators on a routine basis will enhance the principal's position as an instructional leader who is focused on improving student achievement for all students. This process requires planned commitment to serving as a support for teachers and staff, while making the hard decisions that improve the process of student mastery. These suggestions are only a few of the many more you will discover on your own and use to reinforce the teaching-learning process.

A. Communicates expectations to staff and uses multiple data points (e.g., regular observations, walk-throughs, teacher and student data, and other sources) to complete evidence-based evaluations of all staff
- The principal utilizes every means possible to professionally communicate your expectations for student learning and what that means. This includes, but is not limited to:
    1. Producing written documents of instructional mastery expectations with respect to student learning that are directly linked to the vision and mission of the campus.
    2. Discussing these goals in all campus meetings and encouraging staff to publically report the successes they are having.
    3. Using multiple sources of data from teacher-made tests, campus-based assessments and state assessments to determine student performance and identify instructional strategies to reteach material, as necessary.
    4. Utilizing parent newsletters to reinforce learning expectations to your parents and constituents.
    5. Using your campus website to focus on your vision, mission and improving instruction.
    6. Talking to local civic groups to encourage support for your teachers and students in the learning process. (Be prepared to respond to questions regarding needed resources, because civic groups usually will be responsive to the needs of students.)

7. Visiting with teachers and staff in small groups and individually, about what they are doing to move the pendulum of student success in the right direction.
8. Establishing a calendar of walk-through observations on all teaching staff and sticking to the schedule as much as possible. This includes taking time to provide verbal and written feedback to the teacher after every observation.
9. Evaluating individual teacher and student data to stimulate dialogue on how the teacher can improve the teaching strategies and student achievement.
10. Utilizing pre- and post-conferences to help create a culture of teacher development in the evaluation process.
11. Creating generic pre- and post-observation questions to help with divergent conversations. The principal uses those conversations to focus on agreed upon issues and concerns.

B. Coaches and develops teachers by facilitating teacher self-assessment and goal setting, conducting conferences, giving individualized feedback, and supporting individualized professional growth opportunities
- Provides non-threatening settings for conducting pre- and post-conferences.
- Encourages teacher response time to the divergent questions. This allows the teacher to perform reflective thinking on the teaching process and to identify areas of improvement.
- Assists the teacher in identifying teaching improvement goals based on student data, principal walk-through observations and teacher input.
- Includes positive feedback on all informal and formal conferences. The principal allows the teacher to identify what went well in the observation and areas of possible improvement.
- Serves as a resource in helping each teacher to improve teaching skills by providing appropriate staff development, research-based articles and other resources to help develop the teacher's teaching skills.

C. Collaborates to develop, implement, and revise a comprehensive and ongoing plan for the professional development of campus staff that addresses staff needs based on staff appraisal trends, goals, and student information/data.
- Works with PLC teams, leadership teams and other small teacher groups to design and implement staff development that targets the instructional goals for the students.
- Provides a system of on-going evaluation of the staff development. The principal makes the changes as necessary, to improve the staff development presentation.
- Uses longitudinal agreed upon instructional goals to help establish the staff development for the campus. This data to establish the goals includes a review of the essential elements for learning, state assessments, campus-based assessments, teacher-made tests, student discipline data, attendance records, teacher attrition, and the student mobility rate.
- Uses teachers and staff to review the comprehensive staff development through anonymous evaluations and small groups, to make changes in the comprehensive plan.
- Creates a communication process related to the staff appraisal system that enables an open flow of information to from the principal and teachers.

D. Facilitates a continuum of effective professional development activities that includes appropriate content, process, context, allocation of time, funding, and other needed resources
- Assists in creating research-based staff development ideas that focus on the instructional issues and concerns of the teachers.
- Provides the teachers and staff with the opportunity to improve teaching skills.
- Provides time within the school day to offer teachers with appropriate staff development and training.
- Serves as a resource and an advocate for finding the materials needed to allow teachers to present the instructional strategies.

- Finds creative ways to fund teachers who need additional resources to implement the teaching strategies.

E. Engages in ongoing and meaningful professional growth activities, reflects on his or her practice, seeks and acts on feedback, and strives to continually improve, learn, and grow
    - Reads books and articles on how to improve the teaching and learning process. Share those ideas that are appropriate, with teachers in PLC settings and individually.
    - Understands the concepts of the teaching process and is able to hold conversations with the teachers about the instructional delivery.
    - Develops a personal process of reflective thinking and recording that allows for growth over time.
    - Demonstrates through his/her own learning process that he/she is a life-long learner.
    - Shares personal learning growth with the staff and they are able to see the learning in action throughout the day.

F. Seeks assistance (e.g., mentor, central office) to ensure effective and reflective decision making and works collaboratively with campus and district leadership
    - Meets on a regular basis with a trustworthy mentor he/she has enlisted who has the experience and wisdom to assist the principal for guidance and instruction.
    - Establishes good relationships with central office staff. The principal utilizes their leadership on critical issues in their areas of expertise.
    - Works collaboratively with central office staff to create a connection between the campus vision, mission, and goals, as well as the central office's resources.
    - Recognizes he/she is part of a larger team of administrators and works closely with others to achieve the campus goals.

- Serves as an advocate for the campus to the central office to vie for the limited resources of the district.

SAMPLE 268 TExES QUESTIONS FOR COMPETENCY 005

1. Mr. Poppins has just completed a day of working with teachers through several walk-through observations and a full observation that included a post-conference meeting. Although the conversations were good, Mr. Poppins was not entirely pleased with all of his decision-making. He also had parents who were upset because he was not available during the day as a result of his schedule. Before leaving for the day, the last thing Mr. Poppins decides to:
   a. Write a couple of encouraging notes and slip them into the teachers' school mailboxes.
   b. Walk around the building to make sure the building is cleaned and ready for the next school day.
   c. Take some time to complete a personal reflection activity and make some electronic notes on what he could do differently.
   d. Go to the teachers' lounge and visit with any teachers who may be left at school.

2. Ms. Jarratt has been writing emails back and forth with the central office over the past week. There does not seem to be a clear understanding about what Ms. Jarratt is expecting for a fourth grade Reading position at the mid-term. Candidate application résumés have not met the criteria established by the campus leadership team who will be conducting the interviews. Ms. Jarratt's best option is to:
   a. Make a personal visit to the central office and discuss face-to-face with the person identifying applicants, what she and her leadership team are looking for.
   b. Write another email restating the specific details of the campus expectations for the applicants.

    c. Call the superintendent and explain the lack of cooperation she is receiving from the personnel office.

    d. Realize the personnel office is doing what they can and just go with the pool of applicants they give her.

3. Mrs. Graves has been evaluating the data analysis of all the relevant data the campus staff performed prior to leaving for the brief summer break. The goals set were well stated, measurable and they fit into the vision and mission of the campus. The campus staff was excited about the growth over the past year, but understood the importance of the continuous improvement process. Mrs. Graves best next best step is to:

    a. Ask teachers to give up a few days of their summer break to come in and plan for opening activities to begin the school year.

    b. Begin developing an agenda with a list of possible resources that can be used to conduct staff development once the teachers report back to school.

    c. Tell the central office instructional coaching department what her needs are and leave for the summer break.

    d. Begin interviewing qualified teachers for the positions that she has open so her staff will be full for the next year.

4. Mr. Bishop is fully involved with coaching his teachers using the full skillset of instructional tools he has used over the past several years. One of his fourth grade writing teachers approaches him in the hall with a request to complete some action-based action research project she would like to try on her students that is relevant to the instructional goals for the essential elements in writing. Mr. Bishop is aware that the past two projects completed by the teacher did not end up contributing to improved student achievement. He responds by:

    a. Telling the teacher his batting average with action research projects is too low for him to take another chance on this new action research endeavor.

b. Telling the teacher it is not the time and place to be discussing new instructional strategies and for him to set an appointment with the secretary to talk about it more in-depth.
c. Asking the teacher if he has discussed the request with the professional learning community to see if they are in favor of him completing the action research.
d. Asking a few questions about the action research project and encourage the teacher to move forward. Explain he is looking forward to hearing about the results.

5. Mr. Ramirez is the new principal of a struggling campus that has been below expectations on student performance for the past several years. The previous principal who recently retired seemed to let things coast along during his final year. Mr. Ramirez has many instructional changes being applied since the teachers have not been held accountable for student learning. One of the first best steps for him to do during staff development is to:
    a. Assure the teachers and staff he does not intend to replace any of them because of the transition.
    b. Break the staff up into groups and go on a scavenger hunt to find out what is wrong with the building facilities.
    c. Be open and honest. Explain that since this is his first year as principal, he will not be able to assist them much with instruction.
    d. Communicate with the staff his expectations for improving student achievement, how he will utilize walk-through observations, formal observations and feedback to support the process of improving instruction.

CHAPTER 6
DOMAIN III, COMPETENCY 006

WHAT DOES IT SAY?

Competency 006: The entry-level principal knows how to promote high-quality teaching by using selection, placement, and retention practices to promote teacher excellence and growth.

WHAT DOES IT MEAN?

You are beginning to build a knowledge base with professional learning tools to place in your administrative toolbox if you have assimilated the information from the previous chapters. You should begin to see an overlap of leadership expectations for principals as instructional leaders. You should also begin to realize the processes are not always black and white. There will be times, when it comes to making decisions; you will have to base them on the best information available. However, the decisions in the realm of promoting high-quality teachers should always be made using processes put into place that include a planned systems approach and utilizing your campus leadership team. In doing so, you will support your emerging teacher leaders and reinforce a campus culture that values high-quality teaching. Not that high-quality teaching is an end in itself, but that by having high-quality teachers in the right places, you greatly increase your chances for student academic success.

The principal understands high-quality teachers are limited in the pool of applicants. The successful principals have the ability to create meaningful relationships with the central office personnel department, so that your campus has a greater opportunity to interview the small pool of high-quality applicants, whenever available. This also means your campus will not settle for applicants who are not qualified and do not meet the needs of your campus, regardless of who the personnel department wants to refer to you. Their job is to send you applicants who meet the *minimum* state certification standards and have passed the background checks. That does not mean those applicants will add to your campus' culture of improving student academic achievement. Many personnel departments will tell you these are all the applicants. You must choose one from the pool. If there are no suitable applicants, do not settle. If you have to start the year with a suitable long-term sub rather than settling on an applicant you know is not able to grow and develop into a high-quality teacher, then do so.

There will also be extenuating circumstances where the superintendent may call and encourage you to consider hiring the new head football or basketball coach's wife. The political frame in these situations is strong and you need to consider those options when filling positions. If this situation is ever the case, be sure you have had the private, crucial conversation with the superintendent about the challenges this hire may pose to the culture of instructional excellence.

As principal of an instructionally focused campus, you have a selection process in place that utilizes your leadership team. The selection process contains an interview that communicates to the applicants the high performance expectations of the campus as it relates to expected student learning objectives. Each member of the interview team must take their interview assignment seriously and make sure they have thoroughly vetted the applicant during the process.

Teachers have the opportunity to talk with applicants during the interview using agreed upon convergent and divergent questions. The interview allows for the open responses from the applicants and for additional qualifying questions from the campus interview committee. This allows the committee to make a more rational decision toward making a recommendation to hire the most qualified candidate.

The process allows the applicant to provide a brief demonstration of some portion of the teaching cycle that may include the opening, the goals statement, the purpose, the introduction, the modeling, the guided practice, the independent practice, and some sort of formative assessment, to the leadership team. The interview team uses this information to confer after all of the interviews have been completed and the applicants have been vetted. The vetting process includes the references, secondary references, online sites and any other information the interview team can review and investigate. It is important not to consider hearsay. Not everything communicated to the team and viewed on the social websites are necessarily true.

The principal is capable of evaluating the current staff members' strengths and weaknesses. The principal possess the leadership courage to assign and reassign teachers to positions that would provide the greatest success for students. If the culture of the school is strong and the staff has taken full ownership of doing whatever it takes to improve student success, the staff will be on board with the changes. A statement on the wall does not create this type of culture. You create it by establishing a vision and mission statement that has measurable goals. You continue the process by openly talking about the campus culture in small and large groups. This comes with the principal having crucial conversations with the staff members, allowing for what Patterson et. al. (2012), call the pool of shared meaning. As the authors state, "Each of us enters conversations with our own opinions, feelings, theories, and experiences about the topic at hand." The principal is capable of using those shared experiences to make a synergistic decision about placing people in the right places.

Finding good high-quality teachers is only the first step in the process. Keeping them is another. Do not adopt the mentality of some principals who take a laissez faire attitude with high-quality teachers and simply leave them to their own devices. High-quality teachers developed into who they are because someone invested time and coaching into their teaching performances, to help them to get better. High-quality teachers need the same opportunities to grow and get better at what they do. High-quality teachers generally translate into high-quality teaching when the principal serves as a constant encourager and support for their professional needs. This is a form of continuous process improvement for the teachers. They want to work for a principal that values their efforts.

You will want to look for good professional development opportunities for your high-quality teachers; training that enhances their teaching tools and provides for ways to add to their already well-stocked skillset. This is a form of teacher recognition and they will appreciate the opportunities you provide for them to get better at what they do.

Provide opportunities for leadership within the campus and in the district. Be sure that you do not overload them with too many responsibilities, but with enough to help reinforce their leadership skills. This requires some thought on your part. Here are a few ways you can utilize high-quality teachers:

    1. Assign as a mentor.

    2. Serve on the campus leadership team.

3. Evaluate textbook adoptions.

4. Provide informal walk-through evaluations (after being trained).

5. Lead in curriculum design and/or revision.

6. Encourage action research and presentations to the rest of the staff.

7. Develop and present staff development presentations.

8. Lead presentations for new staff members.

9. Make presentations to staff on current research-based articles and strategies.

10. Use high-quality teachers as a sounding board for ideas you have or are considering to implement on your campus.

Hiring, developing and retaining high-quality teachers is a priority for the campus principal. Figure 6.1 gives the reader a pictorial view of the connection of these vital components of this competency. Investment in these areas will save you an incredible amount of time and energy in other areas. In doing so, they will become your biggest supporters in helping to create a culture of academic success. Do not forget, these processes are a means to an end. Your end goal as the instructional leader is improved student success.

Greenwald, Hedges, and Lane (1996) found that high-quality teaching is about five times more effective than typical reductions in class size. This only emphasizes the importance of focusing in on developing teachers into high-quality teachers. It does not just happen. Much of the improved development of teachers comes through well-designed and targeted teacher growth activities.

Miles and Frank (2008) summarize the type of professional development that is most likely to improve student performance. They indicate that strong staff development includes the following components:

1. Evolves out of the analysis of student performance
2. Is organized as school—based, collaborative problem solving
3. Focuses on the implementation of specific content-based curriculum and instructional practices
4. Is scheduled as part of the everyday work of teaching
5. Includes follow-up and coaching
6. Promotes coherent, school-wide design, and

7. Promotes accountability for improved practice and student performance

It is interesting to note that Miles and Frank (2008) also indicate that continuously improving schools and teachers view professional development as a way of life. Staff understands that in order to grow professionally, they must participate in developmental training that will add to their existing tools and skillsets.

Figure 6.1 shows the relationship and importance of the principal to develop teacher excellence and growth. Each of the areas are vital to teacher growth and excellence.

WHAT DOES IT LOOK LIKE? (EXEMPLAR)

Your year as principal of the high school has gone fairly well, to this point. However, you were notified the day before that one of your math teachers found out her husband is being transferred at the end of the month. She has submitted her resignation, effective the last day of the month. She has been a solid teacher for you and you want to be sure to replace her with a quality teacher.

You send out a notification to your campus leadership team and communicate to your entire math teachers you want to meet with them after school for a meeting regarding hiring a high-quality teacher to replace the one leaving. Within the email you send, you attach a list of the generic questions used for interviewing teachers. You ask them to review the questions and provide specific math-related questions that would benefit the hiring of a teacher to fill the specific position.

You also ask the campus leadership team to give you some dates for the following week that they would be available to participate in interviews after school. The other members in the interview team who need to be a part of the process are also included.

Since the coordinator for the math department is already on the campus leadership team, that person will automatically be included. However, you want to provide others in the math department an opportunity to participate in the interview process. You note in the email they may have to adjust their schedule to attend the interviews, but their participation would add value to the interview process.

After sending the email, you contact the personnel department of your district asking for a list of possible applicants. Remind them of the information you gave them when you notified them of the impeding resignation. One of the assistants in the personnel office informs you they have five qualified applicants on file. You ask them to make a copy of all the applications and request they place the information in an envelope. You inform them the campus secretary will come by and pick the packet up within the hour.

During the day, as you complete your scheduled walk-through evaluations, you make it a point to visit individually with all of your campus leadership team and ask for input on the process. You also give each member a packet of the applications your office secretary has prepared for you. Request they do a complete review of the applications, looking for evidence of high-quality teaching experience. You assign each of them references to call to complete a thorough phone call interview, asking them to use the pre-developed list of open-ended divergent questions that may help the committee understand the applicants more completely. You remind them to take notes during the phone interviews and to follow up on any other references the initial references might offer to them.

During the day, you are offering positive encouragement to all your staff (when deserved), making sure you are including your high-quality teachers in the giving positive reinforcement. In fact, you spend a portion of your day handwriting notes to a number of your high-quality teachers, to let them know you appreciate their efforts.

During a passing period, you visit with a teacher who has been engaged in some action research on how to present more effectively, higher order thinking skills in her class. She gives you a brief and informal summary. You encourage her to continue implementing the strategy and to let you know when she is ready to give a report on the strategy used. You can tell she is not pleased with the current results, but she accepts the challenge you give her to continue the research.

At the staff development meeting after school, you have your teachers sign in because those who cannot attend in the afternoon will come the following morning. The staff presentation, by three of your lead teachers, focuses on how to engage lower performing students. The program includes opportunities for staff participation that is research-based. It is a brief presentation, which begins with objectives for the presentations and ends with concrete expectations for the staff and a brief exit evaluation of the presentation. The staff understand that all training focuses on the two or three instructional goals established for the campus this year. There are no administrative concerns covered during this time. You handle those in emails. You provide teachers the opportunity to respond to you during your daily walks through the campus.

You do, however, point out the great action research that is currently going on and communicate to the staff those who are completing this research. You inform the staff the results of the action research will be communicated to the PLC groups. If necessary, the results will be shared with the whole group at one of the staff development meetings in the future.

The following day is similar, except you attend the morning staff development meeting and repeat the same messages to those who could not attend the previous day. The secretary makes you a list of those who were not able to attend either staff development session. You make a note to follow up with each of those during the day. You want to hear about the reasons for not being able to attend and you make any copious notes to their file for future reference. During this process, you bring each staff member up to speed on the information presented in the meeting. You also communicate your high expectations for the staff to commit to achieving the instructional goals set for the campus.

Today is your day to visit several professional learning community meetings and sit in on the discussions they are having. Your teachers have been in training on asking the right questions in these meetings. The questions focus on student learning and achievement. They ask questions that target how to present lessons from start to finish. While you listen, you are quick to point out the high-quality teachers who are utilizing instructional strategies that are research-based and target the learning objectives. You make sure you are writing notes to the teachers and to their files for future reference in the summary evaluations.

You also serve as a support and resource for the PLC teams. You identify areas where they need support and you bounce ideas off your lead teachers to clarify needs and concerns. You make it a point to respond in writing to the individuals on the teams, so they know you will follow-up with your support in the matter of resources.

After school, you meet with your interview team to go over the applications and receive any feedback from the team about the strengths and weaknesses of the candidates for the math position. During this meeting, you ensure that everyone on the committee is clear about the job description for the open math position. You finalize the questions and procedures of the interview committee. This includes assigning different individuals on the committee to call an applicant in advance. It is each of these individual's responsibility to help the candidates feel at ease and as comfortable as possible with the process from start to finish.

The committee agrees on the top three applicants to interview. The person that contacted the applicant serves as the host when that applicant arrives. The host greets the applicant in the main office of the campus and brings the applicant to the interview process. The host has previously informed the applicant about the number of people who will be in the interview so the applicant is not so overwhelmed when he/she arrives in the room set up for the interview process.

You greet the applicant once they arrive in the interview room and individually introduce all members of the interview team. Once everyone is seated, you begin the interview process by trying to put the applicant at ease as much as possible. Questions about the applicant's family and personal background usually help to break the ice for the remainder of the questions. However, these should not include such personal or invasive questions that would compromise the person's privacy protected under constitutional law.

The interview team begins to ask the more focused questions once the informal introductions and comments have been made. The order of the questions have been pre-determined, but the team understands secondary and follow-up questions are permissible if they are related to the primary question. During the interview, the interview team is listening for the applicant's ability to communicate in a professional and acceptable manner, looking for any mannerisms that may signal some issues or concerns, and behavioral traits that add to the interview process. The interview team is trained to look for growth potential, not imperfections.

When all of the questions are asked and any micro-demonstrations have been completed, the principal allows the applicant an opportunity to ask any questions about the position, campus, and community. When those questions are answered, the principal ends the interview by thanking the applicant for applying. The host walks the applicant back to the main office and informs the applicant of how the rest of the interview process works and when the applicant can expect a follow-up call from the principal.

This scenario is repeated with the remaining two applicants.

Now, the real work begins. The principal allows for an overnight recess so the interview team can consider all of the interviewees after having some time to think about each one. This is also the time to make any additional follow-up calls or ask questions on the applicants based on the information provided in the interview process.

At an agreed upon time, the interview team meets to hear summaries of each of the three applicant interviews. This process is more of a question and discussion than just selecting an applicant. This process allows for the synthesis of the pieces of information and gives the team the time they need to make an informed decision.

Two processes are completed during this team meeting. The first one is to allow the team to come to a consensus on their top selection, if there is one. The second process is to decide if either of the other two applicants would be appropriate for the position if the first choice decides to decline the offer. Once these processes have been completed, it is the responsibility of the principal to make the formal contacts to all applicants, either offering the applicant the position or thanking each one for applying.

A LOOK AT THE INDICATORS FOR COMPETENCY 006

The entry-level principal will begin to realize how important and time-consuming this particular competency is. Be aware that you will either spend the time developing good teachers into quality teachers or spend the time fighting battles because you failed to properly invest in teacher selection, placement and retention. Your most challenging responsibility will be teacher assignments. Teachers become satisfied in their comfort zone. It is your job to keep all of the staff engaged in the vision, mission, and goals of the school surrounded by the culture you and your teachers have created.

The indicators listed on this competency and the ideas added to the indicators will help you to develop some of your own ideas in mastering the art of developing quality teachers.

A. Invests and manages time to prioritize the development, support, and supervision of the staff to maximize student outcomes
- Keeps an updated calendar of daily, weekly and monthly schedules to provide time for the development, support, and supervision of the staff.
- Visits teacher classrooms to make walk-through observations for the purpose of teacher growth.
- Conducts brief meetings with teachers concerning walk-though evaluations.
- Seeks participants in creating and presenting professional development training focused on the goals of the campus by using teacher leaders to lead out in the presentations.

- Converses with teachers about how they are progressing in meeting student goals.

B. Facilitates collaborative structures that support professional learning communities in reviewing data, processes, and policies in order to improve teaching and learning in the school
    - Creates a campus schedule that provides time within the school day for teachers to collaborate in Professional Learning Communities.
    - Trains PLC teams on how to conduct PLC meetings using an agenda and minutes.
    - Provides the appropriate data for PLC teams to allow them to complete their assessment of the data and discuss additional strategies as needed to ensure success for all students.
    - Participates in PLC meetings to give input, advice, and support.
    - Serves as a resource to the learning communities for needed instructional strategies, items and equipment.

C. Creates leadership opportunities, defines roles, and delegates responsibilities to effective staff and administrators to support campus goal attainment
    - Encourages teachers to lead professional development presentations.
    - Encourages teachers to perform action research studies.
    - Encourages teachers to lead other teachers and staff members to research best practices for instructional challenges facing the campus.
    - Encourages teachers to create parent involvement programs that are directly tied to improving student achievement.
    - Assigns teacher leadership roles on important committees for the campus and those in the district.

D. Implements effective, appropriate, and legal strategies for the recruitment, screening, hiring, assignment, induction, development, evaluation, promotion, retention, discipline, and dismissal of campus staff

- Includes teachers in designing and developing a master recruitment and hiring process that allows prospective high-quality teachers to grow in a nurturing environment, with support and resources to become successful.
- Creates a campus culture where teachers understand they are in charge of student success and you support them through training, resources and encouragement.
- Hires only qualified and competent teachers and staff who demonstrate a willingness to grow as a professional.
- Completes the appropriate and necessary legal processes to dismiss continually underperforming teachers and staff who are unable or are unwilling to improve. Follows through with the decision to dismiss them.
- Publically praises staff when warranted and privately disciplines staff in writing when also warranted. Be sure to include both in the appraisal process.

SAMPLE 268 TExES QUESTIONS FOR COMPETENCY 006

1. Mrs. Damion, the campus principal, is preparing to interview for a fourth grade math teacher position. She has received several applications from the personnel department and has weeded out the ones that do not qualify for the position. She still has five applications. Mrs. Damion's next best move is to:
    a. Go through the remainder and pick her top two candidates for the interview team to consider.
    b. Ask the interview team to pick the top two to interview by reviewing the applications.
    c. Assign each member of the interview team to review an application, check the references and secondary references, and report to the interview team on the findings.
    d. Review the applications herself so as not to waste the time of the interview team with this part of the interview process.

2. Mrs. Adkins, the principal of Smart Elementary is preparing to meet with the interview team prior to the team interviewing applicants. She has met with the teachers individually, who have completed the application reviews and reference checks. The next best step in this process would be for Mrs. Adkins to:
   a. Ask the lead teacher on the committee to review the initial questions to make sure they are relevant for this particular interview and to assign questions to each of the members to ask during the interview.
   b. Call all of the references just to be sure that she has good background information prior to the interview.
   c. Run off the interview questions. Then, assign teachers and staff on the interview team, the questions they will ask.
   d. Google the names of the applicants, to see if there is any information on the web that might be of additional value to the interview process.

3. Dr. Bishop is the principal of Wilmer Junior High. The school year has ended. All has gone well, but there are a few resignations due to spousal transfers and personal decisions. It is time to consider what positions will be available to interview, and the timeline for interviewing for those positions. Before considering what positions to interview, Dr. Bishop will most likely:
   a. Wait a few weeks before doing anything; to be sure there are no other resignations to consider.
   b. Review the strengths and weaknesses of the remainder of the staff, to consider reassigning current staff to other positions that would provide the greatest opportunity for student mastery.
   c. Begin the interview process by contacting the interview team and getting those members ready to interview.
   d. Meet with the personnel office to determine what applications are available to consider for job openings.

4. Dr. Sena is the principal of a large elementary school and she has been participating in a number of the professional learning community meetings for the day. As she

has taken notes, she realizes that there is a common thread for some specific staff development to address an instructional challenge, which she has verified with the learning communities. Dr. Sena's next step would most likely be to:

   a. Contact her PTA board to see if there is enough money in their budget to pay for the staff development needed.
   b. Review the current budget and shift money around to pay a consultant to come in to make a presentation focused on the challenge identified.
   c. Contact the central office. Tell them to get someone to come and do a presentation on the identified concern.
   d. Meet with lead teachers of the professional learning communities and determine if they can develop some professional development training that would address the instructional challenge. Assure them she will provide the necessary resources to help address the issues.

5. As principal of Harvest High School, Mr. Tomms has established a defined 10-15 minute mini observation where he is observing specific aspects of the lesson and instructional delivery. He makes it a point to briefly visit with each teacher between passing periods to give some verbal feedback and follow-up with a written summary that is added to the formal observation process. One particular observation does not go well. The teacher has underperformed in the instructional delivery process and has been inattentive to student needs. Upon leaving the classroom, Mr. Tomms asks the teacher to visit with him before she leaves the campus at the end of the day. He has taken the copious notes. His next best decision would be to:

   a. Continue about his scheduled day. Wait for the teacher to come in to discuss the concerns he observed in the walk-through.
   b. Contact the lead teacher for the department, inform the teacher, and tell them everything he observed. Let them know he is concerned.
   c. Go to his office, review his notes, and prepare specific questions to ask the teacher that will allow her to respond without feeling threatened when he meets with her after school.

d. Ask his assistant principals to keep an eye on her during the day; to be sure she is okay.

DOMAIN IV – EXECUTIVE LEADERSHIP
(Communication and Organizational Management)

This is a fickle domain in that no one really notices it unless the principal underperforms in these areas. It is what Bolman and Deal (2017) refer to as the Structural Frame of cognition. In this Frame, Bolman and Deal lay out the importance of having a solid foundation in ensuring all structured activities are well organized and being conducted in a manner that provides for a smooth operating organization.

At a campus level, this means there is a well-defined structure to the instructional day. All staff are following agreed upon guidelines for the day. It also means communication structures are in place to keep all constituents apprised of changes in the agreed upon structures.

When you are doing these things correctly, even at a high level of success, most people do not notice or care. However, when your process lacks the needed structure and communication tools, people notice. They are not happy. When people are dissatisfied with the Structural Frame, then the tenure of the principal is short-lived.

CHAPTER 7
DOMAIN IV, COMPETENCY 007

WHAT DOES IT SAY?

Competency 007: The entry-level principal knows how to develop relationships with internal and external stakeholders, including selecting appropriate communication strategies for particular audiences.

WHAT DOES IT MEAN?

A school is not a building; it is an incorporated group of individuals learning to learn together for the betterment of the student population. With that mindset, building healthy, productive relationships is paramount to producing successful academic students. In addition, in order to build those successful relationships, effective communication skills are a necessity (See Figure 7.1).

Building relationships begins with getting to know your staff on an individual level. It requires time invested in listening to individuals and understanding their personal goals and ambitions, as well as getting to know what matters to them. Successful principals in this realm understand that personal files on each staff member helps in creating successful, healthy relationships. Each of those files may look different, but may also bear some commonalties as well. They contain some of the following:

- Birthdays of the individual and information on family members (only if offered).
- Hobbies and personal interests.
- Personal goals (life ambitions and bucket list).
- Concerns, especially if they involve close family members. (It is important to build a level of confidentiality in this area. These concerns are not for sharing with others.)
- Favorite foods, drinks, and snacks (During stressful times, comfort food does wonders for lifting the individual morale of a person).

The number one priority is the success of all students. To get there, the principal must use these ideas and other personal suggestions to create a bond of professional commitment to work together. Teachers and staff want to know they are valued and appreciated. Salaries matter, of course, but they are only a starting point. Teachers and staff place high importance on being recognized and valued for their dedication and efforts in the workplace. Principals must use these opportunities to create a culture of support and success for the teachers and staff.

When teachers and staff have a birthday, take the time to write each one a personal note of gratitude for the work they are doing to help all students achieve success. Wish them a blessed day on their birthday. Maybe you could sing the Happy Birthday Song to each teacher. Yes, it could disrupt the instruction for a moment in the day, but it is an investment in the teacher to let them know they are valued and appreciated. Be creative on this.

The external relationships, although they may be more formal and less personal, are still important. In building those relationships, the principal remains an active listener to the concerns of parents, businesses, and central office staff. Some constituents will not view the campus as a positive place because of personal or previous experiences. It is not the job of the principal to convince those people otherwise. It is the principal's responsibility to listen and be empathetic to those concerns. It is the job of the principal to provide a campus that is open to all constituents and ensure the campus has a warm, welcoming environment.

There are, of course, key stakeholders such as the superintendent, central office staff (who play a direct role on the campus), community business leaders, and parents who want to be engaged in their students' learning. Principals must be prepared to build quality relationships with these individuals and be prepared to address issues that may arise. Like it or not, this is a real aspect of the politics of being a campus principal. Doing a good job in this area may reduce conflict later on down the road.

In building these relationships, communication is tantamount in achieving success. The principal is a communication manager in the sense that you are able to identify the correct tools of communication for the identified group of stakeholders.

Communication is not an on-off process. It is a continuous process of disseminating the correct, appropriate information in a timely manner so that the receiver of the information is able to interpret it, decipher its intended meaning and act upon that information.

Schneider and Hollenczer (2006) provide some great characteristics of the basics for effective communication. They are:

- Be honest. Be direct.
- Talk with your constituents, not to them.
- Be professional.
- Be a leader by listening. Take the time to listen attentively.
- Remember who your publics are. Know them and their concerns.
- Be consistent. Be precise. Be clear with your message.
- Be compassionate. Show empathy.
- Be passionate. Emotion conveys caring.
- Be visible. Be available. Be responsive.
- Elicit help. Let your partners and critical friends help you communicate with others, and
- Be yourself.

Many larger districts employ a Chief Information Officer (CIO). In times of an emergency and crisis such as the Corona Virus (COVID-19) of 2020, it is important to allow these experts disseminate correct, highly sensitive information in as quick and efficient manner as possible. They are experts at constructing the message and can assist local campuses in best processes for getting the message out to constituents in a timely manner.

The principal is not alone. The entire weight of getting the message out should not be confined to one person. However, the principal should approve of any campus-wide messages being disseminated. It is wise to have a communication team who work together to enrich the communication process. A few key campus leaders, active supportive parents, and key central office staff can all play a role in the communication process. They can also help to ensure the information in the message is appropriate for the greater campus population.

The principal should select the type of venue to disperse information depending on the message and who needs to know, as well as the priority of the message. The principal needs to understand how to take advantage of the various methods for communicating the information to stakeholders. This may include, but not be limited to:

- Face-to-face formal and informal settings.
- Large groups such as staff meetings, parent meetings, and assemblies.
- Phone conversations.
- Emails, handwritten notes, letters, and postcards.
- School newsletters and weekly school-to-home notes such as Tuesday Newsday Notes.
- Facebook.
- Texting (professional manner to adults, only in a need-to-know situation)
- Electronic Apps such as Remind 101™ or Class Dojo™ to quickly access parents.
- Local Newspapers and TV stations, and in
- Small groups of formal and informal settings.

[Arrow graphic: Building Healthy Relationships → Strong Communication Skills → Makes a Great Team]

Figure 7.1: A successful principal understands building strong professional relationships by using effective communication skills is a recipe for successful teams.

WHAT DOES IT LOOK LIKE? (EXEMPLAR)

As principal of a large K-5 elementary for the past year, you and your staff have completed a data analysis on the most recent state and campus-based assessments, along with other applicable data. It is clear among the staff and campus administration that a major change in the delivery of the curriculum is necessary to improve student performance. The campus has decided upon several major changes to the school day to bring about academic improvement in the fastest possible manner. Some of the major changes included:

- Lengthening the school day to provide for additional time for reading and math instruction.
- Providing time each week to allow professional learning communities to meet and focus specifically on instructional strategies and student performance.
- Constructing staff development around identified high leverage points of student low performance.
- Rearranging busing schedules to accommodate the longer school day, and
- Generating additional parental support for increased student learning by providing weekly parent make-and-take instructional activities for them to use to support student learning.

Both you and your staff realize the enormity of communicating the message to your constituents. However, before you can begin messaging the information, you must acquire approval of the superintendent and the school board to lengthen the school day. You will need to adjust the bus schedule to accommodate the students who ride the bus to and from school. It is time for the principal to create a plan of action that includes steps to meet the goals of the school and the communication challenge. Fortunately, during this past year, the principal has spent time building relationships with many people in the central office and with the transportation staff. The relationship groundwork has been established to present plans to them.

Before going further into this exemplar, recognize there are many roads to get to the solution, but it is necessary to start at the beginning. The beginning is always communicating with the superintendent. The plan of action might include the following steps that may change as the steps are completed and adjusted according to the previous step progression.

Plan a meeting with the superintendent. Begin with the data analyzed by the staff and what high leverage points were identified. Superintendents are busy. They need a focal point to make decisions. They base decisions on sound information and do not make those decisions in real time unless there is a crisis. Superintendents have a communication ladder they follow. The more sound information you can give the superintendent, the more likely the plan will have a favorable outcome. This meeting with the superintendent should also include all of the carefully designed steps and resources for each step. Information is power and power means the opportunity for a more positive outcome.

This is a time for political etiquette. Do not kid yourself. Politics plays an important part in the school day. The principal is an advocate for his/her campus. The stronger your professional relationship is with your superintendent, the greater the chances are that you may receive approval on the plan with all or most of the resources you need to implement it.

Do not present the plan as critical. Rather, present it as imperative for student academic success. Explain you have the full support of your staff for the recommended changes. Superintendents generally operate from the *Political Frame* and want to know your plans have a high degree of support from your campus staff.

Be open to alternative suggestions from your superintendent. Remember, he/she is the one who will be supporting you 100% if you are allowed to move forward with it. The superintendent may ask you to meet with district instructional staff and transportation prior to making a definitive decision on your requests.

You always finish a meeting such as this on a positive note. Be sure to support the superintendent's recommendations and considerations for changes. Their picture of the success of students is much broader than yours or your campus. It is important that you respect their decisions and position.

Moreover, there is one more point to bring up in this area. Be prepared for you and your leadership staff to present these types of changes to your district's board of trustees. The more the focus is on improving student achievement, the harder it is to argue against such proposed changes. However, you may have Board members offer alternative suggestions. Prepare your leadership staff to be open-mined to those suggestions. Trustees are responsible for the financial welfare of the district as well as the academic success of students. They may be anticipating that other campuses may ask what you are asking for, if your ideas work. That could translate into increased financial investment of the district's limited resources.

Speaking of resources, this would be a good time as a next step, to meet with your Chief Financial Officer (CFO) to determine the monetary impact to the district and campus due to your requested changes.

This next comment is a bit facetious, but there is an ounce of truth in it. CFO's are born stingy. Many believe it is their job to protect the district fund balance and build it up. Do not be surprised if your CFO appears skeptical because they are usually on the defensive when someone needs additional funds.

Again, be positive and continue to build your relationship with your CFO. You are fighting a battle, not a war. When you meet with him/her, be sure to have your draft plan in a format that is easy to comprehend. Explain where any possible increase in finances may occur. Also, point out the areas of the plan that may not require additional resources. This helps to establish a scenario where the CFO understands you are trying to implement changes without additional funding. They will want to know you have adjusted your current funding to meet as many of the new challenges as possible before they consider additional funding.

The next stop is to visit with your district's Chief Information Officer (CIO), if you have one. These people are trained at what they do. Their job is to provide good, strong, systemic communication in a designed, sequential order. You have heard the adage, "Don't put the cart before the horse." This really applies here. They are good at what they do and they want to be a resource for you during this transition time. Fully use their expertise.

At this point, it is important to remember your campus ideas are considerations until you get support from the superintendent, board, and your Chief Financial Officer. CIO's are good at aligning campus considerations into great presentations for the board, parents and the community. Spend some time with this person in creating a proposal of campus ideas that are understandable and clear.

This requires some systemic thinking; who needs to know what and when? It is imperative principals learn to think systemically in situations like this. Being able to do this does not eliminate the problems or issues that may arise, but it helps to be able to respond to them because the principal has had the forethought to prepare for them and to respond with a high emotional IQ.

Now that the principal has begun to establish some support for the campus plan, it is time to return to the campus and brief the staff on the progress. It is important they know and understand the process involves give and take. Decisions always have political ramifications to the populace. Being an advocate does not mean the principal will win every battle. The objective is to win the war and the war is improving student academic achievement.

Use the information your CIO has helped to construct for you. If your district does not have a CIO, use your campus leadership team. Run the process by a trusted mentor for additional advice. The closer to the issue, the more difficult it is to be unbiased about the decisions made. This is especially true when you are the one making the decisions.

Typically, the superintendent is going to give you a timeframe by which you can begin to roll out the proposal to the constituents for consideration. Do not just go by an agreed upon date. The superintendent may ask you for a summary of proposal to send to the board of trustees to allow them to review the information prior to any open discussion they may have on the proposal. More than likely, this will be the first time your constituents will hear of it. That is okay. If you have developed your relationships with them over the past year, they will be anxious to hear how the process will work when you make the presentations to them.

Sometimes, the superintendent may do a weekly information packet to the Board of Trustees with a note that he/she has given you permission to move forward with the proposed changes so you can give an update to the board at a later meeting. Regardless of the process, be sure to make another visit to the superintendent's office. You want to be clear you have the superintendent's blessing prior to going public with the changes.

Once completed, rely on your plan of action to disseminate the information. Your parent base is a great place to start. Provide several options of meetings for parents to attend and have your leadership base at the meetings to be willing to add additional information about the proposed changes.

The first thing you want to do at this point is to communicate the reason for the proposed changes. Essentially, what were the catalysts that moved the campus to propose new changes to the instruction and to the school day? This requires another process of systemic thinking. For instance, one of the proposed changes is for a longer school day. Prior to any meeting, you and your staff will have attempted to generate what questions may be asked during the presentation regarding a longer school day. A list of possible questions and responses needs to be prepared so that the meeting will flow more smoothly. Here is an important point. If you have not prepared for a question and you do not know the answer, say, "I do not know, but we will get the answer to you on a Q and A that will be sent to all parents." Do not try to wing it. You might be right, but you also, might be wrong. If you are wrong, you have created a wedge of distrust in your leadership and your ability to effectively communicate with others.

The best thing you can do is ask the people to hold on to their questions and concerns until after the presentation has been made. Communicate you and the staff will answer all questions at the end of the presentation. You do not have to be the only one presenting or responding to questions. In fact, presentations are more meaningful when they come from the campus leadership. Most parents understand the teachers are at the front line and when they present, most parents listen. This allows you to gauge the audience and be a part of the Q and A at the end of the presentation.

When parents understand changes are being made for the benefit of their children, it is amazing how supportive they become. They just want to be assured their children will be safe and monitored at all times.

Repeat this process as many times as necessary with the identified constituents and the board, if the superintendent deems it necessary. All the while, you are building relationships with students, parents, teachers, staff, and community. This requires one-on-one, small group, civic club, informal and formal interaction with people.

Implementing change requires strong, healthy relationships with an effective process of communication. Change does not come easily for those affected by the changes. Regardless of the outcome, stay positive and if you are able to implement those changes, then they will mean that much more. Sometimes you get your wish. Other times you do not. In either scenario, be positive and keep the relationships open for another challenge.

An example of implementing change that may not happen is moving from a nine-month schedule to year-round school. Once you receive support from the superintendent, you begin communicating with your constituents. Parents have mixed feelings. They are still on board with the proposal when the superintendent calls and explains the board is getting negative feedback because the perception is you are trying to keep minority students off the streets during the summer. You may be disappointed, but understand the politics of education. Know the superintendent is supportive of your efforts. You lost the battle. However, find other ways to help your students achieve academic success. If you do this, you will win the war. That would be student success.

A LOOK AT THE INDICATORS FOR COMPETENCY 007

A wise entry-level principal will seek the counsel of an experienced administrator for examples of building good relationships with teachers, staff, parents, central office staff, businesses, civic organizations and the community. Investing time in people is the number one priority of the principal. You are not a manager. You are a learning leader.

Learning leaders know how to reach out using several forms of communication, sometimes using single sources and other times using multiple forms of communication. Effective communication is the key to successful relationship building. Successful relationship building is the venue for implementing improvement plans that increase student achievement.

Be sure you have background in how to efficiently read body language. This is an important part of communicating and interpreting the message. As the deliverer of the message, be sure to use body language that is welcoming, positive, and receptive to the receiver. You must be able to perceive the message the receiver sends back to you. This is true in both formal and informal conversations. This is an extremely important mindset to revisit every morning before meeting people. It is a part of preparing your emotional IQ for the day.

Here are the indicators for this competency with ideas of how they might look when used by the principal. These suggestions will generate some additional ways you can develop relationships and communicate effectively.

A. Understands how to effectively communicate a message in different ways to meet the needs of various audiences (Here are more ideas than are usually given on an indicator, but these are appropriate.)
    - The use of face-to-face, one-one-one communication, formally and informally.
    - The use of small group communication, formally and informally.
    - The ability to speak clearly and effectively to large groups without having to read notes verbatim.
    - The use of hand-written notes using campus letterhead and commercial cards to all types of constituents.
    - The use of **all** forms of social media including, but not limited to apps such as Remind 101™, Class DoJo™, broadcast text messages, broadcast phone messages, videos, Facebook, and other forms of electronic media.
    - The ability to use the phone with proper phone etiquette.
    - Handshakes and proper body language when doing so.
    - Waving at people.
    - Type-written letters on formal letterhead signed by the principal, and
    - Smiling at people.

B. Develops and implements strategies for systematically communicating internally and externally
    - Create a specific set of guidelines and steps for communicating the message in a manner that is always factual, informative, and professional.
    - Include your campus leaders in the creation of the guidelines and steps mentioned above.
    - Always have another trusted member of the campus or your district Chief Information Officer review information that will be distributed to more than one person.
    - Strategies for communicating important messages should always include the superintendent, and

- Write all messages with the understanding that any information sent out could be reposted on constituents' personal websites. Every constituent will have an opinion.

C. Develops and implements a comprehensive program of community relations that uses strategies that effectively involve and inform multiple constituencies (You should develop the relationships before communicating strategic messages.)
   - Create time to regularly visit businesses located within the boundaries of your campus to begin developing informal relationships.
   - Meet with local civic groups if they are willing to open their doors for you. Introduce yourself and talk about the campus in general.
   - Do not forget to create those healthy professional relationships with key members of the central office.
   - Use the appropriate communication strategy for the group of constituents, and
   - Be willing to be flexible when communicating the message.

D. Establishes partnerships with parents, businesses, and other groups in the community to strengthen programs and support campus goals
   - The purpose for partnerships is to build relationships to help communicate the message. This would include contacting small groups of parents at times and visit with them in an informal setting, to get to know them. The settings could include coffee and donut shops, market restaurants and other informal settings to allow for individual input and sharing of information.
   - Utilize civic groups to give the message of the campus to their organizations.
   - Be sure to communicate with businesses in your area with the formal message of the campus. Seek input from the owners and employees on how the campus can be a good neighbor.
   - Create a list of talking points that include goals to use whenever you are with any person who is a constituent. This would definitely include students, and

- Be intentional about getting the message out 24/7. When you accept the position of a campus principal, you are always on duty, especially if you are in the community.

SAMPLE 268 TExES QUESTIONS FOR COMPETENCY 007

1. Mr. Igo has just completed his first year of serving as the campus principal. The scores on campus-based and state assessments were lower than expected. He and his campus staff have completed two days of data analysis, goal setting and proposed changes to the school day. Sitting in his office, Mr. Igo is contemplating his next step for the process. After some reflective consideration, Mr. Igo believes the next best step is to:
   a. Assemble a small group of trusted parents together to present the ideas to them for approval.
   b. Pull in the leadership team and have them begin working on professional development activities to meet the needs of the new campus goals.
   c. Send out a mass email to all parents about the proposed changes.
   d. Call the superintendent and set up a meeting to discuss the proposed campus changes with him/her.

2. Mrs. Hambrick has just been named principal of a struggling middle school, grades 6-8. She is new to the district and community. As she sits in her office, it is the beginning of the summer long break and she is contemplating what an entry-level principal should do at this point. She has some great instructional ideas that she is convinced will make an immediate impact on the school's academic performance, but where does she begin? After some consideration, she decides to:
   a. Write up a draft of her proposals to present to a full staff meeting as soon as she can get them together
   b. Assemble the campus staff together and introduce herself. Let them know some changes in instruction are coming their way as soon as she can get the ideas approved by the superintendent and curriculum staff.

c. Set up an individual meeting with each campus employee, to create an opportunity to get to know them and begin building healthy relationships among the staff.
   d. Set up her office and unpack her personal items before anyone starts coming to her office.

3. Mrs. Edgington has been the principal for a semester at Corona High School. She has just completed a long and busy day at her campus. Ever since the COVID-19 virus became a pandemic the prior year, the high school name has carried a negative connotation among some in the district and community. She decides to stop by the local market for a few items to fix for supper when she is approached by an irate parent in a crowded store who wants to know why the school has not changed its name. The parent asks her when she is going to do something about it. By now, there is a small group lingering in the area acting as if they are looking for items but actually listening in on the conversation. To top it off, she notices a patron who is videoing the incident on her phone. After pausing for a moment, her best option is to:
   a. Thank the person for being willing to ask the question and inform the person that it is an excellent question, Explain this issue has been addressed by the students, staff, central office, and the administration. Explain that every group mentioned has supported keeping the current name and direct the person to visit the school's website for more information on the subject. Then say, "I don't believe I have had the pleasure of meeting you," and extend your hand.
   b. Ignore the store patron, excuse herself, and move quickly to another aisle. The principal has every right to do this in a public setting and others will understand.
   c. Calmly tell the person she is not on duty at this time. She is grocery shopping for her family and will not answer questions at this time.
   d. Tell the person this is not the time and place to have a discussion on the name of the school. Also, inform the person she was rude and inconsiderate for approaching her after hours and continue shopping.

4. Mr. Motheral, principal of the campus, conducted an intense review of current instructional practices with his campus, superintendent, CFO, CIO, and Board members. They have all supported the current practices as well as the new innovative ideas generated by your campus staff. Although there is some information in the community about the changes because of the Board presentation, there have been no official steps made for disseminating these new changes. Mr. Motheral's next best step would be to:
   a. Wait a week or two to review the proposed information and allow for continued feedback from teachers and staff before getting the message out to the constituents.
   b. Inform each of the teachers to post the new changes on each of their school websites and contact the parents via Remind 101™ or Class DoJo™ to view the individual websites.
   c. Bring the campus leadership team together to review the campus strategies for disseminating the important changes.
   d. Send out a broadcast email and text listing all of the changes to the parents and students.

5. Mrs. Cowan is a first year principal of a large elementary. Mrs. Cowan has had to spend an inordinate amount of time on collaborating with the staff and district administration. Her intent was to develop and implement a more clearly defined Student Code of Conduct. It was communicated to all constituents and implemented with fidelity by the staff. As a result, the campus has become a much safer and inviting learning environment. She has been pleased with the implementation and support from parents and staff. Just about the time she opened her lunch at her desk to eat while checking emails, she hears a commotion in the outer office. A parent is irate and yelling at the assistant principal in charge of enforcing the new discipline guidelines. The parent is accusing the assistant principal of racially motivated decisions regarding the assignment of in-school suspension while other

students did not receive the same "punishment" for class disruptions. As the principal, she decides to take the following step:
- a. Return to her office and allow the parent and the assistant principal to learn from the process. She has assigned the AP to do the job. If she interfered, it would communicate a message the AP cannot handle it.
- b. Instruct the parent to act in an adult and orderly manner or she will call the police and have him/her escorted from the campus. Then, return to her office.
- c. Get on the school radio and instruct the school police liaison to report to the main office. Repeat "code red" several times into the microphone.
- d. She should introduce herself to the parent, explain she was the one who helped create the new discipline consequences and invite the parent into her office to hear the parent's concerns.

CHAPTER 8
DOMAIN IV, COMPETENCY 008

WHAT DOES IT SAY?

Competency 008: The entry-level principal knows how to focus on improving student outcomes through organizational collaboration, resiliency, and change management.

WHAT DOES IT MEAN?

We are still under the umbrella of Domain IV, Executive Leadership. An executive is one who makes decisions, enforces policy, manages, supervises, and accepts responsibility for the outcomes of the organization. With that in mind, we focus on this competency. The entry-level principal should always eye decisions on how they will affect student performance. Student outcomes are job one! Executive leadership is not autonomous and separate from any input from the other campus members. In fact, more times than not, a collaborative process with students, teachers, staff and parents, to determine the best outcomes and processes for improved student achievement increases the chances for success (See Figure 8:1).

The key to understanding this competency is to understand the terminology behind it and not just glaze over the primary descriptor. The three key descriptors are collaboration, resiliency, and change. It is important to understand these terms before being faced with the decision to use them effectively. They can become a bit ambiguous when improving instruction. Executive leaders cannot afford ambiguity. Ambiguity projects a lack of leadership skills to do the job. Be informed and prepared.

The first key word is collaborate or collaboration. Collaboration is the ability of two or more people to cooperate with one another to achieve a common goal. This means there is a process of working together, joining all means of resources to achieve the best possible solution to the challenge the group is attempting to resolve. It is a process of allowing for differences of opinions, to cause the collaborative team to think about all possible outcomes and to work toward consensus on a solution. The goal of collaboration is not total and undisputed agreement with the solution that is deemed the best choice. It is though, an agreement that all will work toward achievement of the solution.

Collaboration creates participation and participation develops ownership in the process. Executive leaders understand one of the keys to a successful outcome is ownership. When people feel their opinions matter, they will invest human capacities to achieve the outcome of the campus goals.

An important component of collaboration is beginning with the end in mind. All staff and constituents want what is best for the student when it comes to academic achievement. The differences occur on how to best reach those outcomes. Effective collaboration is the best vehicle for reaching the most efficient solutions to achieve those outcomes or goals.

Resiliency is another key descriptor in the executive leadership process, not just for the principal, but also for the organization as a whole. To be resilient means to be strong in purpose, toughminded when the goals are challenging to sustain flexibility with the capability to bend but not break in the course of achieving the outcomes. This produces durability. If one is durable, one can outlast the storm of challenges and make it to the finish line.

This is where executive leadership really can make a significant difference when leadership employs systemic thinking. Any goal or outcome worth working toward will have difficult and challenging pushback from others. An entry-level principal is one who understands this will prepare the campus team for the upcoming pushback of resistance. YOU are the captain of this "leader-ship" and if you know a storm is coming, you order the crew to batten down the hatches when a storm is imminent. You are trying to weather the storm and prepare for challenges and pushback.

What causes challenges and pushback during these times? Change causes it! That is our next key descriptor. There are many perceptions about change, but for our purpose, we will say it is a significant modification or transformation in the normal routine of procedures that cause people within and outside the organization to be anxious. They are concerned about that change and its effects on the organization and individuals. The success for change revolves around the effective decision-making used in the change process. Figure 8.1 demonstrates the importance of the decision-making process.

The education of students is the continual process of monitoring and adjusting to the specific needs of the student population in order to achieve maximum academic growth. Usually, small adjustments in processes and procedures go unnoticed by the constituents at large. However, when there are more formal analyses of the data and significant changes are in order that is when change causes upheaval, angst and worry. The principal's responsibility as the executive leader is to be a forward thinker, anticipating the issues so that remedies can be put into place to minimize concern for those changes.

Being a campus principal is a challenging job, but you can do it if you are willing to invest in learning the tools of the trade and you are willing to develop the skills and mindsets to be a leader of learning! That is where we are now in this competency. The competency says you are to use these three key terms to focus on improving student outcomes. Every state has some type of assessment. Based on how each campus performs on those assessments, each campus and district receives a "report card" on how well they met state expectations.

You are focusing on improving student achievement through collaboration, resiliency, and change. What does that look like? Let us look at the exemplar below. This will give you a sample of the knowledge, skills and mindset you will need to be a leader of learning.

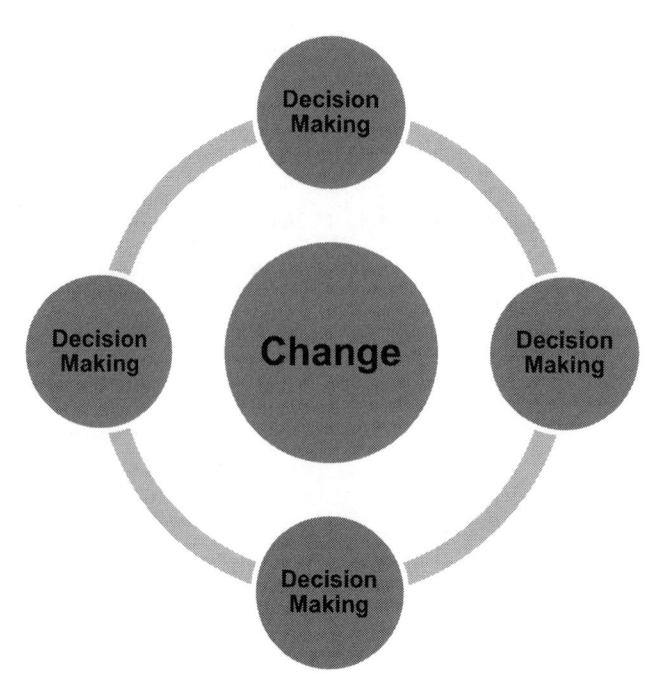

Figure 8.1: Change is a continuous process with improving student academic achievement as the constant focus.

WHAT DOES IT LOOK LIKE? (EXEMPLAR)

You are the principal of Listin High School, an academically struggling school. You were an assistant principal of a middle school in the district until the semester break. The superintendent called and said the principal of the high school retired. The superintendent hire you as principal of Listin.

When you came over to Listin, you had some credibility because prior to becoming an assistant principal, you were a successful math teacher at a high school in another district that was performing well with a high number of minority student populations. You served a high percentage of economically disadvantaged students. However, you realize the frying pan is hot. There is low morale among the teachers and staff because there appears to be a high percentage of student apathy towards academics. The consequence of this is reduced student performance on the state assessments and campus-based assessments. Furthermore, you have begun to notice this apathy moving into the ranks of the staff. You have heard the murmurings of transfer requests among your higher performing teachers who are exhausted.

As the executive leader of instruction, you identify two critical high leverage points as 1) low performing student achievement and 2) apathy toward individual performance. You decide to call a meeting of the campus leadership team to collaborate with them regarding your perceptions. You explain to them that this is just the beginning of a process that will take several months to develop a plan of action. You believe in their leadership and anticipate through a series of collaborative efforts, that the school's culture can be turned around. However, you need their commitment to stay and be a part of the solution.

You seek input from this group and ask for their perceptions. The teachers are emotionally exhausted from trying to coax and coerce students to perform well. They express their frustration. It turns into a good cry session for some of the leadership, but you ask them to give you a year. With their help, things can be turned around. Many of teachers have served several principals and they are unsure of making the commitment for another year. You begin to lay out a plan of action to turn apathy and low student performance into excitement for learning and increased student performance.

Now, you have their interest and you begin to lay out some ideas. Here are some of your proposals for turning things around. This is a basic foundational plan with areas that can easily be adjusted, to begin to turn around student performance and apathy.

1. Contact the superintendent and meet with him to get preliminary approval for the overall plan, which includes two additional days of contract work for the staff.
2. Meet with the staff before they leave for the summer and get them to agree on two consecutive days (at their daily rate) that they are willing to meet and begin collaborating on developing a plan of action. The teachers and staff agree to wait at least three weeks after school is out, so they can all come back rested, refreshed, and ready to work.
3. During the interim, you gather as much longitudinal data from the past 3-5 years over every aspect of the school. This would include, but not be limited to student performance on state and CBA results, student attendance, student discipline, teacher attendance, teacher turnover rate, parental involvement on open houses, student-grading meetings, and any other data that would add to the turnaround.

4. During this same time, you are contacting your leadership team members, meeting with them in groups of 2-3, collaborating with them on the best formats to generate ideas and serve as the catalyst for the turnaround. The leadership team becomes more interested about the possibility of the school becoming a successful learning environment where students WANT to learn.
5. The leadership team and campus leaders decide it is necessary for you to begin the meeting with some type of "State of the Campus" message and finish it with an inspiring challenge to begin the turnaround.

DAY ONE:
1. The day arrives for the two-day professional development to begin. Nearly everyone was able to attend with the exception of three teachers and two aides who had prior commitments and were unable to change their plans. Thinking systemically, you provided for those five the opportunity to attend using the Zoom™ video platform. Four of the five were able to attend using this setup.
2. You begin with a brief overview of why they are there and what your perceptions were from your own observations of the previous semester. You begin by telling them you are honored to be their principal. You have no plans on going anywhere for a long time. Then, you bring up the school's mascot and say, "We are the Listin Lions and I am proud to be a lion! Let's get this place turned around!"
3. Many of the staff are excited and you tell them the first day is a day of soul-searching. You explain we are going to be taking some deep dives into the data and any additional information the staff has to offer to identify the high leverage points that can be used to make a turnaround happen.
4. You explain to them that rather than breaking up in groups by subjects or grades, you have created small groups of five that consists of people who normally do not work with each other. You explain your rationale for this decision as twofold. First, you have noticed that people on the campus do not know each other outside of their subject area or working area and you want to use this activity to allow people to develop relationships among the greater staff. Second, you want to stimulate some more diverse thinking among the staff and you believe this will stimulate creative thinking.

5. Rather than giving all the groups the entire set of data, you decide to divide the data so that no more than 2-3 groups have the same data to allow for the deep dives into the information. You let the group know that you will be participating in the collaborative session as well as using the participants on Zoom™ as your collaborative group.
6. Here is the assignment you give them.
   a. Evaluate the data independently and have each member complete the collaboration questions separately so that each person has an opinion about what the data says and how to make a turnaround with this information.
   b. Hand out this set of guiding questions for each group to use and explain these questions must have a definitive response, but the individual groups may add additional questions if they deem it is necessary.
      i. What pieces of the data show reasons to celebrate?
      ii. What are the two or three areas of the data that with highest leverage points that need immediate attention for a turnaround?
      iii. For each of those two or three high leverage points, create a solution(s) using the following format.
         1. Clearly diagnose and define the problem in easy to understand terminology so that parents and students can understand.
         2. Prioritize and set specific, measurable goals for improving the selected outcome(s).
         3. Identify and define the steps (plan) for implementing and monitoring the steps for success. This would include any possible adjustments that may need to be made to keep the steps moving forward.
7. Explain that all of these steps are to be done individually prior to the groups brainstorming and collaborating over these for a collaborative group solution.
8. The morning session will be used for individual analysis and each collaborative group will be assigned a classroom that is not one of the group member's classrooms.
9. The morning session will be used to complete the individual analysis of the data and the questions.

10. The afternoon session will be for each group to share their ideas and come to some agreement on what the plan of implementation should look like to help with the turnaround. All resources have been provided in the rooms and are ready for use.
11. You inform them the assistant principal will be walking the campus halls in case there is an additional need or clarification on what needs to be done. You also emphasize this turnaround is dependent upon their participation and input. Time is critical. No other discussions or off task behavior is acceptable. This process is mission critical to the turnaround.
12. You explain pizza and box lunches will be provided in the cafeteria at 12:30 p.m. – 1:15 p.m. They are also encouraged to sit at a table with their collaboration members.
13. After lunch, the real work begins with the afternoon collaboration setting. You set some additional guidelines that includes all members must report each portion of their findings one-by-one before attempting to move to mutually agree on next step procedures.
14. The groups are instructed to collaborate until a common plan is adopted using the formatted form you have handed out to be completed by the group. The form is to be submitted to the main office by 4:30 if possible with a group presenter listed in the space provided on the form. In bold lettering on the form, you have added that each member must publically comment in the proposed plan. Yes, this means since there are multiple groups working from the same data, there will be more than one proposed plan for the data sets. That will be explained shortly.
15. Before going home for the evening, all the groups will come together for a brief meeting with you. You give a brief summary of what happened the first day and what to expect for the next day.

DAY TWO:
1. To start the day out, you have the superintendent there as a special guest, to give a few words of encouragement to the staff. The superintendent encourages you to stay the course, to find ways to make a difference in the lives of the students.
2. You instruct the teams that had the same data sets to meet together in identified classrooms, to make presentations of their findings as one collaborative team. Each

team shares prior to any decisions being made about what information would be presented to the large group.
3. Each classroom team would have a plan in place by the noon meal that would be set up in similar fashion on the previous day, with the larger teams meeting at large tables, to get to know each other.
4. For the afternoon session, the larger groups would each present their findings and plan for a solution to remedy the critical issues.
5. (For the sake of print space and reading time, the readers should get the point by now on how the process works for collaboration).
6. To end the two-day professional development, you summarize the solutions with an encouraging message to the staff. You explain the plans of action will be taken to the superintendent for approval. You ask the teachers to be thinking about what problems or issues may arise from these sets of plans and ask them to be prepared to respond on how to address them.
7. The final task for the staff is to break up into their smaller groups and come up with an encouraging statement using the acronym LION PRIDE that reflects high expectations for all students. You communicate there will be no exceptions for student failure.
8. Before each group leaves, they turn in a response to the acronym and you promise to get them out to the entire group for review prior to meeting again on the first day of professional development for the new school year.

FIRST DAY OF INSERVICE AND PROFESSIONAL DEVELOPMENT FOR THE NEW YEAR

1. You review the two days of development with them and explain to them this year will be different with staff, students, parents and constituents.
2. You instruct the leadership team to finalize the acronym for LION PRIDE and the group agrees on the acronym.
3. Once this is done, you tell them the easy part is completed. You can see a collective groan move through the room. You anticipated this because you reflect on what this day would look like and you begin to line out expectations based on what

the plans are for the school year. Here is where you explain that plans do not work unless people work. Students will follow the leading and modeling of the staff knowing all are working toward the students' best interest.

4. Now, you talk to them about big picture pushback from students, and possibly parents. You discuss what you have come up with thinking about the possibilities of next step communication and implementation of the plan. This is a process of systemic thinking. It prepares campuses to become resilient during the tough times. Everyone is willing to get on board until there is a measure of sweat equity required.

5. You break the staff into their original collaboration groups and ask them to formulate possible challenges from constituents to the plan solutions. (There is no need to get too specific for this exemplar, other than it is important to note that a campus needs to have thought 2-3 possible steps out so as to be prepared for responses.) This helps to create a sense of resiliency in the campus staff in knowing they are prepared to respond when pushback occurs. It also puts everyone on the same page. This also helps to create a culture of professionalism and learning. It is not an easy task because most individuals are conflict-avoidant. They do not want to address these issues head on, but this does help prepare them when the going gets tough.

6. You explain to them that it is time to have a communication strategy in place. One that will effectively present the message to the proper constituents that need first-hand knowledge of the plans and expectations. The plan decided upon for communicating the changes and implementing it is:

    a. Present the plan and changes to the board, including why the changes are needed and how the plans were developed. The leadership team should do this presentation with you as the lead presenter.

    b. Plan for four different open house presentations for parents based on student grade level. Parents are welcome to attend all presentations.

    c. Provide a clear overview of the plan on the school website for the parents, students and community to see.

    d. Meet with the student council before school starts to present the plan to them and ask for their support. (Note: With each meeting, systemic thinking needs to take place based on the feedback received from the meeting, to prepare for the next meeting.)

e. Send a notice out to all students listing the plan and new expectations for the changes.

f. Meet with the students by grade level on the first day of school and explain in more detail how the plan and changes will be implemented and enforced.

g. Allow students to discuss the changes at a designated time in their school day with a teacher in classroom settings, to provide follow-up response by the staff.

h. Principal establishes meetings with local civic groups to communicate the message.

i. Implement the plan and changes with fidelity. Monitor the consistency of the changes made. Be an encourager to all involved and hold all accountable.

j. Monitor, monitor, monitor.

The result of your leadership and planning will be a change in the culture of the school. This will not come without some pushback as stated earlier, but the apathy among the students and staff will be greatly reduced. The campus will enjoy some renewed success in academic achievement because you have improved student achievement through collaboration, resiliency, and change.

A LOOK AT THE INDICATORS FOR COMPETENCY 008

Most readers have looked through either binoculars or a microscope. One of the first things you need to do is to determine on what you are trying to focus. Then, you adjust the power of the instrument to be able to obtain a more clear focus. That is what these indicators do for you. They help you to bring your objective into focus and your focus is improving student performance.

The less ambiguous the entry-level principal can make student performance, the higher the possibility for student success and continuous improvement. These indicators and examples will assist you in bringing clarity to the process. Remember, this competency includes collaboration, resiliency and change as you use your fine and course adjustments on a microscope. You use them as needed to bring into focus the ways to improve student achievement.

A. Demonstrates awareness of social and economic issues that exist within the school and community that affect campus operations and student learning
    - Review the demographics and changes in the last 3-5 years using the reports from the state assessments.
    - Become familiar with your campus attendance zone by driving around the community and visiting with people.
    - Visit with local pastors to get to know the various cultures you are working with during the school day.
    - Read and get to know major cultural celebrations and be able to talk about them.
    - Talk to students.

B. Gathers and organizes information from a variety of sources to facilitate creative thinking, critical thinking, and problem solving to guide effective campus decision making
    - Use websites to see how others are addressing the same challenges you are experiencing.
    - Create a think tank using principals from other campuses that have similar demographics.
    - Use all forms of data such as most recent state assessments, attendance and discipline records, observation records, and attrition records to make informed decisions.
    - Become an expert on the steps used in solving a problem or a challenge. These would include being able to diagnose the problem, prioritize and set goals, establish plans, and implement and monitor the plan.
    - Learn to lead the campus in various collaborative efforts.

C. Frames, analyzes, and creatively resolves campus problems using effective problem-solving techniques to make timely, high-quality decisions

- It is important not to wait for problems to occur, but to find them before they become an issue. The way to identify problems is to monitor your plans and goals that are in place.
- By framing the problem, you are defining the issue in clear terms that can be easily understood and addressed.
- Today's challenges require creativity. Sometimes, the solution is more than one answer. Encourage teachers to be creative in their solutions to improve student achievement.
- Be knowledgeable of problem-solving techniques. These can be different but generally follow this pattern:
    - Identify the issues.
    - Be clear about what is the problem.
    - Understand everyone's interests.
    - List the possible solutions (options).
    - Evaluate the solutions.
    - Select a solution or solutions.
    - Document the agreement(s), and
    - Agree on contingencies, monitoring, and evaluation.
- Be able to make decisions in a timely manner.

D. Develops, implements, and evaluates systems and processes for organizational effectiveness to keep staff inspired and focused on the campus vision
- Create a calendar of instructional walk-through observations.
- Implement expectations of behavior for both students and staff related to student success.
- For every goal and plan implemented, there is an evaluation piece in place to clearly and effectively monitor the success of the goals.
- There are specific assignments for staff members to be accountable for the success of the changes implemented.
- Talk about the campus vision and mission every time there is a meeting.

E. Uses effective planning, time management, and organization of work to support attainment of school district and campus goals
- Keep a "Things to Do List" to begin each day. Prioritize the list.
- Wait until lunch or the end of the day to respond to emails.
- Allow the secretary access to your email account in case there is an urgent email that needs to be addressed by you. (This also helps to maintain the integrity of the account.)
- Complete paperwork before students and staff arrive. You can do this after they leave school, as well.
- Monitor the attainment of campus goals on a daily basis by visiting professional learning communities.

SAMPLE 268 TExES QUESTIONS FOR COMPETENCY 008

1. Mr. Engle's work as the first-year principal during the summer and the beginning of school as has been successful. The plan for making some significant changes has begun to be implemented. He has energized the staff about the plan. However, he is not sure if everyone is on the same page with the changes. Mr. Engle's next best step is to:
    a. Send out an email. State all portions of the plan for improving student achievement should be in place.
    b. Develop and implement a process that will keep the staff inspired about the changes, which include verifying the plan has been implemented with fidelity.
    c. Trust his staff is completing the correct processes. Allow them flexibility to make the needed changes.
    d. Walk the campus halls and peek his head in the doors of the classrooms. Give the teachers a nod to let them know he is in the hallways in case they need him.

2. Mrs. Wallace has just successfully completed a goal-setting process, which requires several changes in the routine of the school day. The staff and students have adjusted to these changes for the most part. However, two teachers from one professional learning community approach her about a concern they have, but neither one can clearly frame the issue. After listening to both of them, she decides to:
   a. Utilize some problem-solving techniques to get a better understanding of what the issue is with the two teachers.
   b. Suggest the teachers return to their PLC and bring the concern up with them.
   c. State that she needs some time to think about the issue. She lets them know she will get back to them in a couple of weeks.
   d. Ask them to talk to some other teachers about it to see if they might have some suggestions that would help remedy their concerns.

3. Mrs. Stagner, the principal at a large inner city elementary is monitoring the halls. During a passing period, she overhears two teachers discussing a student's performance when one of them says, "She just sits there hugging her stomach and won't pick up her pencil to do the work." After hearing the comments, Mrs. Stagner decides to:
   a. Ignore the small talk because there are plenty of students in the same situation.
   b. Ask if they know where the student is at this time so she can discipline her for not completing her work
   c. Request the teachers not talk about students publically, because that might be breaking FERPA laws.
   d. Suggest to the teachers to talk to the student, to see if she has had anything to eat recently because she is aware the student lives in a high poverty government housing.

4. A teacher comes into Mr. Williams' office after school in February on the verge of tears because a couple of her parents have complained in person to her this week

that the rigor of the coursework is too demanding. She is asking too much by asking her students to learn that much information. Mr. Williams discusses with her what she is doing. Next, he concludes she is right where she needs to be based on the agreed upon goals and plan of implementation. The teacher also adds the other members of the PLC team have experienced the same types of responses from parents as well. Given this is not an isolated issue, he decides to:
   a. Call a full faculty meeting. Instruct the teachers and staff to ease up on the plan for improving student achievement until he can get a handle on why the parents are so upset with the level of rigor.
   b. Thank the teacher for letting him know about her concerns and let the issue play out by itself.
   c. Assemble the teachers together and show them the data from the campus-based assessments that indicate the changes made at the beginning of the year are showing positive results. Remind the staff they completed a systemic process to anticipate this very type of feedback. Encourage them to stay the course and keep up the good work.
   d. Ask for the names of the parents who have concerns, call them individually, and reprimand them for complaining to the teachers about doing their best to help their student achieve maximum performance.

5. Since being assigned to be the principal of a struggling junior high in a large city district at the beginning of March, Mr. Hogue has observed there is no system of consistency in the delivery of the curriculum. Teachers are teaching the Essential Knowledge and Skills, but the order is random. It is inconsistent with curriculum guidelines and the scope and sequence. He has observed all the PLC meetings. There is no continuity in the manner any of the meetings are being held. The PLC leaders do not have a full grasp of how to conduct a PLC meeting. Additionally, they have not been held accountable for student performance. In fact, many of the meetings focus on campus discipline problems rather than student academic performance. After some reflection on the issue, Mr. Hogue decides the best strategy to use is to:

a. Issue a directive memo from his office as Executive Director of Instruction for the campus, all PLC's will be run in a manner consistent with district policy.
b. Pull the leadership team in for a full training session on how to conduct a PLC meeting with a focus and consistency of delivering the instruction in a manner consistent with one another. Explain to them that this is not a suggestion, but an expectation for all PLC teams to adhere to the remainder of the school year.
c. Sit back and remain an observer for the rest of the year. Next year, he will include staff training in how to run an effective professional learning community.
d. Invite the district curriculum specialist to come in and make the necessary corrections to the PLC meetings so the teachers get back on track with delivering the curriculum in a manner acceptable to the district.

DOMAIN V – STRATEGIC OPERATIONS (Alignment and Resource Allocation)

There is a stark difference between managing and being a strategist. Managing is the process of accomplishing or succeeding in an objective. A strategist is one who identifies the operations needed to achieve those goals. The entry-level principal should be able to become a strategist, a planner, an organizer of detail in policies, and a plotter. The principal must be *able* to manage the identified goals and objectives of the campus.

The entry-level principal must look at the big picture. The principal must face the challenges and issues confronting the campus and identify the proper solutions, structures, and policies that will move the campus forward. You will use the resources to improve student achievement. Every plan, every objective must have a means of being able to get from the starting point to the ending point. Think of the plan and objectives as the vehicle and until you put wheels on it, it is going to be tough to drive. The principal should be the strategist in leading the way to formulating the details of the plan so the campus will achieve those goals.

You will notice even more in this domain how closely it connects with some of the other domains. Do not become confused, here. The more you can identify structures and policy in as much detail as possible, the better the opportunity you will have of achieving your intended goals listed in your mission and vision.

Let us review those competencies.

CHAPTER 9
DOMAIN V, COMPETENCY 009

WHAT DOES IT SAY?

Competency 009: The entry-level principal knows how to collaboratively determine goals and implement strategies aligned with the school vision that support teacher effectiveness and positive student outcomes.

WHAT DOES IT MEAN?

Stay focused on this one. The competency has some more notable terms in it than you have seen before but it is how you apply them that gives a slightly different connotation to it. Notice also there is a close connectivity to them. The principals who can keep the main thing, the main thing, throughout all the chaos and disruptions that come through a normal school day, will be the ones who realize the greatest improvement in student achievement.

Our country has experienced a global pandemic from the corona virus (COVID-19). Talk about a disruption! This is not a once in a lifetime occurrence. It is more like once in every 100 years. Principals who are collaborating closely with their staff are providing the essential elements of the knowledge and skills needed for students to progress during these challenging times. These principals have a healthy grasp of this particular competency. This will change the face of how schools do business once the pandemic subsides. Those who are working together about how to address this issue will be miles ahead of the others. The solution is not about having the technology. It is how the campus principal strategizes with others to develop effective learning practices during those crazy disruptive times such as a pandemic.

Let us look at the key terms and phrases in this competency to see how they connect to improving student achievement. Focus on the end in mind and work backwards to see if we can obtain a different perspective of what this competency is saying. It is time to dive in to this competency.

What is the ultimate end goal? You want student outcomes. What kind of student outcomes? You want *positive* student outcomes. How do you acquire positive student outcomes? You acquire positive student outcomes by supporting teacher effectiveness. How do you support teacher effectiveness? You start by implementing strategies that are aligned to the goals of the campus. How do you determine the correct strategies? You begin by establishing goals. In addition, how do you establish goals? You ensure they are aligned to the vision and mission of the campus. How do you align the vision and mission of the campus? Here is the magic word...*COLLABORATE!* (See Figure 9.1)

By now, if you have been reading through this textbook, you have read some form of this word, collaborate, well over one-hundred times. If you expect to be a successful principal for any length of time, you must embrace the process and learn from it each time.

Briefly, you are an educational strategist who is willing to take the most recent data and collaborate with staff and constituents to identify the high leverage points of challenges in the data. You will use the information to create clearly defined, measurable goals that connect to the vision and mission of the campus. You will also work together to determine the appropriate instructional strategies that will engage all students to reach these goals. How do you do that? By starting with the end in mind.

Figure 9.1: The foundation of any lasting student academic success begins with a solid core of continuous collaboration.

WHAT DOES IT LOOK LIKE? (EXEMPLAR)

As the campus principal of a middle school, you have been pleased with the implementation of your new vision and mission, along with the campus goals for the year, improving student achievement. However, as with everyone else, you have been concerned about the rising number of students who are missing school because of an extremely strong strain of the flu. In fact, the entire region is experiencing the same thing among their students. The challenge is that it is the third week in February. Your staff is entering crunch time. It is a Tuesday morning. The superintendent calls to inform you the entire district will be closed the next week to try to stem the tide of rising illnesses.

Approval to close the district for a week was granted by the state agency as long as the district and campuses are able to verify continued instruction during the closure. The final words from the superintendent gives each campus the authority to pursue learning as they deem is appropriate, but it will need to pass approval from the state agency through a district submission. The plans must be on the desk of the superintendent by the end of the day on Thursday, for his review and approval prior to submitting the plans on Friday.

You begin the process by communicating with your entire staff and students of the impending brief break in school attendance, but not in student learning during the break. You officially announce to the students that learning will continue through online technology that has been provided to all students.

Then, you begin to execute a strategy to continue the process of learning while students remain at home the following week. You make the following plans for the continuation of student learning.

1. You send a personal message to lead teachers in the building to make plans to meet with you the last two hours of the school day that day (Tuesday).
2. You identify staff to cover in those classes during your collaboration meeting with the teachers for the last two hours of the day.

3. You review your student outcomes for the following week, using the Year-At-A-Glance information agreed upon by the instructional leadership teams for each grade and subject area.
4. You target the specific learning goals for the campus and connect the instructional lessons for the next week to those goals, to ensure the high leverage learning indicators will be addressed appropriately.
5. You create a format that will be used consistently throughout the subjects and grade levels so students will get a sense of continuity throughout the campus. Included on the format will be a list of "hot spots" where parents and students may go if they do not have access to internet in their home.
6. You execute some non-negotiables for the week students and staff will be at home.
    a. Once the week's assignments have been developed through collaboration, reviewed by the lead teacher for each professional learning community, all formatted assignments must be verified that students can access the material and resources through the existing technology.
    b. The teachers must be available to all students each day, from 9:00 a.m. – 11:30 p.m. and from 1:00 p.m. to 3:00 p.m. each day.
    c. The venue the students or parents will use to contact teachers will be through the remote learning platform used by the school. All students and parents have enrolled in the learning platform and have access to it during the year.
    d. Teachers will prepare and present videos over new information. They place those videos on the internet platform being used. Those videos will be noted in the daily formatted assignments along with what is being introduced.
    e. Any written assignments will be submitted through the internet platform. Students who are underperforming or do not demonstrate mastery on assignments will be retaught those skills when school resumes.
    f. Students who do not appear to be participating will be contacted and encouraged to participate through the online platform being used for instruction.
    g. Students who have the flu will be temporarily excused from completing the work until they are well enough to do so.

    h. All teachers in each grade and subject are to provide a description of evidence of learning during the week students are away from the campus.
7. You create a schedule for the staff of each grade level and subject area to meet for two hours on Wednesday. You schedule to use existing staff, substitute teachers, and a few volunteer parents to assist by covering the classes during this time.
    a. Reading and math will meet from 8:30 a.m. – 10:30 a.m.
    b. Social studies, science, and fine arts will meet from 1:00 p.m. – 3:00 p.m.
    c. Any assignment for the following week that needs to be addressed will be addressed by the lead teacher in making a decision to meet at the end of the day on Wednesday, if necessary.
8. All lead teachers will have a substitute for the morning meeting on Thursday, to verify the assignments address learning objectives. All materials and resources are accessible to the students listed in the plans.
9. All plans are to be submitted to you by 1:00 p.m. on Thursday, for your review and submission.
10. To execute this strategy, you meet with your lead teachers at the designated time to cover your non-negotiables to be implemented. You do ask your lead teachers to work with other teachers in their respective disciplines at the scheduled times. You do this to verify the instructional strategies are used to present the information in a way that the students can understand. Additionally, parents are able to assist in the learning.
11. Remind the lead teachers if there are any additional resources needed, to let you know as soon as possible so you can assist in locating those for the staff.
12. Encourage the lead teachers to keep the focus on the planning, reminding them the objective for the PLC meeting to be held on Wednesday, is to provide consistent learning with continuity, with a focus on student mastery of the learning.
13. Let them know you will be sitting in on all meetings for a time to observe and to be there to answer questions.

Once you have established and communicated the expectations for learning, allow your lead teachers to do their job. You will be available to help with questions as they arise during the planning sessions. If any changes are made that influence what has been communicated, make sure the other PLC teams receive the information.

Since this is a district-wide process, there will be a communication sent out from the Central Office. Be sure to be consistent in communicating the message of the district to the parents when they call or email for clarification.

Keep the focus on learning. Communicate that message with every student, teacher, staff member and parent during the temporary transition to online learning. A change in environment does not have to mean a loss in instructional learning and mastery.

A LOOK AT THE INDICATORS FOR COMPETENCY 009

Teachers and staff want to be valued. At this point, the reader should understand the importance of establishing goals based on the vision and mission of the campus. It would be fairly easy and even time saving for a principal to write some measurable goals and be done with it. However, the intent here is to generate goals that will create ownership by working together. Collaboration allows people to express their own opinions even if they may not be considered in the final decisions for the direction the campus eventually decides to move toward.

When people's opinions are heard, they feel they have a part in the process. They are more likely to develop a sense of ownership in the process and the outcomes that are agreed upon. It is the principal's responsibility to create that atmosphere of teamwork among the staff. Remember, this whole process is about the end game. That end game is improving student performance. The best way to do that is to get as many people as possible on board with the campus mission, vision, and goals.

A. Assesses the current needs of the campus, analyzing a wide set of evidence to determine campus objectives, and sets measurable school goals, targets, and strategies that form the school's strategic plans
- Reviews all forms of data gathering including, but not limited to campus-based assessments, state assessments, PLC agenda notes, student discipline, student absenteeism rate, teacher absenteeism rate, teacher return rate, parent and

community surveys, student surveys, and staff surveys to determine highest leverage points for improvement.
- Identify the objectives for the following year using collaboration among the staff by creating measurable descriptors.
- Use the goals to identify specific instructional strategies to address the objectives created.
- Verify the strategies and address the measurable objectives, that they are aligned to the state and local instructional standards.
- Develop a plan of implementation.

B. Establishes structures that outline and track the progress using multiple data points and makes adjustments as needed to improve teacher effectiveness and student outcomes
- Create a calendar of implementation through staff collaboration for all to follow.
- Identify *how* and *when* the identified measurable objectives will be assessed.
- Identify what observable measures will be used to determine success.
- Create assessments to measure objectives through specific analysis questions.
- Make adjustments using PLC teams when assessments show little or no growth toward achieving those objectives.

C. Allocates resources effectively (e.g., staff time, master schedule, dollars, and tools), aligning them with school objectives and goals, and works to access additional resources as needed to support learning
- Contact curriculum specialists to determine effective available resources.
- Provide time in the school day for professional learning communities to meet.
- Create a master schedule that focuses on providing additional time in reading, math, science, and history.
- Adjust the budget to allocate specific funds for resources identified by the staff to improve instruction to meet the stated goals.
- Be an advocate at the central office for additional funds and/or resources to meet the instructional goals of the campus.

D. Implements appropriate management techniques and group processes to define roles, assign functions, delegate authority, and determine accountability for campus goal attainment
- Identify key systems for implementation.
- Ensure *each* member of the staff understands their role in meeting the goals of the campus.
- Develop leadership through training and delegating authority to lead teachers. Allow them the freedom to do their job.
- Each meeting starts with a review of the vision and mission. The campus reviews the goals and ways the campus is in meeting them.
- Continuously look for databased, research-based instructional strategies that align with the campus goals. Communicate those to the staff for consideration.

SAMPLE 268 TExES QUESTIONS FOR COMPETENCY 009

1. Mr. Hedlund was beginning his first year as a principal of a high school in a suburban district. In reviewing the data over the first part of the summer, it was apparent the students' performance in several areas were not matching expectations. He was previously a part of a successful campus as a high-performing teacher. He was disappointed in the campus' performance and where to begin to improve the state scores. Mr. Hedlund's first option would most likely be to:
    a. Contact the curriculum specialists. Ask them to identify the poor performing teachers and prepare to contact them for individual conferences.
    b. Call in all of the lead teachers from the previous year who are returning. Ask them to explain why their scores are below what they should be for the student population.
    c. Create a plan of action that includes implementing specific strategies that address the high leverage points he has identified.
    d. Begin with the end in mind. Use the data to determine where the two or three highest leverage points are to begin planning staff development.

2. After sitting in on a math PLC, it becomes apparent the group lacks leadership. There is no focus on the agenda for improving student scores in the two high-leverage points identified in the previous month's staff development at the beginning of the year. Much of the discussion is even off task. As principal of the campus, Ms. Walton has to make a decision to help the group return to focus on instructional strategies that improve student achievement. She decides to:
    a. Make an executive decision to bring the group back on task for the moment. Make a mental note to pull in the lead teacher for some intentional training on how to conduct a professional learning community using the campus-designed agenda.
    b. Hold the group accountable for not staying on task and following the agenda of the professional learning community. Make an executive decision that their evaluations will reflect their lack of coordination and cooperation as a team.
    c. Ignore the conversation for the time being and return in a couple of weeks to see if they have been able to get on track with meeting the goals established in the professional development prior to the start of school.
    d. Politely enter the conversation, but does not change the course of the conversation. The group will know she is not a threat to them so they feel comfortable in their setting.

3. As principal of a large inner city elementary with a high number of low social-economic students and a mix of various cultures, Mrs. Shipley is pleased with the progress of the staff development. The teachers have identified the two major high leverage points that need to be addressed. The staff has created sound measurable goals for the coming school year. Then, one of the teachers asks how the money for the additional resources are going to be found? After carefully considering her question she explains to the staff that the first step in finding additional money to achieve the goals will be to:

a. Make an executive decision to eliminate two aides to garner enough money so the teachers will have the resources they need to meet the campus goals for the year.
   b. Indicate to the staff that based on the goals established for the year, the current budget will be scrubbed. The budget will be realigned for any excess funds to help with the necessary resources needed to meet the stated goals.
   c. Make an executive decision to meet with the district Chief Financial officer. Request additional funds to help with the purchase of the necessary resources.
   d. Explain to the staff that the campus will hold a fundraiser to raise the necessary funds in order to purchase the resources needed. She will contact the school's PTA once school has begun.

4. The teachers are excited about the two-day staff development that has just been completed. The high leverage points have been identified and address the challenge in very tight and measurable goals. There is a measure of enthusiasm that has not been felt since Mr. Rammage was selected from the campus administrative staff, to lead the school for the next year. Now that there are measurable goals in place for the year, the next best step for Mr. Rammage is to:
   a. Write an individual note to all staff members, encouraging them to have a great year. He wishes them well on helping the campus to obtain the stated goals.
   b. Contact the curriculum department of the district. Ask them to identify specific instructional strategies the campus needs in place to meet their goals so that the campus will have some ideas in which to begin the year.
   c. Ask the staff to meet in their PLC teams to establish specific roles and routines for ensuring the success of implementation of appropriate instructional strategies. Each team will be instructed to be prepared to report to the group.

d. Dismiss the group. Then, go to the office to prepare a directive on how the goals will be met through the PLC groups. Dictate the exact roles and responsibilities to follow in order to meet those goals.

5. Mrs. Murphy was selected to be the principal of an elementary campus located in a semi-rural district with a mix of cultures, socio-economic status, and ethnic groups. However, her campus has done an excellent job of identifying the appropriate high leverage points of concern. They have established reasonable, yet challenging goals for the students. The teachers have begun to plan for the year. Despite her best efforts at scrubbing the current budget, her teachers need more resources for reading and math. They need more manipulatives to teach the necessary skills required to master the learning objectives tied to the goals. She is two weeks into the first nine-week grading period. After some reflection, she decides her next best step is to:

   a. Decide to call a meeting of the lead teachers from each of the subject areas to collaborate on the need for more time for reading and math, as well as the need for more manipulatives. Ask them to help come up with a schedule and review their budgets for any additional funds for manipulatives.
   b. Call the superintendent. Explain that the campus will not be able to meet their stated goals without additional help from the district in the form of increased funding in order to support the purchase of math manipulatives. She clarifies she needs the superintendent's help in convincing the CFO to increase the campus budget.
   c. Be open and honest with the staff. Tell them the budget and schedule are set. They will have to do the best they can with what they have for the time being.
   d. Contact the curriculum department to see if they can come up with a better schedule for the campus that would include more seat time for the students in reading and math. Request additional funds for manipulatives.

CHAPTER 10
DOMAN V, COMPETENCY 010

WHAT DOES IT SAY?

Competency 010: The entry-level principal knows how to provide administrative leadership through resource management, policy implementation, and coordination of school operations and programs to ensure a safe learning environment.

WHAT DOES IT MEAN?

This competency seems harmless until something goes awry. This happens when a campus principal fails to make the necessary changes to provide the resources needed for an efficiently run campus. Hidden within this competency is the principal's capacity to provide leadership while ensuring the campus is well maintained. The faculty is working in safe conditions. The students are learning in a safe environment. The air conditioning and heating systems are working. All lights are working properly. Restrooms are kept clean and are in good condition. Classrooms are inviting places to learn with relation to the physical plant. The floors and rooms are properly maintained to meet high expectations of a safe learning environment.

Policies of the school are being implemented and administered in a fair and equitable manner towards all staff and students. They are reviewed regularly with adjustments made as needed and approved by the campus leadership team.

District policies are implemented and administered equally across the board. Everyone is treated with respect, regardless of race, religion or ethnicity.

This competency means as the campus leader you will not show any favoritism whatsoever toward the dissemination of resources to your campus staff. If your budget calls for the replacement of six classrooms of student desks, the principal will replace the desks of the classrooms who have had the same desks the longest period of time. He will disburse the better-maintained desks to other classrooms, if that is what is needed to be done. (See Figure 10.1)

The principal is responsible for communicating the message that the school is a place of learning. Everyone should be held accountable for creating an environment that promotes learning. Students should be taught to pick up after themselves, to keep restroom areas clean after use. By executing this, it helps students to create a sense of pride in their learning environment.

It is about having a safe learning environment. The principal should be scheduling regular and routine maintenance walks with the custodians to evaluate the condition and safety of the school. This should include but not be limited to an evaluation of the following systems in a building:

- Entryways should be clear of all clutter. Doors should be working properly as well as kept clean of any debris upon approaching the entryways.
- Check all windows to ensure they are clean, working properly and are not cracked or damaged.
- Check for clutter such as extra campus furniture that should be stored in a safe place away from the normal school traffic and out of sight.
- Check all restrooms for plumbing, graffiti, cleanliness and adequate toiletry items.
- Ensure the heating, ventilating, and cooling systems are functioning properly in each area of the campus.
- Inspect for proper drainage issues around the building that could cause water to seep beneath the building and cause foundation problems.
- Inspect and ensure that all entryways have handicapped accessibility according to state and federal laws.
- Ensure that waste cans are emptied; floors are swept on a regular and routine basis.
- Confirm that all classroom doors work properly and can be secured during shelter-in-place drills.
- Develop a yearly painting schedule so that the classrooms are painted on a rotating basis over a five-year cycle.
- Regularly praise the custodial staff in campus meeting when their work warrants recognition.

A campus cannot run efficiently without having an efficient discipline management policy that is implemented in a fair and consistent manner. Students want to learn in an environment that is safe from chaotic disruptions, where general student misbehavior is addressed in a consistent and orderly fashion. Strong discipline management programs have a short list of classroom expectations that are implemented and administered by all campus staff regardless of whether the student is in class, in a passing period, the library, the cafeteria, the gym or any other place in the building or on the campus grounds. The consistency of the entry-level principal builds compliance. Following the rules and guidelines develops an atmosphere for a more safe and secure environment.

The discipline management plan should include all state mandated consequences for those selected offenses. Those are non-negotiables. They are implemented as stated in Texas Education Code and in the Texas Administrative Code. It is always a good idea to have the most recent copy of these in your office for reference. When in doubt, always consult your district attorney in matters of discipline related to school law.

Additional minor offenses should be clearly outlined. The consequences are implemented on a fair and equitable basis to ensure the compliance needed for a safe and orderly environment.

There is not a one-size-fits-all discipline management plan that works successfully for every campus. The principal must take into consideration the needs of the campus and the culture of the community before collaborating with the school to develop a plan that works for that learning community. Be consistent, fair, and equitable in every situation. The way to do that is to have a system in place that is very clear about what the consequences will be when certain misbehaviors occur. You communicate the plan effectively to all of the constituents, including the students and the parents.

Policy implementation does not start or stop with students. The principal must ensure all staff are following district and campus policies regarding their working environment and expectations for following those policies as they are stated. Staff are expected to show up at a designed time and to remain until a designated time. Anyone in education knows most teachers and educators put in vastly greater hours than stated on their contract. However, as a matter of safety, teachers are expected to be on campus and in their classrooms at specific times to support the safety of the learning environment.

Very few educators start out intending to be late or make a conscious decision to let students off the hook "just this one time," but all habits begin with the first incident. Over time, it becomes easier to slide into those habits unless all are held accountable for their behavior. The principal must have the leadership courage to address and confront those concerns as they arise. This competency addresses all of the district and campus policies implemented to assist in creating a safe and professional environment.

A topic of importance in this area is Special Education. Although Special Education is an aspect of the instructional learning environment, there are many specific school laws tied to providing students who qualify, with the same opportunities as children who do not qualify. The principal is responsible for the integration of students into the Least Restrictive Environment that will provide them with the best setting for success. Principals and teachers do not get to do whatever they want to do. The law requires Individual Education Programs (IEPs) for each student who qualifies. They are not suggestions. The overarching purpose is to provide a platform whereby every child can experience success while mastering the identified standards. The principal is to be the campus advocate for all students, especially for those who qualify for Special Education.

Another topic the principal needs to be keenly aware of is the campus budget. The principal is the custodian of the campus finances. There may be others on the campus such as a campus secretary who may assign the appropriate funding numbers when disbursing funds and establishing purchase orders, but the campus principal is the Chief Financial Officer for the campus. A regular review of purchases and amendments to the budget should be made to serve as an accountability check for the proper disbursements of funds. Communities do not like for their hard-earned tax dollars to be mismanaged and misappropriated. Be knowledgeable and diligent about expenditures in this area.

This particular competency cannot be covered in total, but just keep a keen eye on non-instructional processes. The one area where management is so important is this competency. If you pay close attention to it, then you are more likely to eliminate time-consuming problems and issues down the road. That will allow you to focus on the main thing, which is instruction.

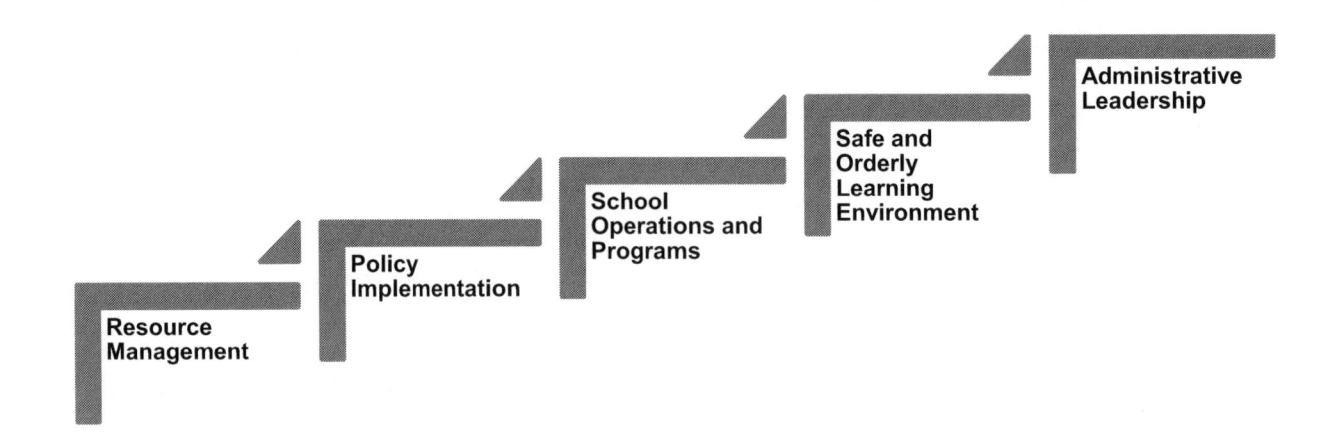

Figure 10.1: Effective Administrative leadership involves ensuring all of the steps of campus and district requirements are in place and administered appropriately.

WHAT DOES IT LOOK LIKE? (EXEMPLAR)

You have just successfully completed your second year as an assistant principal in a large inner city high school when the superintendent calls. He informs you to come to his office to meet with him. When you get there, you find out that you were selected from a pool of applicants who applied and were interviewed for the principal's position at another high school in the district.

The superintendent congratulates you and gives you a directive. He tells you to bring some discipline back into the school. He explains you will be approved at the next Board meeting, but wants you to get started right away.

He proceeds to tell you that the school has been in disarray the past couple of years. He has had his fill of teachers and parents complaining about the lack of discipline. The campus is on the verge of becoming an unsafe place to learn. He explains that one of the reasons you were selected was because of your ability to "run a tight ship" at your current campus.

Aside from being excited about being named the principal, you are already thinking about the next steps to help your new campus to gain back control of the campus, to establish a more safe and orderly environment. For one, you need to finish your responsibilities at your current high school so you can set up your office as soon as possible at your new assignment as the principal. During this time in the transition, you make some notes of steps that need to be taken to meet the directive of the superintendent. Obviously, your goal is meeting his directive, so you begin to take some copious notes to begin changing the culture and environment of your new assignment.

Here are a few items, but not an exhaustive list of steps you have written down to begin making an impact at your new campus so you can provide a safer and more inviting learning climate:

1. Meet with the current office and administrative staff separately. Introduce yourself. Explain you will meet with each of them separately to begin getting to know each of them. Ask for their help in the transition. Make a note to yourself to be a good listener, to take notes on each person's comments. Also, be prepared to write a handwritten letter to people you talk to and thank them for their time and commitment.

2. Meet with each of the office staff starting with your secretary. *As with ALL of these meetings it is of the utmost importance that you have at least one other person in attendance. This is especially true during the summer hours when the building is sparsely populated. This provides the stage for complete professionalism during these meetings.* Once you have passed the greetings and concerns, ask her to construct a sign-up sheet for all staff to schedule a meeting, to come in and visit individually with you. Make each meeting 30 minutes in length, but schedule 45 minutes between the meetings to allow for longer meetings. You will use any extra time to summarize notes, to write letters to each individual, and mail letters the next day.

3. Be prepared to receive a few responses from teachers and staff that they are either unable or unwilling to meet with you during their time off the contract. Try not to formulate any preconceived ideas about these respondents. Have the secretary make a note to schedule them in your calendar after they have reported for their contracted days of service. Once you start meeting with the teachers and staff, the other staff will begin hearing about the feedback. Their curiosity will get most of

them. They will contact the secretary for a meeting, because most will want to be a part of the solution.

4. Begin meeting with each person and stay on the schedule. Listen for the red flags that need to be addressed other than the improvement in the discipline management and school safety.

5. Keep a running list of concerns of who expressed what. This will help to establish a preponderance of evidence for the challenges listed. Also, ask your secretary for a classroom map of where teachers are located to determine if there is a physical part of the school that shows more of a concern than other areas. It may be this might be a place where advocating for security cameras may come in handy if requesting additional funds to meet those needs is necessary.

6. Be sure to give each person the same amount of attention and time when you meet. Most people will be grateful for the opportunity to get to know you and to share their concerns. With today's instant media technology, social visiting will spread the word quickly that you are interested and intent on serving the staff.

7. Be honest during these meetings. Do not to promise anything you are not 100% sure you are able to deliver on during the course of the school year when teachers return from the summer break.

8. Have your secretary identify key parents in the community and do the same with them. Keep the number between 5-8 parents so you can begin building those relationships and coalition of support in the community. These need to be parents who will pass the word around once they have met with you.

9. Review all of your staff comments. Identify the concerns related to discipline management and school safety once you have completed your introductory meetings.

10. Begin using this information to map out a two-day staff development training to address the issues and concerns.

11. This staff development begins with you talking about the main challenges the school has from the meetings held over the summer. You explain you are there to be a part of the collaboration process. You will do everything to provide a safe and orderly environment. You want teachers and students to learn in a safe environment.

12. There needs to be a review of the campus vision and mission statement, if there is one. Every goal established must have an end in mind. Use collaboration to have teams describe what they want their school to look like. Once each team has shared, you ask the hard questions such as:
    a. What do WE have to do to get from point A to point B?
    b. What needs to be in place for us to experience this new environment and culture?
    c. What agreed upon written classroom expectations and policies need to be in place for this to happen?
    d. What are the expectations for the school administration and office staff?
    e. What are the expectations for the students?
    f. What are the expectations for the parents?
    g. How will we communicate the changes to all?
13. You have teachers and staff separated in groups where they do not normally work. Ask them to respond to each of these questions.
14. Prior to the beginning of the staff development, you establish a rough draft of a new discipline management policy that needs local campus consequences put into place. The discipline management plan will include expectations for all constituents.
15. After the first day of collaborating over the questions, coming to some agreement of expectations, you insert those into your rough plan that evening. You prepare a draft document to be discussed for the next day. This document includes a list of common classroom rules of five or less expectations the teachers agreed upon on the first day.
16. During the second day of finalizing the draft of a discipline management plan, you explain that the whole purpose is to change the culture from one of fear and confusion to safe environment that can focus on learning.
17. As a review, go over the list of concerns that were brought up during the individual summer meetings. Ask each PLC team if those concerns have been addressed. Do not move on to the next one until everyone believes they have been properly addressed.

18. Once you have a firm sense that all of the issues have been addressed, explain that words on a page have good intentions, but do not get the job done. It is putting feet to the plan and providing a comprehensive implementation of that plan which includes constant monitoring and vigilance toward working the plan. This includes the absolute commitment of every employee. Attitudes do not change behavior. Behavior, which is easily evaluated, can influence and change attitude.
19. Clearly communicate that everyone is accountable for maintaining a safe and orderly climate, inside and outside of the classroom. Once the staff all understand that this is a team effort, the real work begins.
20. Ask a few people on the staff to clean up the rough draft about grammar and spelling. Prepare the document for presentation to the students, staff and parents.
21. Inform the superintendent of the progress and that communication of the new staff and student expectations will be disseminated through all media sources available.
22. Plan for parent meetings prior to the start of school for parents and students to attend, to explain the changes being made. Be prepared to answer the hard questions about the previous climate of the school.
23. Implement the plan. Be sure to have administrative staff who will follow the stated consequences consistently and fairly, regardless of the student.
24. Evaluate the progress of the discipline management plan on a regular basis to check for inconsistencies or unforeseen gaps in enforcing the policy.
25. Be visible in the building and the classrooms, as well as the cafeteria to be a deterrent to student misbehavior.
26. Get feedback from your students, teachers, parents, and community on a regular basis.

There are a number of other steps that can be taken in this process, but the intent of the exemplar has been met. The principal is focused on being the learning leader of the campus, but until the non-instructional issues and concerns have been addressed properly, instruction will continue to take a back seat. If instruction takes a back seat for too long, scores will begin to decline and so will your expectation for maintaining your principal position. Take care of your business, so you can take care of THE business…improving instruction.

A LOOK AT THE INDICATORS FOR COMPETENCY 010

If there is ever a place that can get an administrator in trouble in a hurry, it is this competency. If the administrator is allowing district policy or rules to be skirted on the campus, trouble is coming. If the administrator is misappropriating funds in the campus budget, trouble is coming. If the administrator is not following carefully outlined state and federal laws regarding students with special needs, trouble is coming. If students and staff are not held accountable to a fair and equitably designed discipline management policy, trouble is coming. If the administrator does not properly take care of the physical plant and its surroundings, yes, trouble is coming.

Taxpayers want their children and property to be cared for in a manner where they would expect safety for the students and proper upkeep of the school facility. When those expectations are not met the administrator's time as the campus leader will be short. However, this competency can be conquered by a principal who willing to face the non-instructional issues. One who works to create that safe and secure environment parents and community members expect to have on a campus. Here are the indicators for this competency and some ways the administrator can show these indicators are being implemented.

A. Implements strategies that enable the physical plant, equipment, and support systems to operate safely, efficiently, and effectively to maintain a conducive learning environment
- Create a calendar to regularly review all physical plant systems.
- Create a calendar to review regularly, the work processes of the assigned custodians.
- Place work requests in to the central office in a timely manner when there are needs for equipment or supply replacements.
- Take notes of all issues and concerns with large-purchase systems such as HV/AC and make sure they are included on the district budget for repair or replacement as needed.
- Complete impromptu evaluations of building safety and cleanliness.

B. Applies strategies for ensuring the safety of students and personnel and for addressing emergencies and security concerns, including developing and implementing a crisis plan
- Develop and implement an updated crisis management plan that includes a communication piece to the central office, the Public Information Officer, the parents and the community.
- Conduct all state-required drills based on the requirements for each drill. Schedule these on the calendar so they will not be overlooked.
- Implement a safe and secure discipline management program that is fair and equitable to all parties.
- Ensure the building is well-maintained with good lighting with no "dark" spots that may encourage inappropriate behavior.
- Install hallway security cameras as deemed necessary by your leadership team to help detour any unacceptable behavior in the hallways of low-traffic areas.

C. Applies local, state, and federal laws and policies to support sound decisions while considering implications related to all school operations and programs (e.g., student services, food services, health services, and transportation)
- Check periodically to ensure that Foods of Minimal Nutritional Value are being served using the correct proportions in the cafeteria.
- Review campus policies to ensure they are meeting requirements of district and state laws.
- Evaluate implementations of policies to ensure they are being implemented with the intent of the law in mind.
- Serve as an advocate for students with special needs.
- Review bus routes to ensure students are not spending an undue amount of time on the bus in route to and from their residence.

D. Collaboratively plans and effectively manages the campus budget within state law and district policies to promote sound financial management in relation to accounts, bidding, purchasing, and grants
- Become comfortable with using the different budget codes used for expenditures.
- Monitor the expenditures of the budget so the amount does not exceed the allotted amount for any particular budget code or fund.
- Guard against using money from a different account that does not legally apply to the expenditure unless the account has been amended with the money approved for transfer per district and state guidelines.
- Work with teachers to determine the budget needs for the coming year, based on the vision, mission, and goals of the campus.
- Meet regularly with the district Chief Financial Officer to determine any inefficiencies or amendments that need to be made in the budget.

E. Uses technology to enhance school management (e.g., attendance systems, teacher grade books, shared drives, and messaging systems)
- Review the attendance policies to ensure the teachers are appropriately taking attendance for each class.
- Review teacher online grading systems to ensure the grading policies are being followed per the district policy.
- Determine technology needs of the teachers and students as it relates to the campus goals. Additionally, ensure the technology is available and up-to-date.
- Teach email etiquette for all staff. Remind them all correspondence on the email system is professional and relates to student learning.
- Encourage the use of instructional technology with students.

F. Facilitates the effective coordination of campus curricular, co-curricular, and extracurricular programs in relation to other school district programs to fulfill the academic, developmental, social, and cultural needs of students
- Works with each of the subject area professional learning communities to ensure the state standards are being met through the instructional delivery design.

- Work closely with fine arts departments to verify Essential Knowledge and Skills are being taught. Equipment should be safe and in proper working order.
- Meet with extra-curricular staff to determine equipment used is safe and reliable. All participation areas are clear of any hazardous issues or concerns.
- Ensure that all cultural norms are respected in the delivery of curriculum and extra-curricular activities.
- Review policies being used by curricular, co-curricular, and extra-curricular programs to ensure the fair and equitable application with enforcement is being used in an appropriate fashion.

G. Collaborates with district staff to ensure the understanding and implementation of district policies and advocates for the needs of students and staff
- Create a calendar where there is a certified administrator present for all Admission, Review, and Dismissal (ARD) meetings.
- Ensure that state and federal laws are adhered to during the meetings.
- Ensure that all parties affix their signature during the ARD meetings.
- Ensure that all Individual Education Programs (IEPs) are being carried out by the teachers and support staff.
- Serve as an advocate for the student with special needs.

H. Implements strategies for student discipline and attendance in a manner that ensures student safety, consistency, and equity that legal requirements are met (e.g., due process, SPED requirements)
- Review current discipline management policies for fair and equitable administration of consequences.
- Ensure teachers and staff are enforcing the discipline management policy in a consistent, fair, and equitable manner. It is important to let them know you will support them when they enforce unpopular policies.
- Ensure students sent to the office on a disciplinary referral are treated with respect. They are allowed to tell their side of the incident prior to assigning disciplinary action.

- Contact parents of students who are sent to the office. Inform the parents of the infraction and the consequences.
- Safeguard that all laws related to regular education students and students with special needs are adhered to in a professional manner.
- A good procedure to have in place is to have female teachers address female dress code concerns to avoid any accusations from students or parents rather than male teachers addressing the issue.

SAMPLE 268 TExES QUESTIONS FOR COMPETENCY 010

1. Mr. Thomas has just finished an informal walk-through of his high school campus where he was newly assigned over the summer. He had been focusing on establishing the goals with the teachers using collaborative strategies. They appeared to be going well. However, during this walk-through of nearly all of the classrooms, he has noticed a significant difference in classroom rules. This was evidence of a lack of consistent enforcement of the campus discipline management plan. Mr. Thomas' best next step is to:
    a. Review current discipline management policies for fair and equitable administration of consequences to make plans for a review of the expectations at the next staff meeting.
    b. Allow the teachers to continue to work their own plans until there is an issue with students sent to the office not based on the discipline management plan.
    c. Ignore the concern since it did not come up in the staff development prior to the start of the year.
    d. Direct his assistant principal to complete a walk-through on the classrooms and perform a write-up. The assistant principal will submit a note to file for teachers who are not following the discipline management plan.

2. Mr. Kello was selected the principal of the middle school. He previously served as the assistant principal for three years at the same campus. His main responsibilities included discipline management and building maintenance. Mr. Kello hired a new

assistant principal with no administrative experience who was a teacher on another campus. Two weeks into the school year, Mr. Kello began to get phone calls from parents who were complaining about the assistant principal because he was not contacting them about the issues in which their children were involved. Mr. Kello decides to:

   a. Inform the parents, the school is not responsible for contacting them. Tell them the students need to behave themselves so they do not put the parent in that situation again.
   b. Let the parents know he will take care of their concerns, and then quietly monitor the situation for another week to determine the issue.
   c. Let the parents know it is the responsibility of the school to contact parents about students sent to the office on disciplinary referrals, to inform the parents of the infraction and the consequences. He additionally will give some immediate training for the assistant principal on expectations of communication with parents whenever students are sent to the office on a referral.
   d. Listen politely to the parent concerns, then call the assistant principal in and issue a written warning for not following school and district policy.

3. Mrs. Parker was recently selected the principal of a large junior high in a high economically disadvantaged area of the school district. At one of the first ARD meetings six weeks into the year, she learned from the diagnostician, that there was one teacher in particular for this student, who was openly refusing to follow the IEP as written because it was too much trouble to implement. Mrs. Parker decides that her next best step is to:

   a. Ask the diagnostician to meet with the teacher. Have her instruct the teacher to resume the requirements of the IEP in full. Ask her to observe the classroom regularly to verify the student's IEP expectations are being met and to report to her in a month.
   b. Review the IEP to see if the teacher is correct in that it is too much trouble to implement the student's IEP.

c. Remind the members of the ARD committee that it is the responsibility of the school to implement all requirements of the ARD and the student's IEP.
   d. Explain to the teacher we are all here to ensure the students' IEPs are implemented as written and that she will ensure that all Individual Education Programs (IEPs) are being carried out by the teacher and support staff as approved in the ARD.

4. Mrs. Lynch is serving as principal of her first campus. The year has gotten off to a great start. There appears to be good collaborative meetings, and classroom instruction is going well. When she returns to her office, the secretary has placed the Public Information Education Management System (PIEMS) report on her desk to sign for the first nine weeks of class. As she thumbs through the pages, Mrs. Lynch notices that there are some discrepancies in attendance reporting from a few of the teachers. When she asks the secretary about the issue, the secretary comments that the teachers in questions usually say they were too busy to take roll at the designated time. After a more careful review of the PIEMS report, Mrs. Lynch identifies the teachers who have not correctly submitted their attendance. Her next step is to:
   a. Meet separately with the identified teachers. Remind them to accurately take attendance for each class at the designated time. Inform them that student attendance is how districts and campuses are allotted money the following year. It is important to follow those procedures closely.
   b. Send an email out to the entire campus reminding the teachers of the seriousness of not taking attendance properly. Explain that not doing so will affect the financial status of the district and campus if the average daily attendance drops.
   c. Call in each teacher individually, write them up on a warning and place the warning into their evaluation files. Inform each of them if they continue to remain flippant about taking attendance, they will be non-renewed for the next year.

d. Sign the PIEMS report and ask the secretary to inform her if the problems persists.

5. Mr. Hadley is the principal of an elementary school with most of the students being bussed to the campus. They live further than two miles from the campus. At the end of the day, Mr. Hadley returns to his office to complete some paperwork when he receives a phone call from an irate parent. The parent is complaining that her second grade daughter is only spending thirty minutes on the bus going to school, but spending an hour and a half on the bus before she arrives home. Mr. Hadley takes her name, the student's name, the home address of the student and informs the parent he will look into the length of time the student is spending on the bus to get back home. Mr. Hadley's next best step is to:
   a. Put the information aside for a few days until he can get more important work done. Then, look into the issue in a few days.
   b. Call the transportation department and complain to them for establishing routes that allow that much time for a student to have to remain on the bus. Then, call the superintendent to complain. This should resolve the issue.
   c. Calmly tell the parent that with the start of school, there are always a few glitches in the transportation with students. Ask the parent to give the process a few weeks for the issue to resolve itself and tell her it just takes time.
   d. Thank the parent for bringing the concern to his attention. Then contact the transportation department and explain the concern. Ask that the department to review the student's transportation home, to find a quicker route to delivering the student home in a reasonable amount of time. Mr. Hadley calls the parent to inform her of what has been done and that the concern will be corrected as quickly as possible.

DOMAIN VI – ETHICS, EQUITY, AND DIVERSITY

In simple terms, ethics can be summarized as a system of moral principles that are good for individuals and society in general. It is about doing the right thing in all situations. Doing the right thing all the time, frees the individual from worry about whether or not he/she has made the right decision. Ethics surpasses personal opinions and beliefs. A person grounded in ethical decision-making does not have an on/off switch. One must demonstrate ethical behavior in all situations.

You are expected to be ethical in all situations. You are required to follow a Code of Ethics found in the Texas Administrative Code (19 TAC §247). See the Appendix B for the full list of the Code of Ethics for Educators. Read these codes thoroughly to be sure you understand them prior to assuming any educator responsibilities. Of the many domains we have talked about, all of them are cause for a principal to be potentially fired or reassigned depending upon the performance of the principal in those areas. This domain can cause you to be fired, lose one's educator licenses and possibly be charged with some sort of criminal violation. Your actions or lack thereof could also include some time in prison.

Equity means to demonstrate fair and impartial decisions in all aspects of life. Make all decisions in the best interest of students and teachers regardless of the situation. Guard yourself against making any type of decisions based on favoritism or cronyism. The continuous misalignment of equity results in a dysfunctional campus, low morale, and the decrease in student performance.

A principal who demonstrates diversity is one who is willing to hire quality teachers and staff members who do not look, think, or act like one's self. This process offers a wide variety of opinions, ideas, strategies, and solutions for serving the student populations on the campus. The staff should mirror the student enrollment whenever possible. The principal must have a mindset that having different opinions does not mean in opposition to the norm. Diversity develops the strength of the solutions to close the learning gaps in ethnically diverse campuses. Principals who strive for that will find out this will become the strength of a positive learning culture.

CHAPTER 11
DOMAIN VI, COMPETENCY 011

WHAT DOES IT SAY?

Competency 011: The entry-level principal knows how to provide ethical leadership by advocating for children and ensuring student access to effective educators, programs, and services.

WHAT DOES IT MEAN?

Leadership is a learned and earned trait, not to be confused with charisma. Learning leadership traits takes time, dedication, commitment, and effort. Principals must create a knowledge base of information from which to be able to make well-informed decisions. Leaders also earn the trust of their followers by continuously making good, sound, ethical decisions for their students and staff. Teachers will not always agree with the leadership decisions, but typically follow and entrust their personal commitments to leaders who they genuinely believe make sound moral decisions for the campus. (See Figure 11.1)

ALL students should have the same opportunities as their peers, regardless of their learning strengths, ethnicity, religious beliefs or economic situation. The principal is to be the advocate for all students to have access to effective educators, programs and services. Sometimes, being an advocate means reaching beyond the walls of the campus to enlist the help of central office staff. You always want to ensure students have equitable resources for academic mastery and learning conditions.

Provide services in a fair and equitable manner for all students who qualify for those services. This also includes teachers serving all students in the same manner regardless of any personal differences. To do otherwise would be a breach of the Texas Educator's Code of Conduct.

Figure 11.1: Every educator is expected to abide by a written code of ethics for the educational profession. Administrators must adhere to an even a higher standard.

WHAT DOES IT LOOK LIKE? (EXEMPLAR)

As your day begins, you receive a short list of teacher applicants, one of which does not have the requisite certification for hire. However, the leadership team is highly recommending the applicant. After a phone call to the applicant and clarifying that she has no plans in the near future to meet the certification requirements unless she is hired, you make the decision not to consider her. You communicate with the leadership as to why the applicant has been removed from the interview process.

You meet early on with your campus secretary to review the previous week's budget expenditures, which indicate a large sum of money earmarked from one particular function. The funds are not allowed for that type of purchase without an amendment to the budget. The district board of trustees must approve it. You instruct the secretary to delay the purchase of the item until an amendment to the budget is approved.

While meeting with your secretary, she reminds you that the campus Parent/Teacher Organization has scheduled to present you with a plaque. You and your wife will also be given flowers. Additionally, you are given a gift card that meets the limits of allowable amounts. The card is to a local favorite restaurant, in appreciation of your first year of service. The PTO is supportive of the great strides you have made in improving student achievement over the past year. You ask the secretary to provide you with a list of the names and mailing addresses of each of the PTO officers so that you can write a personal note of thanks for their thoughtfulness.

After completing your meeting with your secretary, you meet with your PEIMS secretary. She is asking you to sign the PEIMS report for the previous nine-week period. She must submit it to the district office by the end of the day. You ask her if the information is correct. She states she had to make a couple of changes to the attendance form because one of the teachers failed to take attendance on a particular day. You ask her to verify that each student was in class for other teachers that day. Additionally, you require the classroom teacher to complete a handwritten note to verify the students who she identified were in fact in her class. You also require a copy of the signed hand-written note to be included in the PEIMS report submission.

Just before you walk out of the office door, the assistant principal in charge of conducting all of the campus drills informs you that he failed to complete the tornado drill and the shelter-in-place drill scheduled for the previous month. He asks you what to do. You reply by saying to leave the documentation forms blank for that month. You remind the assistant principal of the importance of completing those required drills on the timeline identified in the state statute.

You are finally able to begin your daily walk in the halls prior to the start of the first bell when you overhear two staff members discussing marital issues of a third staff member who has been out for two days on personal issues that you are aware of, but have not divulged to anyone. You quietly and respectfully remind the two staff members that it is inappropriate to be discussing someone else's personal issues and that it is unprofessional conduct to be doing so. You ask them to refrain from talking about another professional's personal troubles. You wait until you receive an affirmative response from both staff members before continuing your walk down the hallway.

As the bell rings, you step into a classroom to make a formal observation on one of your beginning teachers who is showing improvement by the day. Once you have observed, you will make some informal comments to her directed toward the objectives outlined in her lesson plans and remind her that the observation evaluation will be ready tomorrow. You ask her to schedule time during her conference period to review the comments in more detail. You remind her you will come to her classroom for that conference.

The principal's day is always full of on-the-spot decisions. Being informed as an entry-level principal, the easier it is to react and respond to those decisions in a fair, ethical, and professional manner. Thus, success will be more likely. Be aware of the expectations of the Texas Code of Ethics. Stay within those guiding boundaries. They are not there to restrict you, but to guide you into making ethically correct decisions.

A LOOK AT THE INDICATORS FOR COMPETENCY 011

Many of the indicators in this competency are lighthouses for you to guard yourself against ending your administrative dreams by failing to comply with societal expectations for a leader of a campus full of the communities' children. It is one thing to unknowingly break an ethical rule. Based on your past performance the staff and community may forgive you. However, if you recklessly disavow a known statute or community expectation, there will be consequences.

It is always good to revisit the Code of Ethics on a regular basis, just to remind yourself of the community and state expectations placed upon you as an educator. When in doubt always check with a trusted mentor or even better, your superintendent.

A. Implements policies and procedures that require all campus personnel to comply with the Educator's Code of Ethics (TAC Chapter 247)
- Hand out a copy of the Texas Code of Ethics. Have each staff member read and sign the form stating each agrees to abide by the code.
- Have the members turn in the form to you after making a copy for their own keeping.
- Post your copy in your office in a place that can be reviewed on a regular basis.
- Review the code often to remind yourself of your own personal expectations.

- Follow them.

B. Models and promotes the highest standard of conduct, ethical principles, and integrity in decision making, actions, and behaviors
   - Demonstrate appropriate professional language at all times.
   - Refuse to do anything with children or staff that could be perceived as unprofessional.
   - Always use unbiased decision-making in all decisions regarding students, staff and children.
   - Behave in a manner becoming to a principal, not performing actions that would lend themselves to suspicion of wrongdoing.
   - React in a way to opposing views or comments that would communicate you are open to differing opinions.

C. Advocates for all children by promoting the continuous and appropriate development of all learners in the campus community
   - Periodically review students' IEPs and confirm the plans are being implemented as stated.
   - Look for signs that individuals or groups of students are not being included in classroom discussions or activities.
   - Ensure that students from diverse backgrounds are being treated fairly and equitably.
   - Review discipline consequences to verify students are being discipline in a fair and consistent manner without regard to race, religion or ethnicity.

D. Implements strategies to ensure that all students have access to effective educators and continuous opportunities to learn
   - Review the procedures of assigning students. Confirm all students are being treated the same with regard to assignment of teachers.
   - Complete periodic walk-throughs to ensure that no students are being overlooked in the teaching process.

- Review participation procedures with teachers so they are cognizant of including all students in the learning process.
- Implement guidelines for students to redo assignments when they do not achieve instructional mastery.
- Seek feedback from teachers and staff on how the campus can continue to provide equitable and continuous opportunities for students.

E. Promotes awareness and appreciation of diversity throughout the campus community (e.g., learning differences, multicultural awareness, gender sensitivity, and ethnic appreciation)
- Create opportunities for celebrating the cultural diversity of your campus.
- Provide cultural awareness seminars for your campus and staff.
- Communicate with staff members that students with learning disabilities are capable of learning. Celebrate the small victories as they come.
- Reinforce the idea that every student has the right to learn and grow, regardless of his/her learning differences and gender preference.
- Seek to know and understand how cultural differences can be used to support learning in the classroom.

F. Facilitates and supports special campus programs that provide all students with quality, flexible instructional programs and services (e.g., health, guidance, and counseling programs) to meet individual student needs
- Provide solid health initiatives for students based on the School Health Advisory Committee (SHAC) recommendations.
- Recognize the importance of counselors' main job description. Protect the integrity of their work as they counsel with children.
- Train teachers in recognizing the signs of child abuse or neglect. Provide them with the knowledge of how to report abuse when it is suspected.
- Encourage student support groups led by the campus counselor regarding the needs of the students.

- Ensure that all students begin the school day having had a meal so they can focus on learning.

G. Applies legal guidelines (e.g., in relation to students with disabilities, bilingual education, confidentiality, and discrimination) to protect the rights of students and staff and to improve learning opportunities
- Ensure that all IEPs are being followed as prescribe by the ARD committee.
- Ensure that all English Language Proficiency (ELP) learners are being taught according to state and federal guidelines.
- Safeguard the privacy of student information. Periodically remind staff of the Family Education Rights and Privacy Act (FERPA).
- Ensure that ARD and Language Proficiency Assessment Committee (LPAC) meetings are following the federal guidelines for meetings.
- Ensure that when a student is being disciplined who falls under the Special Education umbrella, that the ARD committee properly reviews the Behavior Manifest Determination.
- Review Special Education and bilingual meeting notes for discrepancies in meeting requirements.

H. Articulates the importance of education in a free, democratic society
- Celebrate with students and staff, the concepts of being able to live in a society where there are more freedoms here than in any other country in the world.
- Encourage reading and English Language Arts classes to write about how our country's freedoms allow us to participate in a democracy.
- Encourage art students to create projects that demonstrate the freedoms of our country.
- Encourage the music classes to sing patriotic music and make presentations to the campus PTO.
- Create a "Celebrate Freedom" week to emphasize the importance of the freedoms we have in a democracy.

SAMPLE 268 TExES QUESTIONS FOR COMPETENCY 011

1. Mr. Foote is six weeks into his first year as principal. He has begun to get to know many of his students, the background from where they came and is excited to learn more about them. However, it is apparent the staff members are uninformed of the traditions of the various cultures represented on the campus. After some careful consideration, Mr. Foote decides to:
    a. Issue a directive to the staff that they need to become more culturally informed about the student campus population.
    b. Think about how the campus could magnify the cultural differences for the next school year. Then, write down ideas and suggestions on how to achieve this goal.
    c. Begin to perk the interest of the staff by asking individual members to answer questions about what he has learned so they will want to know more.
    d. Call a meeting of the leadership team to ask them how the team can collaborate to come up with ways to recognize the diversity of the campus. Encourage them to develop a plan to organize a week of diversity celebration and pull in some parent representation from each of the ethnic groups.

2. Mrs. Styne, the principal of a large elementary, is about to enter an Admission, Review, and Dismissal meeting when she realizes there is no teacher representation at the meeting. The parent is noticeably concerned the teacher is not present for the meeting. Mrs. Styne checks with her secretary. She informs Mrs. Styne the teacher had to leave the campus at the last minute because the daycare had called. Her child was running a fever. After reviewing the situation, Mrs. Styne's best option would be to:
    a. Inform the parent the teacher had an unexpected emergency in her family. Suggest that the meeting be postponed until another day when the teacher can be present to give a full report on the student's progress.
    b. Inform the parent the teacher had an unexpected emergency in her family. Suggest the meeting continue as scheduled.

c. Express how upset she is when the teacher did not show up and apologize to the parent. Explain she will deal with the situation later. Then, begin the meeting.
   d. Begin the meeting and let the parent know the teacher will email her a full report of the progress the student has made.

3. While standing in the main office, Mr. Murdock, the high school principal is approached by the secretary who asks for a private conference. She explains that the parents of a student are requesting all of their son's records because they are considering placing him in a private school to complete his degree. The 18-year-old boy has been a persistent behavioral problem since he entered three years ago as a freshman. The parents explained that they are not withdrawing him on that day, but may do so later once the private school has had an opportunity to review all of the records. After some deliberation with the secretary, Mr. Murdock's decides his next best step is to:
   a. Approve the records request on the condition that the parents must plan to meet with him prior to making the decision to withdraw their son.
   b. Approve the records request since the parents are only considering the move, understanding that the student has been a behavioral challenge since he began high school.
   c. Greet the parents in the main office. Wish them well on trying to move their child to a private school and offer to make calls to the potential receiving school if they think that would help in the transition.
   d. Call the parents into the office. See if there is a way to keep the student at the high school. Clarify with them that since the student is 18 years of age, the Family Education Privacy Act will not allow the school to release records to anyone until the school receives a signed released from the student, who has been called to the office to do so.

4. Mr. Neff is the principal of a high school with a winning tradition in football. All head coaches are given a conference period and a period for coaching responsibilities.

While sitting in his office, the secretary announces that a parent is here to see him regarding the head football coach refusing to meet with the parent's child during his assigned conference period because the coach is busy with coaching concerns. He meets with the parent. She explains the same details while at the same time, Mr. Neff calls the student down to answer any clarifying questions. After meeting with the student and the parent, it appears that the coach is dedicating both periods to football. Mr. Neff thanks the parent for coming. He explains he will call her once he has had a chance to meet with the coach. After some reflection, Mr. Neff decides to:

   a. Send an email to the head football coach reminding him that he is to be available for students during the designated conference period. Request that he abide with the district policy in the future. Thank him for his cooperation.
   b. Set up a meeting with the head coach during his conference period. Inform him that he will meet with the coach in his classroom. At that time, bring up the concerns by the parent and ask the coach to clarify. If in fact, the coach is using the instructional conference period for coaching, instruct the coach to stop using the instructional period for coaching responsibilities. Reiterate it is to be used for instructional planning, PLC meetings, and working with students who are requesting additional help.
   c. Schedule a meeting with all of the head coaches the next morning. Remind them they have been given an additional period for coaching responsibilities. They are to use the instructional conference period for instructional planning, PLC meetings, and working with students who are experiencing difficulty with the material.
   d. Contact the district Athletic Director and inform him/her of the issue that is brewing. Ask him/her to address the issue with the head football coach as soon as possible. Explain to the Athletic Director that he will be calling the parent in the morning to explain the issue has been resolve.

5. Ms. Gains is the principal of an elementary school. She has noticed on several occasions where students are asking a group of kids why they are always covering their faces and dress differently. After taking an informal survey of the staff, it is

apparent there is no integration of information about the different cultures that exist on the campus. Ms. Gaines decides that her next best step is to:

    a. Check out several books on the various cultures to become informed of the cultural differences so she can make a presentation to the staff at the next available meeting.

    b. Request the students not to ask questions about other students because it may hurt their feelings and could turn into a bullying situation. Explain that this could cause the students to lose recess time or a more severe consequence.

    c. Bring the leadership team together to share what she observed. Ask them to begin planning ways that the campus could celebrate with the students, staff and community about the diverse cultural practices demonstrated on the campus.

    d. Begin planning a week of cultural diversity celebration. Ask a number of parents to come in to help her with the planning and the presentation. The presentation will be during one of the PTA meetings later on in the year.

PART II – THE KNOWLEDGE, SKILLS, AND MINDSETS FOR THE PRINCIPAL

Every trade requires a unique set of knowledge, skills, and mindsets in order to complete a specific job. For instance, if a carpenter wants to build a nice finished dresser, he would need to have the knowledge base on exactly what materials and tools he would need to complete the project. He would start by developing a set of plans that met the design of the cabinet he wanted to build. He would understand the need for the specific tools required to complete the job. He would use each of those tools to create a piece of furniture to the exact details of the plan. Finally, he would need to be prepared mentally (mindset) to achieve his task of building a dresser. Once he has decided to build that dresser with specific measurements in mind, he would not spend his mental capacity wondering what a table would look like; he focuses on completing his agreed upon task.

Educators are no different. The entry-level principal must become aware of the knowledge, skills, and mindsets needed to complete the tasks before him. These KSM's (Texas Education Agency, 2017) are the minimum tools and experience needed to be successful at completing various tasks and achieving success as a principal. A carpenter would not walk into his woodshop without having the knowledge of what he needed to do, the tools he needed to complete the task, and the commitment to finish the job that shows the skills and quality of his craft. You are no different. You would be wise to review, reflect upon and assimilate these knowledge, skills and mindsets to prepare you for success in the leading learner role of a campus principal.

Mindset is having the appropriate mental understanding, the capacity to use your knowledge and skills to the benefit of others. Nothing comes easy in the education of learners. You must be mentally prepared to do the task well. This will not happen unless your mindset fits your capacity to know and ability to do. For many, it may be a process of backward design by starting with the expected mindset. Then, it is about understanding what you need to do to get there. Finally, what do you need to know to get the task done? If you major on the minors (indicators) with the foundation of the KSM's, then you will have a better chance of becoming a master carpenter in education, building a foundation of success for all students. However, to do that, you must first develop your own KSM foundation.

Administrative leadership is a fluid, flexible, and interlocking process. These knowledge, skills, and concepts are not compartmentalized into a specific isolated competency or indicator. However, some of the KSMs may play more of an important role in one particular competency and indicator than another, just as some tools of a master carpenter can be used for many tasks. They play more important roles, depending on what is being built. You are building for instructional success.

Here are some basic *knowledge, skills, and mindsets* you will need to have to be successful as a principal. It is a long list, but it is not an exhaustive one.

CHAPTER 12
KNOWLEDGE: CANDIDATES DEMONSTRATE AN UNDERSTANDING OF BASIC KNOWLEDGE

It is vitally important for entry-level principals to have a working knowledge of information related to success as an instructional leader. This is a list of Basic Knowledge (BK) statements that will enable you as an entry-level principal to enter the campus with some measure of confidence. Read them with the intention of assimilating these into your professional skillsets.

BK.1 Effective stakeholder group composition based upon the context

You will need to have the knowledge to identify the specific stakeholders needed to perform the task of developing, creating, and implementing an effective vision and mission statement or any other task before you. Every campus is unique because of the make-up of the staff, students, parents and the community. This is a critical step in making sure you identify the correct people to serve on the group. It does not mean only people who agree with you, but people who are willing to initiate change that will create a culture of high expectations for all students. A careful analysis needs to be done here.

BK.2 Systems for gathering input and feedback and purposes for each system

Every step of the process requires a system for information gathering, analysis and decision-making. Understanding what type of system to be used and how it is to be used are paramount to keeping the group moving forward on the task.

BK.3 Effective strategies to systematically gather input from stakeholders

Once you have the systems in place, you will need to have knowledge of the strategies to gather input. It could be the use of electronic media via email and surveys. It could include phone calls or personal meetings with individual members. It could include hard data from state assessment exams, campus-based assessments, student discipline records and a host of other data-rich programs.

BK.4 Communication strategies which support innovative thinking

You must develop the knowledge needed to encourage creative thinking to allow your group to consider possibilities. The knowledge tied with the skill of supporting all ideas is a tremendous tool that may open the doors for more creative solutions through individual action research projects. These communication strategies should lean heavily on supporting teachers who are willing to try new instructional ideas to improve achievement.

BK.5 Communication strategies which support inclusive cultures

Everyone is welcome to be a part of the group process in developing a vision and mission statement that is open to all cultures and nationalities. Cultures should have no barriers when the focus is on helping all students achieve high academic success.

BK.6 Consensus building strategies

You must gather knowledge to build consensus among the group. Patterson et al. (2012) state that, "Consensus means you talk and listen until everyone honestly agrees to one decision." They add that, "Consensus building should only be used with high-stakes and complex issues or issues where everyone absolutely must support the final choice." Upon reflecting on this comment, instructional strategies and concept standards are included in the process.

BK.7 Conflict management strategies

You must have the applied knowledge to handle differences when they arise in the group process. There is a fine line between encouraging input, valuing input, and guiding the group to a resolution when opinions are offered from opposite ends of the spectrum. Conflict management strategies help the group to understand that differences of opinion do not equate to arguments. Conflict management strategies help to shed more light than heat on reaching the solution.

BK.8 Information gathering strategies

This process can quickly become cumbersome with all the information flowing in from different constituents. You must be able to gather the information in an orderly fashion for quick reference and retrieval. Typically, an electronic system where you have ordered the material in files, based on the type of information with the constituent and a timestamp for records purposes, will help you keep the information in a logical fashion.

BK.9 Collaborative processes to develop campus vision and mission

You must be able to identify and define your steps. There is no one specific process that will get you to a defined vision and mission statement. However, having identified a clear process will improve your chances for success. Lezotte and Snyder (2011) give some insight into what those steps should include. They believe that clarifying your belief system, involving the stakeholders, making the mission clear and specific, is done by keeping the focus on the mission. These steps are critical elements of a successful process.

BK.10 Appropriate communication strategies to meet the needs of different stakeholders

You must be able to find a way to communicate with your constituents who do not have English as their primary language. You must overcome this barrier. You do this through translating both verbal and written communication. "Inclusive" means you will include everyone and provide the means for helping everyone to participate in the communication cycle with an understanding of what you are communicating.

BK.11 Best practices in communicating internally and externally

You must have the knowledge to communicate effectively with your immediate staff through direct verbal communication, written communication and repeated communication. The external communication to parents, businesses, and the community is just as strategically important. You must have the knowledge and speaking skills to present to various groups about your campus' vision and mission statement, with a sense of urgency and commitment.

BK.12 How parent and community members' home language impact communication

You must be able to go into the community with a commitment to communicate will all constituents. You have to know your parents' language preferences and be willing to overcome those language barriers with appropriate translations.

BK.13 Forms of written and verbal communication

You must have the knowledge of when to use the formal register or when to use the informal register with parents. Typically, the formal register is used in all written communication to constituents, but many of your parents and constituents will use the informal register of their culture. You must listen with the same concern and professional attitude as you would with anyone else.

BK.14 The connection between ethnic and cultural norms and effective communication

You must be familiar with the different nuances of ethnic and cultural norms and be willing to consider these differences when your constituents are participating in the group discussion.

BK.15 Proactive approaches to home-school communication

You must be willing to use all the formal communication and informal processes to communicate with parents. You need to be trained in the electronic media while continuing to use the traditional forms of communication with parents such as the phone, email, and postal mail.

BK.16 Who to include during communication process

You must have the knowledge of who is to be included in specific pieces of communication and when to include different participants in the group. Not everyone needs to be informed about every piece of information but everyone does need to be informed some of the time.

BK.17 Best practices in facilitating two-way dialogues

You must know that dialogue is taking part in a conversation, discussion or negotiation. Patterson et al. (2018) describe dialogue as the, "free flow of meaning between two or more people." You must have the knowledge to facilitate this type of dialogue to create forums for open discussions and be able to read the non-verbal messages from the receiving person.

BK.18 Aligned standards (TEKS, Pre-K guidelines, ELPs, CCRS, etc.) for each course

It is not enough to have the curriculum expectations sitting on a bookshelf in your office. You are to be knowledgeable of what your teachers are expected to teach and what your students are expected to learn. These standards are important to know because they are what you will use to help your teachers. The standards will be broken down into primary components to understand how to teach and learn them.

BK.19 Construction of standards (content and how the content is being assessed)

It is important to have a triangulation of the state standards with what is being taught by teachers, as well as the many different types of classroom formative and summative assessments used. This triangulation can only occur by communication and developing strong curriculum delivery systems at the campus level using professional learning communities.

BK.20 Construction of assessment questions

Assessment questions must be directly connected to the curriculum and instructional strategies. The principal is responsible for guiding teachers in developing high-quality formative and summative campus assessments that are directly assessing the student mastery.

BK.21 Rigorous end-of-course assessment and aligned formative assessments

Students will only clear as high as the instructional bar is set. End-of-course or EOC assessments should be aligned to the highest end of the instructional standards spectrum for each instructional discipline.

BK.22 Use of daily formative assessments

Principals must lead in the development of ongoing daily, high-quality formative assessments. These types of assessments allow for the teachers to gauge student learning and mastery levels. Principals must also ensure these daily formative assessments are used to adjust future next-day instruction and provide for corrective feedback.

BK.23 Rigor is defined as the expectations found in the end of-of-course assessment

Principals work with instructional staff to begin with the end in mind. Principals collaborate with teachers to ask the questions, "What do we want students to know on the EOC? How do we need to teach the standards in a way that will help students achieve mastery? How will we know when they achieve mastery? What will we do differently to help students achieve mastery?"

BK.24 Culturally responsive teaching best practices

Principals must help staff understand student learning is impacted by cultural influences. Campus staff must understand what those influences are in order to know how to best reach students to achieve maximum academic success. It is not about changing the students' cultural background and beliefs. It is about understanding where they are, then figuring out how to use their cultural influences to engage the students in a more effective learning process.

BK.25 Cultural self-awareness (experiences, knowledge, skills, beliefs, values, and interests) including biases and blind spots

Principals help all staff members reflect on possible personal biases. They work to embrace cultural differences and to use those differences to help all students achieve academic success.

BK.26 Student cultures (experiences, knowledge, skills, beliefs, values, and interests)

Principals help staff learn about the many cultural values, skills, beliefs, and interests of students so those cultural influences can be celebrated and embedded into the students' learning processes.

BK.27 Staff cultures (experiences, knowledge, skills, beliefs, values and interests)

Principals must have an understanding of the various differences in staff cultures. The principals use these values and experiences to promote diversity learning among the staff and students.

BK.28 Components of quality assessments, including alignment and rigor

Principals understand the many different components of quality assessments and check to ensure those components are being implemented to provide rigorous high-quality assessments. The principal meets with the professional learning communities (PLCs) individually to assess the quality and rigor of the questions being used to monitor student mastery. This includes the alignment of questions to the standards and the instructional delivery.

BK.29 Multiple forms of assessment

The principal collaborates with each of the PLCs to have discussions on the types of mastery monitoring used to determine student understanding of the instruction being delivered. The principal uses walk-throughs to observe continuous assessments such as quick checks with thumbs up or thumbs down and various other evaluative monitoring tools teachers can use to quickly assess student understanding. It is important for teachers and students to understand when the process of checking for understanding occurs there is in essence a safe zone where people are free to admit what they do not know.

The principal also verifies in the collaborative process that various types of formative and summative assessments are being used to determine student understanding of the material being taught.

BK.30 Definition of "highest leverage"

Highest leverage points are the one or two critical indicators identified collaboratively by the teacher and principal that could make the greatest impact in improving the teacher's instructional delivery and student mastery. Highest leverage points may also apply to identifying the campus' greatest needs or attention to achieve significant gain over a period of time.

BK.31 Qualities of a strong student exemplar aligned to the standard

These exemplars are the characteristics of teaching that are closely aligned with the state standards, the established curriculum, what is being taught, and what is being assessed. These qualities are demonstrated in an example that can be clearly understood by the student. It also includes making adjustments to the exemplar based on student understanding and alignment to the standards.

BK.32 Components of a strong reteach plan

The components of a strong reteach plan include research-based and action-research that specifically addresses the students who are not mastering the prescribed curriculum using the initial teaching strategies. It includes reteaching the material using different learning modalities that help students see the learning process differently.

BK.33 Data collection tools and analysis protocols

This is the process of being able to identify and use correctly the different sets of data to help analyze the results of student achievement. It is learning how to interpret data to make action-oriented goals for improvement. Those data may include, but not be limited to teacher-made tests, checks for understanding, formative quizzes, tests, state assessments, student attendance, teacher attendance, teacher turnover and retention rates, parental involvement, resource allocation, etc.

BK.34 The impact of high performing teachers on student learning (they can generate 5-6 more months of student learning each year than a poor performer)

The principal must understand that high performing teachers are those who are able to monitor and adjust, seek additional instructional strategies, collaborate with others and set rigorous high expectations for students. Then you must provide the support and resources for teachers to achieve learning goals.

BK.35 The impact of high performing teacher attrition (when high-performing teachers leave the classroom, they are virtually impossible to replace: a 1 in 11 chance)

The principal must understand that it is important to help the high performing teachers feel valued and appreciated. This might help keep them from leaving.

BK.36 The impact of low performing teacher attrition (when low performing teachers leave the classroom, they are likely (3 in 4) to be replaced by a higher performing teacher, even in difficult to hire subjects)

The principal must understand that low performing teachers are those who are unwilling or unable to monitor and adjust, seek additional instructional strategies, collaborate with others or set rigorous expectations for students. Low performing teachers are unable use the guidance and support they receive to make improvements.

BK.37 The research that demonstrated low performing teachers that do not improve within one year, are unlikely to improve at all

The principal must have the leadership courage to non-renew a low-performing teacher who is unwilling or unable to make the necessary improvements within the first year. The principal will use the state and district adopted processes to support those decisions.

BK.38 Protected classes that cannot be discriminated against during the hiring process

The principal must understand that the Civil Rights Act of 1964 enumerates protection against discriminating for hiring purposes because of race, national origin, religion, or gender.

BK.39 Profile of a quality teacher

There is no one profile that encompasses the complete description of a quality teacher, but Southern New Hampshire University (2019) staff enumerated on observable characteristics. They include, being an effective communicator, being a good listener, focusing on effective collaboration, having the ability to monitor and adjust, engaging with students and other staff members. They also have the ability to be empathetic, demonstrating patience, engaging in teachable moments using real-world learning, collaboration, sharing of effective instructional practices, and being life-long learners. There are other characteristics, but if you can help teachers to become quality educators by incorporating these effective attributes, the principal will have a much greater opportunity of developing quality teacher traits.

BK.40 Quality candidate pools and sources of talent

The principal is engaged in creating quality pools of candidates by working with other teachers, the district personnel office, and higher education.

BK.41 Talent pipelines

The principal engages with the district, with recruiting agencies such as institutions of higher education to publicize your campus, its culture, and the positions available. Continuous relationship-building in these areas promotes greater opportunity for securing high-quality applicants.

BK.42 Best practices in teacher selection, including a demonstrated record of accomplishment of student achievement and concrete demonstration of teaching skills

The principal understands there are indicators used to hire teachers. This includes evaluating prior teacher performance and observation reviews. The principal observes the prospective teacher in mock mini-teaching sessions. The principal seeks input from other teachers as to the potential effectiveness of the teacher using well-organized teacher hiring committees from the campus.

BK.43 Standard criteria for teacher performance on a continuum of proficiency

The principal understands what proficiency looks like using all of the walk-through and observation instruments available. The principal is able to discern quality teaching from poor teaching.

BK.44 Developmental process of acquiring pedagogical skills in terms of both management and rigor

The principal understands the structural frame of administration includes skills in how to direct employees in formative tasks. The principal sets an expectation of completing those tasks at a high standard. This includes providing the teachers and staff with the appropriate training to allow them to achieve success at a high level.

BK.45 Characteristics of high-quality action steps

The principal understands that quality action steps for teachers and staff are clearly defined, measurable, and in a chronological order. These steps have a reasonable completion date agreed upon by the staff member and the principal.

BK.46 Qualities of a strong exemplar

The principal understands the expectations of any given instructional assignment. The principal can discern the difference between a low-performing exemplar and a quality exemplar. A quality exemplar will include all of the instructional steps to assist the student in obtaining mastery of that particular instructional standard.

BK.47 Qualities of strong reflective questions

The principal understands strong reflective questions cause the teacher or staff member to identify the highest leverage point of the lesson. The principal provides an opportunity for the staff member to respond with improvement ideas.

BK.48 Teacher needs and areas for growth

The principal is capable of identifying the highest instructional needs of the teachers based on the lesson presentation. He/She is able to provide suggestions for improvement using reflective questioning.

BK.49 Types of professional development

The principal understands that professional development typically is associated with one or more of the following processes: focus on content, creating opportunities for action-learning, focus on collaboration, modeling best practices as well as allowing for coaching and support activities. The principal is capable of creating aligned professional development with the campus goals by delivering the information in a way that improves student performance.

BK.50 Tools to support the design and development of professional development

The principal is capable of ensuring all of the necessary resources needed to present staff development are available and in place.

BK.51 Forms of data, which inform the identification of professional development content

The principal is able to bring in all forms of data analysis and collaboration necessary to analyze the professional development needed.

BK.52 Best practices of adult facilitation and learning

The principal is capable of facilitating adult learning. Egle (2009) lists several best practices when working with adult learners. They are:

- Use multi-sensory learning strategies. The more senses used, the greater the opportunity for learning.
- Keep the adult learner actively engaged in the learning by using problem solving, discussion and other activities that would require action on the part of the learner.
- Utilize first and last experiences. Learners tend to remember more of the first and last parts of any learning session.
- Tell them what you are going to tell them. Tell them. Tell them what you have told them. This is a form of "chunking" information.
- Give adult learners immediate and continuous feedback. Participants need feedback on their progress. Similarly, facilitators need feedback on whether they are meeting participants' needs.
- Reward success. We all feel better if our efforts are rewarded. Training must include tangible results for participants to feel positive and satisfied.
- Practice and repetition reinforces the learning taking place.
- Give the big picture to the adult learners (holistic learning). Provide the learners with the big picture context. Then specific detail that provides a logical framework for the thinking process.

BK.53 Best practices in professional learning communities

The principal understands the professional learning community is an active, engaged, committed group of learning professionals who seek to improve student achievement for all students. DuFour, DuFour, Eaker, and Many (2006) define a professional learning community as, "…composed of collaborative teams whose members work interdependently to achieve common goals linked to the purpose of learning for all. They go on to say there is:

- A focus on learning,
- A collaborative culture with a focus on learning for all,

- A collective inquiry into best practice and current reality,
- Action orientated (Learning by doing.),
- A commitment to continuous improvement, and
- Result oriented.

BK.54 Practice-based facilitation design

The principal is capable of assisting/coaching teachers on improving the delivery of content using a well-designed format. This allows principal/teacher collaboration and success in the delivery of the instructional content.

BK.55 Research-based resources for professional development content

The principal possesses the skills to digitally access research-based information, resources on various websites and is knowledgeable on the use of resources in a professional development setting.

BK.56 Group learning techniques

The principal understands there are specific group learning techniques that are more successful than others are. He/She understands how to use those techniques in group situations. A few of these processes are think-pair-share, roundtable discussions, and peer questioning.

BK.57 Indicators of adult engagement

The principal understands the characteristics of adult engagement such as remaining alert, listening, tracking the presenter with their eyes, and taking ample notes. The principal is also asking questions, answering questions on a knowledge and comprehension level, and can respond promptly to directions.

BK.58 Multiple learning styles

The principal understands that learners have multiple learning styles. He/She recognizes there is no one single learning style better than another one. The major learning styles are visual auditory, verbal, logical, physical (tactile-kinesthetic), social, and intrapersonal.

BK.59 Alignment of professional development to instructional coaching and other school systems

The entry-level principal is capable of aligning the professional development activities to his/her ability. They can use those activities in an instructional coaching setting. This means being able to break down the professional development information into its smallest components to assist the teacher to know, understand, and implement the new strategies.

BK.60 Data that measures the effectiveness of the professional development (throughout the session, at the end of the session, after the session)

The principal is capable of creating a data measurement instrument that measures the effectiveness of the professional development. This includes a way to monitor teacher and staff understanding so the professional development can be adjusted in real time. This will allow the professional development to have a higher opportunity for success and rate of return.

BK.61 Factors that should inform campus initiatives and goals

The principal understands the leverage points in data, teacher instruction and student performance that drives the campus initiatives and goals. This allows for the constant tweaking, improvement of the goals and the delivery points for each lesson.

BK.62 Criteria and characteristics of a safe campus

The principal understands what a safe campus looks like. An orderly, purposeful atmosphere is free from the threat of physical harm. The atmosphere is not oppressive. It is conducive to teaching and learning. The discipline management process is clear and followed consistently by all staff. The physical facilities are kept clean. All repairs made as quickly as possible.

BK.63 Components of a measurable goal

The principal is capable of defining the chronological, observable, and measurable steps in obtaining a campus goal. The broad question to ask the staff in developing these steps is, "What do we, as a staff, need to do to achieve this goal?"

BK.64 Definition of equity and equality

The principal understands equity is giving everyone the tools and skills they need for each task in order to be successful. This means providing them in a way the learner best learns. Equality is treating everyone the same regardless of their culture, ethnicity, gender, religious preference or mental capacities.

BK.65 Elements of a high quality school vision and mission

The principal understands the mission statement is a description of what the principal and staff want the school to achieve, not necessarily, what it is. Once decided upon, then the elements of a high-quality school vision and mission can be created and implemented. A few of those elements may be:

- Teachers and staff set rigorous expectations for all students and provide the support for student success.
- Teachers and staff create a culture of professionalism among themselves. They can hold each other to a high standard of dress and behavior.
- Professional learning communities continually focus on improving student achievement.
- All staff are supportive of all students, while keeping expectations high for all.
- Failure is not an option. Students are required to learn the material regardless of the amount of re-teaching necessary for the student to achieve mastery.
- No one gives up or quits on any student.
- All successes are celebrated.

BK.66 Process of creating a vision, mission, goals, priorities, etc.

The principal understands the process of creating a vision, mission, and goals always begins with data analysis of relevant and applicable information. Personal egos and preferences are checked at the door so a real analysis of why students underperformed is addressed in a professional manner. It is not about identifying people. It is about identifying strategies. The right questions are asked about the data.

Once the strategies are identified, then the strategies need to be written in the form of concrete, measurable goals. The steps to achieve those goals must be created and clearly defined. The goals are also concrete, observable, measurable, on a chronological calendar for monitoring, adjusting, evaluating, and accountability purposes.

BK.67 Elements of effective student culture routines

The students have been trained in systematic academic routines in each class with expectations of behavior for any changes of classes during the day. Teachers teach students that their job is to be a successful learner. The teachers and staff are here to support the learning process. This may include clearly defined expectations for all learners that do not change from the moment they step onto the campus.

BK.68 Practices that develop and sustain a strong staff culture

The principal understands the symbolic frame includes the principal as an encourager for strong staff culture and sustainment. The principal understands high-quality teachers value sincere recognition. The principal works to recognize teacher and staff success during meetings. He/She writes personal handwritten notes of thanks for jobs well done. The principal understands high-quality teachers are provided with the tools and resources necessary to allow them to be successful at a high level of rigor.

BK.69 Root cause analysis process

The principal understands a root cause analysis is an approach for identifying the underlying causes of why students are not learning the standards. Effective solutions can be carefully chosen to correct the learning challenge. This requires the principal to keep asking the hard questions until the instructional staff is able to clearly identify the root cause for learning deficiencies.

BK.70 Types of data that can be collected in order to inform a root cause analysis process

The principal understands that observation data, informal checks for understanding, formative assessments and walk-throughs can all be used to triangulate the root cause of low-performing student achievement. This is coupled with reflective questioning exercises by the principal with the teachers.

BK.71 Research-based problem-solving techniques

The principal understands there are many sites, people, articles and forms of data that can be identified for use in help to identify the best research practices for a given instructional standard.

BK.72 Phases of a continuous improvement cycle

The principal understands there are steps to a continuous improvement cycle. They may appear something like this:
- Identify the highest leverage point of a teacher's lesson using data and observation tools.
- Use reflective questioning to help the teacher identify the same issue the principal has identified.
- Brainstorm ways the information can be presented differently to improve the chances for success.
- Implement an action plan with measurable steps and defined expectations.
- Allow the teacher to practice the changes while the principal is observing.
- Implement the action plan with the principal observing the changes in the presentation.
- Evaluate the outcomes against the measurable goals.

- Repeat. Although this is one simple word, the step provides continuous growth in the teaching-learning process. This translates into improved student achievement.

BK.73 Strategic planning processes

There is no one way to complete a campus strategic planning process, but some of the steps may be familiar. They may look something like this:

- Begin by having an initial meeting that uses data to identify where your campus is in the continuous improvement process. This step includes a deep dive into the data to identify key high leverage points for discussion later.
- Allow for teachers and staff to provide insights on the results of the data analysis. Record those insights on large poster paper where participants can see.
- Discuss the results of those insights openly.
- Begin to identify two or three of the highest leverage points in order to establish the clear, measurable objectives to improve upon student academic achievement.
- Develop the steps that needed to implement those objectives.
- Develop a calendar of expected implementation with measures of accountability. In other words, who is going to do what, and when?
- Identify the support, training, and resources to achieve the objectives.
- Identify the concrete measures of accountability for the reporting process.
- Communicate the plan to all constituents. Stick with the plan, making continuous adjustments as needed.

BK.74 Components of a strong action plan

Components typically consist of S.M.A.R.T goals. They would look something like this:

- Specific – The goals would be laser-like in its focus on improving an identified highest leverage point.
- Measurable – The goals would be clear, concrete, and measurable.

- Agreement – The people who will be working to meet the goals need to agree on the goals with the expectations of achievement.
- Realistic – The goals need to be rigorous, yet achievable.
- Time Specific – The goals must be able to be reached in a reasonable amount of time that is agreed upon by all who are a part of the solution.

BK.75 Characteristics of strong goals and vision statements

The characteristics of strong goals and vision statements are that the goals are S.M.A.R.T. Construct the vision statement in a way that unites the campus and provides stable transcendental goals.

BK.76 Characteristics of a high leverage action

There is no one set of high leverage actions. Here are a few ideas of what high leverage action may look like:
- There is an observable use of cognitive and metacognitive strategies.
- The teacher provides high levels of scaffolding in the beginning and knows when to begin to deconstruct the scaffolding.
- There is good use of appropriate technology.
- The students are actively engaged in the learning process.
- The teachers uses flexible grouping when it is applicable.
- There is continuous positive and constructive feedback.
- There is explicit instruction for students.

BK.77 Characteristics of effective progress measures and benchmarks which measure progress towards the goal

The principal understands there is a tight triangulation between the standards (the curriculum), what is being taught (the lesson), and what is being tested (formative and summative assessments). All benchmarks align to the instruction. The instruction aligns to the curriculum, and the curriculum aligns to the benchmarks. There are in place effective learning checks along the way to validate instructional strategies used.

BK. 78 Characteristics of effective data tracking systems

An effective data tracking system is one that has clearly identified the campus goals with what steps need to occur in achieving those goals. The principal validates the alignment of the instruction to those goals. Data is collected from each teacher in a timely manner to help with tweaking and planning adjustments.

BK.79 Purpose and use of various forms of data

The principal fully understands how data is collected, used, and where to access that data. He/She understands data comes from many different sources.

BK.80 Effective systems for time management and organization

The principal keeps a campus calendar that is available to the staff. The calendar is kept current with only one person able to input changes and additions. The principal uses a "To Do" list on a daily basis and attempts to adhere to the list as closely as possible. The performance of the principal is focused on the principal as the leader of learning.

BK.81 School personnel dynamics and influencers in the root cause and strategic planning processes

The principal understands that personal influences and biases may come into effect when implementing and completing strategic planning processes. These need to be resolved by the principal by redirecting off-task behaviors and beliefs to meet the needs of the students.

CHAPTER 13
SKILLS: CANDIDATES DEMONSTRATE AN ABILITY TO...

These Basic Skills are learned and developed through gaining an understanding of the skills, knowing when to use them, and increasing confidence through experience. Experience takes time. It is important for the entry-level principal to internalize *what* these skills mean to advancing instruction and *when* to use them. As you read them, visualize how you would implement each of them as a campus principal.

Basic Skills.1 Deliver clear expectations and rationale to all stakeholders

This skill takes some reflective thought on your part. It is the first personal action you will take before beginning an activity. This is true when creating a vision and mission statement. These are non-negotiable expectations. You have outlined the specific process you want to use. This also includes the list of expectations and norms you expect all to follow during this process. These need to be clearly communicated to all participants.

Basic Skills.2 Implement effective strategies to involve stakeholders in campus planning processes

Investigate appropriate participation strategies. Have them ready to use when you begin the process of creating and implementing a vision and mission statement. Participants who are not a part of the staff are going to be reluctant to jump into the discussion because educators tend to use educational terms that can be intimidating to outside group participants. Be ready to call on non-volunteers and allow for wait time before calling on someone else to participate. Create an inclusive atmosphere by having educators sit *with* constituents. Give positive responses to input and encourage everyone to participate.

Basic Skills.3 Integrate parents and community members in campus culture

This can be a tough process. There are campus cultures where staff verbally indicate the desire for inclusive participation but the atmosphere displayed is a culture that communicates a different message to parents. It promotes a culture that parents and community members are not welcome to the campus. The entry-level principal must take steps to create a welcoming atmosphere to parents and other constituents to be on the campus. A couple of suggestions would be to train your office staff to be more pleasant when parents visit, simply by smiling and communicating with guests. Some campuses have provided a parent learning center where parents can visit with others or even learn about what the campus is doing and how students are learning.

Basic Skills.4 Build relationships with internal stakeholders

When you are altering the vision and mission of a campus, you are changing the culture. You cannot do this in a vacuum. The best leverage you can have is to build relationships with your staff. There are a number of activities you can do to build these relationships. You begin by listening to your staff. They have much to say about the "state of the campus," but they will not be willing to speak unless they know you are willing to listen. Listening is a skill that needs to be developed by entry-level principals. It is not about repeating information back to the teacher who is sharing with you, but genuinely showing some concern by communicating with them later, about their concerns and your intentions.

Write personal professional notes of gratitude for how staff members are teaching in the classroom. Teachers want to be appreciated for their efforts in the classroom. When you notice and respond, they remember and report. They tell others. When they tell others, the culture begins to make a change because behaviors begin to change. Others want the same affirmation, so they will begin to emulate the characteristics that are being praised. They want to be noticed as well. This practice begins to influence the professional culture of expectation. It raises the level of expectation and professionalism on the campus. People appreciate genuine recognition and change.

Basic Skills.5 Build relationships with external stakeholders

Building relationships with external stakeholders means making time for them to express their opinions and concerns. There are many administrators in leadership positions who have given ear, nodded to comments made by a sincerely concerned constituent, but they did not "hear" the person. It was evident on the constituent's face when they were not being heard. BE IN THE MOMENT when you are with constituents. Give them your full attention. Even if you do not agree with them, most will respect and value you for your time.

Basic Skills.6 Use effective strategies to communicate in order to meet the needs of specific stakeholder groups

You will use different strategies for different stakeholders. An email to your staff may be perfectly fine, whereas mass emails to stakeholders may lose the impact of your intended message. When meeting with parents, businesses, and community members, you are more likely to get the message across with face-to-face meetings in smaller settings. This takes time, but you are investing in changing your culture. Make sure your message is appropriate for your constituents you are addressing.

Basic Skills.7 Communicate consistently with all stakeholders using best practices

The message may be delivered in different ways, but the same message must be communicated repeatedly. When you are changing the methods in which you deliver the message (email, Facebook, Twitter, and other electronic messages, including video) review your message prior to communicating it to your stakeholders. Additionally, this is not a one-and-done process. Communicating the message of your campus that emphasizes education for all at a high level has to be ongoing and repetitive.

Basic Skills.8 Employ effective strategies to communicate effectively with stakeholders who speak another language in order to ensure that they feel included in the school community

Nothing will turn off a stakeholder more quickly than to feel they are not valued. It takes people, time, and money to invest in accurate translation systems with quality software, but that is money well spent. Hire good translators who can translate on the spot, who can translate from written to written and verbal to written form. Electronic software programs are good to a point, but there are occasional mistranslations made.

It is generally a good idea to have someone who is proficient in the language to review all communication.

Basic Skills.9 Seek consistent input around important decisions

You are not in a Lone Ranger process, leading the charge for change all on your own. The more participants you can bring in for real dialogue to help in getting the message (the same consistent message), the greater the opportunity for continuing success. Remember, this is a continuous process, so you want continuous input. This also reinforces the idea that your resolve to bring about success for all students at a high level is for real. It is not just a mantra posted on the wall.

Basic Skills.10 Collaborate with parent organizations

To collaborate means to work in cooperation with others to achieve a collectively agreed upon decision or solution. Parent organizations have the best interest of the students and staff in mind. These organizations work *with* the administration to assist teachers and students succeed. In many cases, this is a vastly underutilized group of supporters who are willing to help with the process. The entry-level principal should tap this resource with a listening ear in mind. They have been around a lot longer than you have been. They have acquired some pertinent information regarding the campus if you are willing to collaborate with them in the process.

Basic Skills.11 Facilitate systems for both proactive and reactive communication

Communication is a fast-paced process in this day and time. Positive information is much slower to make the rounds than negative. Electronic media can be a boon or a bane for the campus administrator. Treat this with respect and high regard. You must have a communication system set up to reach your parents on a moment's notice. You must get out ahead of misinformation related to the vision and mission development process. This type of proactive engagement sends a subliminal message that you value the message, the process, and the person receiving the message.

Basic Skills.12 Break down standards into component parts

The entry-level principal is able to understand and provide examples of what Essential Elements look like when those EE's are applied to learning. The principal is capable of breaking the Essential Elements into their simplest components to understand the full learning value of the standards.

Basic Skills.13 Break down standards into the content it is assessing (both knowledge and skills)

The principal has the ability to assist in formulating curriculum documents with the standards, and align strategies that are connected to one another. This makes the implementation of the TEKS seamless.

Basic Skills.14 Identify the rigorous end-of-course assessment and align questions on rigorous end-of-course assessment to standards

The principal is able to make direct connections of the end-of-course assessments with the identified curriculum and teaching strategies used throughout the year. The principal can make a clear connection between what is being tested with what is being taught.

Basic Skills.15 Break down rigorous assessment questions into content and how it is being assessed.

The principal can assist in analyzing content on the assessments; collaborate with others as to the effectiveness of the question as well as whether the question appropriately assesses student mastery.

Basic Skills.16 Break down rigorous assessment questions to include requisite skills, vocabulary, and other non-content specific skills

The principal can assist in analyzing content on the assessments and collaborate with others to make sure the questions are effectively assessing the learning skills and vocabulary. Students must master these to be successful at the next level.

Basic Skills.17 Compare/contrast assessment breakdown to standards breakdown

The principal can assist in analyzing content on the assessments and collaborate with others as to whether the assessments are evaluating what is being taught.

Basic Skills.18 Utilize assessment and standards breakdown to guide unit planning calendar of objectives (sequencing and pacing)

The principal can collaborate with others to loop or spiral previous learning objectives that need to be retaught or reinforced with additional curriculum to be taught.

Basic Skills.19 Utilize assessment and standards breakdown to guide daily lesson plan objectives and key points

The principal can review the information from the analysis of the assessment standards. He/She can use the information to collaborate with teachers to restructure the learning for students through changing guided daily lesson plans to meet the immediate needs of the students.

Basic Skills.20 Analyze and identify additional aligned assessment questions that can be used formatively

The principal is capable of creating and evaluating assessment questions that may be used to further assess student mastery. Additionally, the principal serves as a resource to help with the collaboration of aligned assessments within the individual professional learning communities.

Basic Skills.21 Utilize assessment and standards breakdown to create additional aligned formative questions

The principal can assist in creating a formative assessment bank of questions teachers may use to check for understanding of the students' learning levels by recycling summative questions into formative assessments.

Basic Skills.22 Incorporate formative questions into daily lesson plans and other formative assessments

The principal is responsible for ensuring teachers are establishing a routine of checking for understanding. By using appropriately developed formative questions, learning will take place daily in the classroom. The principal ensures the teachers are monitoring and adjusting their lessons in real-time, according to the overview of the checking for understanding.

Basic Skills.23 Facilitate vertical alignment across curricular resources

The principal is capable of working collaboratively with teachers in different grade levels, to align vertical curriculum into a seamless transition for student learning.

Basic Skills.24 Analyze curricular resources to ensure scaffolding and spiraling of critical content across grade levels

The principal can work with teachers and central office staff to locate appropriate academic resources that will align with the vertical curriculum while supporting student academic learning.

Basic Skills.25 Share focus of bringing equitable practices to the school community and hold cultural competence to be a key component of the school's culture and practices

The principal is the banner carrier for ensuring that all students are presented the standards through instructional strategies that address cultural differences.

Basic Skills.26 Communicate and maintain high expectations for all students

The principal is an expert in communication, being able to use all the communication tools available to accurately, adequately, and appropriately communicate high expectations to all campus constituents. This includes all staff, students, parents, businesses, central office, and board members. All constituents need to understand the campus leader and staff are focused on improving academic performance.

Basic Skills.27 Facilitate the development and integration of culturally responsive teaching

The principal leads out in the development of appropriate instructional lessons that focus on the students from varying cultures. This includes taking an active role in collaborating with professional learning communities to promote culturally responsive teaching.

Basic Skills.28 Lead conversations with staff about inequities and about honoring diversity

The principal leads the discussion about identifying any inequities in honoring diversity in teacher and staff behaviors as well as lesson presentations.

Basic Skills.29 Lead teachers through a process to identify students' strengths and assets as a bridge to new learning

The principal assists the teachers in identifying the correct data analysis tools to help them recognize student strengths and weaknesses. Use those as a guide to create learning strategies to help with bridging students' new learning with what they already know.

Basic Skills.30 Communicate and maintain positive perspectives for all parents and families

The principal keeps a positive demeanor and outlook with parents related to student learning and outcomes. The principal serves as an encourager. He/She is a resource for parents, students, and teachers.

Basic Skills.31 Facilitate the development of culturally competent educators by institutionalizing cultural knowledge

The principal is the lead learner and facilitator in developing culturally competent educators by embedding cultural knowledge of the diverse campus.

Basic Skills.32 Model cross-cultural communication, recognize when an adjustment is necessary and adjust as needed

When applicable, the principal is able to communicate to a diverse culture. The principal knows when to provide appropriately developed means of communication modes for the purpose of providing the needed information to that diverse culture.

Basic Skills.33 Analyze and recognize instances and outcomes that represent misalignment of cultural competence and inequity

The principal understands when instruction is not addressing the appropriate alignment of cultural diversity. He/She is able to lead changes in instruction to allow for such diversity.

Basic Skills.34 Address and correct instances that represent a misalignment of cultural competence and inequity

The principal acts upon the knowledge of misalignment of cultural competencies. They provide the resources to remedy the challenges.

Basic Skills.35 Implement consistent systems for the collection of student achievement data at regular intervals (formative and summative)

The principal possesses the requisite skills to implement routine data collection systems using common, formative, summative assessments, also anecdotal teacher comments, observations, and student feedback to make course corrections on strategies used to deliver instruction.

Basic Skills.36 Intentionally plan all components of the data meeting, including anticipated teacher responses

The principal understands the importance of preparing and implementing an agenda that addresses data meeting objectives. This includes an action agenda including next steps, adjusting teaching delivery systems, and re-teaching curriculum standards. The principal is capable of systemic thinking in preparation for teacher responses.

Basic Skills.37 Establish strong systems and protocols to ensure that all teachers have a clear understanding of their role, in order to ensure participation and timeliness.

The principal understands the importance of the structural frame of administration. He/She can outline specific responses for teachers as they address the required business of the school day. This also includes the role of the teacher in establishing high expectations for students and themselves.

Basic Skills.38 Deeply understand the focus standard and define the aligned exemplar response

The principal is capable of articulating each focus standard and present the information to staff in a manner that can be understood by the staff. He/She can verify the validity of the exemplar against the standard.

Basic Skills.39 Create or identify an exemplar response so that all can see the bar for rigor

The principal is capable of creating and identifying exemplar responses so that the expectation for learning is established at a high level of rigor for staff and students.

Basic Skills.40 Analyze student work to identify the gaps between student performance and the exemplar, to identify the highest leverage misconception

The principal is capable of examining and evaluating student work to determine student gaps as they relate to the exemplar. He/She is able to identify instructional leverage points to improve student achievement based on those gaps.

Basic Skills.41 Leverage reflective questioning to support the teacher in uncovering the highest leverage error and conceptual misunderstanding

The principal becomes effectively trained in guiding teachers in using reflective questions that allow teachers to identify the gaps in instructional presentations. The principal is able to identify what actions or highest leverage points make the greatest gains towards student mastery.

Basic Skills.42 Identify the most appropriate approach to teach highest leverage misconception

The principal understands what questions to ask to help the teacher identify and use the highest leverage actions. He/She can recommend instructional strategies to overcome academic challenges by students.

Basic Skills.43 Plan intentional practice to support teachers in their ability to address the misconception during the reteach

The principal has the teacher practice the presentation to receive constructive feedback prior to the teacher presenting the information.

Basic Skills.44 Provide in-the-moment feedback to support teachers in ensuring their reteach effectively addresses the highest leverage misconception

The principal uses walk-through and observation opportunities to help the teacher reteach the highest leverage point once the teaching misconception has been identified.

Basic Skills.45 Leverage current relationships to source quality teacher referrals

The principal uses all the strategic resources based on prior and current relationships to identify quality teachers. He/She uses these resources to hire them as quickly and efficiently as possible.

Basic Skills.46 Communicate proactively to potential candidates expectations for the selection process

The principal has a process in place that clearly identifies the hiring procedure to all prospective candidates when they seek application. This is communicated to each one in a clear and professional manner.

Basic Skills.47 Communicate accurately the expectations of the school

The principal has a clear set of expectations of the learning community regarding student mastery. This includes prospective candidates being informed of those expectations prior to applying.

Basic Skills.48 Give opportunities for candidates and school to ensure fit

The principal allows the candidate/teacher to be introduced to the current staff and student populations using informal gatherings.

Basic Skills.49 Differentiate between high performing and low performing teachers

The principal has the ability to identify high-performing teachers and low performing teachers. High-performing teachers have been identified in an earlier skill. Here are some characteristics of a poor teacher from *The Nassau Guardian* (2015):

- They do not allow children to grow and change.
- They solve all their problems for them (students).
- They find a teaching method that fits them and expect their students to adapt to that method.
- They play favorites.
- They think they already know everything they need to know.
- They lack subject knowledge.
- They have poor classroom control.
- The act unprofessionally.
- They cannot diagnose learning problems.
- They are obsessive about using the same method to present information.
- They focus on the wrong goals.
- They have no goals at all.

There are more characteristics. If the principal has a teacher demonstrating these characteristics, then this should be a red flag and is a potential cause for non-renewal.

Basic Skills.50 Clarify roles, accountabilities, and decision-making among team members

The principal needs to have the capability to assign roles on teams to ensure team members understand what is expected of them.

Basic Skills.51 Demonstrate respect and appreciation for teachers by empathizing, valuing time and contributions, and being available and responsive to their needs

The principal should understand teachers invest a number of hours outside the school day to help students succeed. Therefore, the principal should find continuous ways of identifying and honoring teachers through campus recognition activities and personal hand-written notes. He/She should also find other ways to give teachers the credit for long hours past the normal school day.

Basic Skills.52 Consistently coach others toward goals providing constructive and positive feedback that is both timely and relevant

The principal is capable of identifying highest leverage points. The principal can use that information to coach teachers who may need improvement in delivering instruction.

Basic Skills.53 Evaluate performance regularly, helping teachers identify areas for development

The principal should be in teachers' classrooms on a daily basis, offering constructive feedback and providing resources as needed.

Basic Skills.54 Recognize accomplishments publicly

The principal should always praise in public and correct in private. Public recognition goes a long way with teachers who have a lot of time invested with students and the outcomes are successful. That public recognition reinforces the appropriate direction to change attitudes and mindsets of the campus culture.

Basic Skills.55 Inform high performing teachers that they are high performing

The principal should not only recognize that high performing teachers are high performing, but the principal should ask what makes them high performing. Most teachers are reluctant to talk about themselves, but they appreciate it when the principal wants to know about their attitudes, behaviors and mindsets.

Basic Skills.56 Provide leadership opportunities for high performing teachers

The principal needs to walk a fine line with providing leadership positions for high performing teachers and overextending their capacity to be high performing because of too many responsibilities.

Basic Skills.57 Delegate tasks to appropriate individuals or groups

The principal understands it is good practice to delegate as many non-instructional tasks to other staff members in order to focus on being a learning leader.

Basic Skills.58 Allocate classroom resources to high performing teachers

High performing teachers will continue to be high performing if they are provided the appropriate resources to continue the rigor of high student success. This is a delicate process of allocating resources without generating a dip in morale with other staff members. To reduce this possibility the focus must always remain on the vision and mission of the campus.

Basic Skills.59 Discuss performance with teachers candidly

The principal must understand that this is a learner-centered process. The egos need to be checked at the door. Student success is the focus and all staff need to know there is room for improvement.

Basic Skills.60 Manage out poor performers that do not meet expectations

The principal must have the leadership courage to non-renew or terminate staff when it becomes evident the staff member is unable or unwilling to make the required improvements.

Basic Skills.61 Manage calendar to observe quality of instruction in individual teachers' classrooms directly

The principal must have an accurate calendar that allows for walk-throughs, observations, and information observations throughout the entire year.

Basic Skills.62 Ensure that least effective teachers receive the most support

The principal needs to redirect people, time, and resources to those staff members who are experiencing low or ineffective performance.

Basic Skills.63 Set and communicate a high bar for instruction

The principal needs to be able to use the most recent available data to collaborate with staff members to set high expectations for both students and staff.

Basic Skills.64 Measure efficacy of instruction in terms of student outcomes

The principal must be able to possess the skills to discern whether the instructional strategies used by teachers are effectively addressing student mastery for the identified standards.

Basic Skills.65 Protect school and students by documenting all personnel interactions that could impact retention

The principal keeps excellent written notes to document all conversations regarding staff performance with the action steps that have been enlisted to promote growth.

Basic Skills.66 Develop structures to support the scheduling and implementation of observation and feedback cycles

The principal schedules periodic walk-throughs, informal and formal observations with the intention of always providing feedback to the teacher for the purpose of professional growth.

Basic Skills.67 Develop systems to track teacher action steps

The principal, in collaboration with the teacher, creates a set of action steps that are clearly defined that are able to be completed within a specific time frame. The principal and teacher agree on that time frame. The principal makes periodic observations and holds conferences to achieve the goals established.

Basic Skills.68 Observe instruction through the lens of standard criteria for teacher performance

The principal will weigh student mastery based on the curriculum standards taught. Teachers can present great lessons that do not necessarily address the standard that needs assessed. The principal ensures there is a tight correlation between the standards, the instructional strategies, and the assessment process.

Basic Skills.69 Collect low inference data throughout the observation

Identify those areas where the students are not making a connection between what is presented and what needs to be learned. This information is valuable in helping teachers see where they need to adjust their teaching strategies to help students understand the connection between prior and future information.

Basic Skills.70 Identify the highest leverage gap in teacher performance in relation to standard criteria for teacher performance

You are finding the largest gap in the student learning process and investigating the reasons for that gap. Meeting with the teacher is a good way to identify the leverage points and to develop instructional strategies that will bridge that gap.

Basic Skills.71 Develop an aligned action step which is bite-sized, high leverage, and observable and clearly "name it" in plain language

The principal works closely with the teacher to develop the incremental, systematic action steps that will provide the greatest opportunity for student success. The plan's steps are observable. There is a written, observable and measurable goal.

Basic Skills.72 Identify or define the exemplar implementation of the highest leverage action step, so that the teacher can "see it"

Provide the teacher with examples of what exemplary implementation and results look like for the highest leverage action step so the teacher can begin to understand what instructional success looks like when the appropriate strategies are implemented.

Basic Skills.73 Leverage reflective questioning and low inference evidence to support the teacher in identifying the key elements of the exemplar

The principal understands how to ask the right questions to encourage the teacher to complete some reflective thinking and responses as to why students may not be making the connection to the new learning. The principal helps the teacher, through reflective questioning, to identify the important elements of what an exemplar should possess.

Basic Skills.74 Analyze teacher actions in relation to the exemplar to identify the highest leverage gaps in the teacher's performance

The principal is capable of understanding the actions of the teacher presenting the lesson based on the exemplar. The greatest learning gaps can be corrected through reflective questioning based on the exemplar.

Basic Skills.75 Leverage reflective questioning to support the teacher in uncovering the highest leverage gaps in their performance

Similar to the previous skill, the principal is capable of initiating the appropriate types of questions that will guide the teacher into a reflection of the lesson presentation. You use this process to identify the largest gaps in the student learning process.

Basic Skills.76 Intentionally plan for the practice, with the teacher, ensuring practice aligns to stated action step and the exemplar

The principal has the teacher practice the exemplar while observing to verify the teacher is aligning the action steps developed in the exemplar. The objective is to agree on the intended outcomes.

Basic Skills.77 Facilitate teacher practice in alignment with the stated action step

Another word for facilitate is to assist. The principal will assist and support the teacher practice to ensure alignment with the target instructional goals.

Basic Skills.78 Provide in-the-moment feedback to the teacher to ensure that practice aligns to the stated action step and the exemplar

The principal will provide real-time feedback so the practice aligns with the exemplar.

Basic Skills.79 Intentionally plan for a follow-up observation to ensure implementation of the action step

The principal holds himself and the teacher accountable by verifying the action step agreed upon is implemented as stated in the reflective questioning meeting.

Basic Skills.80 Develop a coherent professional development scope and sequence aligned to campus and teacher needs and root cause analysis

The principal is capable of collaborating with the teachers and staff using all of the available data to analyze and assess the underlying causes for the highest instructional leverage points. This collaboration results in working closely with the staff to pinpoint the specific instructional standards needed for professional development. The principal collaborates with staff to create staff development that directly addresses these issues.

Basic Skills.81 Develop professional development sessions based upon identified areas of need, as indicated by teacher and student outcomes, aligned to best practices in the field

This sounds like the principal creates the professional development calendar and that is it. Not so. The principal must have the ability to verify the areas of need that are the greatest leverage points. The principal is able to locate or assist in developing the targeted training necessary to provide the best practices in the field to achieve the intended goals for staff development.

Basic Skills.82 Develop clear objectives for professional development sessions

Every professional campus development activity must have defined, measurable objectives that relate directly to the campus goals and improving student achievement. Each campus will also have required state-mandated training at the beginning of the year. The general overarching purpose for these is for the safety of staff and students.

Basic Skills.83 Clearly communicating rationale and purpose of professional development

There is nothing wrong with the principal beginning the staff development by stating the rational and purpose of the professional development. The more activities are goal-oriented, the more the focus is on improving student achievement, and the higher the likelihood toward reaching those goals.

Basic Skills.84 Create or find exemplar models aligned to objective

Similar to other basic skills mentioned in this section, the principal is the point of reference for providing a path to create exemplar models that align to the standards of the curriculum. The principal collaborates with teachers and staff to develop those goals.

Basic Skills.85 Design scaffolded learning activities aligned to the objective

Scaffolded learning activities are not exemplars. They are opportunities for students to practice the new learning with the critical learning steps clearly defined and shown in the practice. Then, students can safely navigate the student action portion of the learning process.

Basic Skills.86 Integrate opportunities for participant practice throughout professional development

The best staff development is one where staff are actively engaged in performing and practicing the actions of the staff development before using in a classroom setting.

Basic Skills.87 Integrate authentic resources to support the understanding of new content

The principal is capable of providing reliable resources to support new learning content when needed.

Basic Skills.88 Create a culture conducive to adult learning

Students typically do not learn unless the teachers and staff are engaged in learning as well. The principal should be presenting articles and books to the attention of staff that reflect the goals and objectives of the staff. This helps to create an environment of professional learning.

Basic Skills.89 Respond to adult engagement and formative assessments

The principal needs to ensure teachers and staff are engaging in assessing. They must be engaged in analyzing the formative assessment results in two critical areas. First, is the student mastering the information? Second, are the questions formatted in such a way so as not to create ambiguity or cultural bias? Then, the teachers and staff make the necessary adjustments to reteach the critical elements of the lesson when necessary.

Basic Skills.90 Develop and collect indicators of effectiveness such as survey, classroom observations, student outcomes

How will you know if students are successful? Of course, the state assessments are one way but that is not the only way. The principal must identify and create multiple forms of surveys to determine student success.

Basic Skills.91 Reflect and adjust after collection of indicators of effectiveness

The principal and staff must have the flexibility to adjust to the information collected from the indicators so that the opportunities for student achievement are increased.

Basic Skills.92 Create a clear and compelling mission, vision, and set of values (or communicate a pre-existing mission, vision, and set of values)

The principal and staff must come to a collaborative agreement on what the mission, vision, and goals are of the school. Ownership into these sets of beliefs and values create the learning culture, which in turn provides a springboard for learning in the classroom. These are non-negotiable.

Basic Skills.93 Establish campus goals in alignment with the mission and vision

The campus goals (no more than 3-4) are clearly defined, measurable, and can be implemented in a timely manner. These goals are established with high expectations and rigor in mind.

Basic Skills.94 Inspire and gain the commitment of others towards the mission, vision, values and goals

The principal serves as the symbolic frame encourager. The principal models and supports staff in their commitment to fulfilling the vision, mission, values, and goals of the campus.

Basic Skills.95 Model organizational values

The principal emulates what is expected of others with regard to setting a level of high expectations, rigor and professionalism.

Basic Skills.96 Translate vision, mission, and values into concrete behavioral expectations for adults and students that are described, taught, modeled, and reinforced

The principal collaborates with the staff to determine what the vision, mission, and values look like when put into action on a daily basis. This includes how teachers and staff behave and how the staff will hold each other accountable for student success.

Basic Skills.97 Respond to breaches in culture effectively

The principal is willing to address those who are unable or unwilling to promote the campus culture. This would include documentation and written action plans with a timeline that addresses the issue. *One cannot control beliefs; however, one can control behavior.* The principal is willing to make the leadership courage decision when a teacher or staff member needs to be non-renewed or terminated.

Basic Skills.98 Maintain emotional constancy in the face of conflict

Maintaining a high emotional IQ throughout the day, especially during times of crisis, helps to set the tone and mood for the entire campus. You cannot control how others act, but you can control how you react. That will make all the difference in the atmosphere of conflict.

Basic Skills.99 Create systems that foster relationship building

The principal is the servant leader. Therefore, it is important to earnestly develop healthy relationships with all staff because all staff are important. The broader sense of developing relationships extends beyond the confines of the building into the community and with the central office staff.

Basic Skills.100 Implement consistent systems for the collection of teacher feedback on working conditions at regular intervals

The principal needs to know the teachers feel safe and comfortable within their classrooms and in the building. The principal must be intentional about soliciting feedback to that effect. Then, act accordingly using the results if they call for action.

Basic Skills.101 Create structural opportunities for student leadership and community input

Create positions of graduated leadership for students in a way that promotes student leadership development. Student council, hall monitors, office staff, and principal round table discussions are a few ideas of many to generate student leadership cohorts.

Basic Skills.102 Collect and analyze data, both quantitative and qualitative

The principal should be continuously collecting data on student achievement. The day should be evaluated using teacher walk-through evaluations, teacher and student absenteeism, and other factors to determine root cause for low performance.

Basic Skills.103 Identify common trends within and across data sets

The principal uses the data to identify current and longitudinal indicators to pinpoint any cases of low performance areas in need of improvement.

Basic Skills.104 Identify causal and correlated actions

The principal is capable of observing and identifying root causes when students do not understand the lesson. The principal understands the actions of the teacher may not be connecting the old learning to the new learning.

Basic Skills.105 Determine root cause of causal actions with justification

The principal is capable of identifying the underlying causes for the lack of student understanding in lessons. The principal can justify those underlying causes by giving examples of what the teacher has said or done to initiate the disconnection in the lesson.

Basic Skills.106 Develop campus level goals and benchmarks in alignment with root cause analysis

The principal and staff identify root causes (the underlying causes) for lack of student mastery through analysis of the data in comparison with teaching strategies.

Using this information, they establish clear campus goals that will raise student performance to align with the campus benchmarks.

Basic Skills.107 Identify the highest leverage action, using data as justification

The principal understands the highest leverage action is the point in the lesson where the teacher can make the greatest gain in student comprehension. The principal uses data to justify the highest leverage action.

Basic Skills.108 Research best practices in alignment with the intended goal

The principal is capable of researching all available areas of information sets to identify best practices for the instructional activities needed to assist teachers in helping students to obtain mastery of the intended goals.

Basic Skills.109 Develop an action plan in alignment with root cause analysis and goals

The principal is capable of developing a clear and measurable action plan that meets the needs of correcting the learning issues identified using a root cause analysis. This includes a process of identifying the underlying reasons for struggling student learners.

Basic Skills.110 Develop systems to track progress towards implementation of action plan and goals

The principal must be able to create a sound observation process that identifies each teacher's areas of improvement and measurable instructional improvement plans. A calendar would help verify improvement toward reaching the individual teacher and campus goals.

Basic Skills.111 Develop structures and schedules to support implementation of action plan

The principal collaborates with teachers to create specific action steps used to implement the action plan. These steps should possess some sort of chronological order for implementation so they are observable and measurable.

Basic Skills.112 Determine key supporters and allies to invest in action plan

The principal builds coalitions of teachers, staff, students, parents and community who have ownership in the process. They are willing to implement the action plan with fidelity.

Basic Skills.113 Allocate human and material resources based on action plan

The principal works continuously as an advocate for identifying, soliciting and providing the necessary resources to allow the teachers and staff to meet the goals of the action plan.

Basic Skills.114 Develop and deliver critical communication to key stakeholders

The principal masters the art of carefully constructing the messages that need to be communicated to constituents. He/She communicates the messages multiple times in various venues while using the appropriate body language.

Basic Skills.115 Collect and analyze benchmark data, tracking progress towards goals

The principal understands collecting multiple forms of data is a continuous process. The principal also understands the results of the analysis of the data is used to make course corrections throughout the year.

Basic Skills.116 Reflect and adjust action plan based on data collected

The principal and staff understand the action plans are not set in stone. A series of monitoring and adjusting are made based on the most recent data analyses.

Basic Skills.117 Ensure consistent alignment of goals, resources, and action plan

The principal understands there is a continuous triangulation of the goals and resources against the action plan. Nothing is permanent. Once one area changes another area may need to be tweaked to meet the goals of the action plan.

CHAPTER 14
MINDSETS: CANDIDATES DEMONSTRATE THE BELIEF THAT...

Having the appropriate mindsets for students, staff and teachers, begins with the principal. Developing and incorporating these mindsets is a learning process that begins with behavior. There must be a conscious decision by the principal to want to learn and grow as an individual and as a professional. This may require a change of behavior before the mindset can be developed, ingrained and incorporated into the principal's toolbox of professional skills.

How you think determines *what* you think. If you are quick to come to a conclusion about issues, you may be more likely to miss value-added information. You will be given ideas to develop these mindsets, but do not allow yourself to be limited to one way of accomplishing tasks.

What we think determines what we *do*. Do not limit your scope of information on a subject or topic. The more information you have on an issue, the greater the chances for a more successful resolution. Incorporating these mindsets will allow you to see a bigger picture and increase your success as a learning leader.

What we *do* determines who we *are*. Your actions as a learning leader will be enhanced by developing each of these mindsets to the point they are second nature to you. They are the bedrock of your ability to be a successful instructional leader.

Basic Mindset.1 Multiple perspectives are valuable

When you as the principal have developed this particular mindset, you will have a tendency to be more open to suggestions, recommendations, and ideas that may be different from yours. However, maintain your goal of improving student achievement for all students and creating a culture of high expectations. What is a multiple perspective? It is similar to a baseball player hitting a homerun. Depending on where you are sitting, you are going to have a different perspective. Someone sitting behind home plate will view the hit differently than a fan in left field. A fan sitting midway down the first base will view it differently as well. When all of the descriptions of the hit are shared, you end up with a more complete picture of the home run where each fan has benefited from others' perspective.

The creation of a vision and mission statement (or any other task) is very similar when considering others' thoughts and opinions. You have teachers, students, parents, and community and business members standing on different corners who will be giving you a much different insight of what the vision and mission should be. You must be willing to have a multiple perspectives point of view, open to their corner of perception.

Basic Mindset.2 Community input is valuable

When working with the community, understand they can interpret your information, actions, and body language very quickly. This is why this mindset is so very important to construct prior to any meetings with parents and the community. You might have the right agenda and the right questions, but the manner in which you respond and body language will sound louder than your introductory speech for them to be a working partner. It is important to express your interest in how much you value the community responses by giving uninterrupted listening time. You do this by displaying a posture that demonstrates openness to the community and that you are willing to listen to their comments. Valuing community members mean you have a genuine interest in what is communicated by them. In the end, not all ideas and suggestions will be used, but what the community WILL remember is you valued their input.

Basic Mindset.3 Proactive communication to engender trust and foster strong school-community relationships is essential to building school culture

To be proactive means you have established a mindset of continuously being prepared to anticipate problems, needs, concerns or issues. You are willing to get out in front of those through effective communication systems and actions available to you. This includes an open and honest dialogue when the news may not be particularly in your favor. When you do this on a consistent basis, you develop constituents who trust and respect your leadership as well as the process. This mindset helps to create strong relationships with your stakeholders.

Basic Mindset.4 Quantifiable, academic outcomes for students are the primary measure of quality of instruction

The principal is able to decipher, through concrete measurable student outcomes, the ability of students to master the identified curriculum and the quality of instruction taking place. This information is ascertained through the processes listed in the Basic Skills section of this domain. This calls for the principal to be fully participatory in collaborative sessions and with data analysis meetings.

Basic Mindset.5 Retention of high performing teachers and counseling out low performing teachers is a top priority

Again, this is where the leadership courage of the administrator must be prevalent. The principal must have the ability to recognize high performing teachers in a manner that distinguishes their performance from others and the professional IQ to counsel out low performing teachers while keeping their dignity intact.

Basic Mindset.6 Achieving ambitious goals needs to be a team effort. It is the principal's responsibility to define roles, motivate action, and monitor progress for the campus team

This process involves clear, concise, and correct communication to students, staff, teachers, parents, and the learning community. Everyone wants to feel successful. The best way to do that is to present the roles and responsibilities related to all committees, groups and learning teams. This includes the students understanding their roles and responsibilities in the learning process.

Basic Mindset.7 Finding, developing, and keeping high-quality teachers are the highest leverage actions a principal can take to ensure student achievement

The principal understands that leverage actions are processes implemented by the principal to locate high-quality teachers. This includes developing good relationships with other high-quality teachers. You do this by encouraging them to keep a watchful eye for potential high-quality teachers. It also includes keeping a good working relationship with the personnel office, so they can serve as an early notice for potential high-quality teachers.

The principal must find continuous ways to provide opportunities for high-quality teachers to develop their craft. This includes, but is not limited to encouraging high-quality teachers to take risks, complete action research on their own that would benefit improved student achievement and to share the results with other staff members. You aggressively search for quality training that would add to the teachers' high-quality skill sets. You provide the high-quality teachers with educational material that lends itself to targeting improved student achievement.

Basic Mindset.8 A campus where teaching and learning is prioritized will naturally attract and retain quality teachers

This mindset serves as the rudder of the campus instructional ship. The principal must daily point all students, staff, teachers, parents and the learning community to the vision and mission of the campus. This requires the commitment of the principal to focus on teaching and learning as the number one priority. You might want to incorporate the vision and mission statement into the time allotted for morning announcements such as the Pledge of Allegiance and a Moment of Silence. This may help keep the focus on student learning.

Basic Mindset.9 Quantifiable, academic outcomes for students are the primary measure of quality of instruction

The principal must understand the importance of establishing realistic, measurable outcomes that are rigorous, yet achievable. These quantifiable measures are used to correct courses and keep the campus moving in the right direction. Everyone on the campus agrees to these accountability measures and seeks to fulfill those to the best of their ability.

Basic Mindset.10 An effective principal accepts and respects all cultural backgrounds, customs, traditions, values, and communication as assets

There are no negatives when it comes to cultural backgrounds. These influences are used to shape the overall culture of the campus and community. Diversity helps to create unity when all members understand the importance of accepting different customs, traditions, values and how we communicate those differences.

Basic Mindset.11 All members of the school community must hold unwavering high expectations for all students and families

This is a non-negotiable mindset. All staff understand that all students can and will learn if given the time, support and resources they need to achieve academic mastery. This demands extraordinary effort by all staff members to determine that failure is not an option and by providing additional learning opportunities as needed.

Basic Mindset.12 Equity is a school-wide belief, attainable goal, and daily practice

All students and staff will treat each other with the same high regard and respect regardless of a student's or a staff member's age, gender, religious preferences or cultural beliefs.

Basic Mindset.13 Cultural competence is a core belief and practice

The principal understands and is able to communicate and effectively interact with people across cultures. The principal is aware of how the world is viewed by other cultures and their differences. It is by gaining an understanding of those differences and using those differences that we help all students achieve academic success.

Basic Mindset.14 A conceptual adjustment involves the need to know each student's mastery, or lack of, after every lesson and concept has been taught

The principal ensures teachers and staff are monitoring student mastery of learning concepts by adjusting the teaching learning process as necessary, to achieve that success. This is a priority of the learning process.

Basic Mindset.15 Leaders should push teachers to develop a better understanding of why students are not performing well on content that has been taught and what action is needed

Teachers are taught how to use reflective self-questioning to identify learning gaps. They do this to further identify highest leverage points to allow for the greatest gain in academic mastery by adjusting the teaching methods and strategies to reach more students.

Basic Mindset.16 The use of rubrics containing a progressive continuum of performance expectations that better supports teacher reflection and development is best practice

The principal uses a personally developed rubric that contains the identified performance expectations of each teacher on a growth continuum. There are periodic checkpoints whereby the principal and teacher collaborate on perceived growth and expected growth. Principal-guided self-reflection questions are used to identify highest leverage growth points.

Basic Mindset.17 Data driven instruction can serve student achievement in multiple formats – it should look different to support different ages and ability groups

The principal understands there are multiple data points used to determine the performance of students. The data points may be different, depending on the age of the student and measures of student performance.

Basic Mindset.18 To effectively address student errors and misunderstandings, students should receive feedback and practice until they demonstrate mastery of the skill entirely on their own

This mindset is often overlooked because of time constraints, but it is one of the more important ones. The principal understands that the staff is in a continuous monitor and adjust mode of the teacher checking for real-time understanding of the standards and mastery. When challenges are identified, staff understands that scaffolding is used until the students can demonstrate independent mastery.

Basic Mindset.19 Teachers deserve consistent feedback around their practice to fine-tune their skills and to improve

Walk-throughs and observations are viewed as prospects for improvement with opportunities to implement self-reflective questioning and constructive feedback. Teachers understand the process is used for improvement of instructional delivery and personal growth.

Basic Mindset.20 Feedback is most effective when it includes concrete action steps, which can be implemented within a week

The principal and teacher understand that feedback is used for constructive improvement in the teaching process. Action steps are created that are measurable, specific, and contain a timeline for improvement. These steps are developed in a manner that allows the teacher to practice within a short period of time.

Basic Mindset.21 Short-cycle, bite-sized feedback allows teachers to develop knowledge and skills rapidly

The principal and staff understand that small incremental learning called "chunking" serves the students' best interest in the learning process. This provides an easier identification of where students may be struggling when teachers implement continuous monitoring and checking for understanding.

Basic Mindset.22 Practice is the most impactful component of the coaching conversation in supporting teachers in the development of new skills

When giving feedback through self-reflection questioning, once an action plan has been developed, the teacher practices the new behavior until the teacher demonstrates mastery.

Basic Mindset.23 Learning is best retained when it is applied and practiced over multiple intervals

This mindset applies to both the teachers who are on an action plan and students who need to master the learning. Repetition helps to develop myelin around the synapses in the brain, allowing for a more fluid recall of the skill. Myelin is a mixture of proteins that form an insulating sheath around the nerve fibers, increasing the speed at which impulses are conducted. The myelin affect is created when correct mastery is practiced routinely. This produces automaticity.

Basic Mindset.24 The effectiveness of professional development should be measured by effective teacher implementation of the knowledge and skills taught

Professional development is viewed as an opportunity for growth and the PD is developed around the vision, mission and goals of the campus. The professional development success is evaluated against the success of the teachers and staff successfully implementing the new information based on the PD expectation. This is a form of accountability, but more importantly, a reinforcement of the professional culture.

Basic Mindset.25 Effective teaching is the cornerstone of a strong school vision and mission, and therefore have a low tolerance for ineffective teaching

The principal and staff understand that student performance is the priority of the teaching process. Walk-throughs and observations are used to improve student performance and teaching. Teachers who are unwilling or may be unable to improve their teaching skills to the point of improving student performance understand they will be non-renewed or terminated from their position. This requires leadership courage on the part of the principal and the staff. When teachers or other staff members are underperforming, they understand it is imperative they be willing to exhibit teachable habits and change.

Basic Mindset.26 Great teaching should be consistently recognized

The principal consistently and publically recognizes great teaching. This is not a "pass the recognition around" process, but a real recognition of excellence in teaching.

Recognitions can also be acknowledged with personal handwritten notes and in other creative ways.

Basic Mindset.27 High expectations for all teachers strengthens a school's instructional culture

The principal sets the standard for high expectations for all teachers and staff by modeling those expectations. When students see a consistency of high expectations, they tend to rise to the occasion and produce higher quality work.

Basic Mindset.28 Positive adult relationships are the foundation for student academic growth

All students have an adult or two on campus who serve as their instructional advocate. This is one in whom they can confide when necessary without feeling embarrassed or ridiculed. Adults are responsible for building those healthy relationships over time. Students should feel like they can approach the staff to get any kind of help they need.

Basic Mindset.29 In order to thrive, students' basic needs must be met

Students cannot learn until their basic needs are met. A significant percentage of students may experience some sort of neglect or abuse at home or even qualify for homeless services. Campus staff need to be mindful of students requiring help with food, clothing, a place to stay, and a desire to feel safe at the campus. The campus must attempt to meet those needs as much as possible.

Basic Mindset.30 All students come to school with unique histories, values, and strengths

The principal and staff understand that each student is a unique individual with unique needs. The campus recognizes those differences and addresses them in the learning setting with a master design of reaching all students.

Basic Mindset.31 Stakeholders will be more invested in maintaining a culture they feel they helped to create.

All staff and a representative body of students and parents are included in the development of the culture of the campus. Therefore, the more people who have ownership, the more likely there will be a positive culture based on helping all students achieve mastery.

Basic Mindset.32 Routine feedback is an integral part of building a positive school culture

The principal provides on-the-spot real-time feedback on what is going well and what needs to be improved upon. This is the norm for campuses that are in a continuous improvement process mindset.

Basic Mindset.33 Only effective plans with clear initiatives and responsibilities, that are consistently reviewed and updated throughout the year, lead to improved results for students

The principal spends the time up front to establish clear, measurable and effective S.M.A.R.T goals with all staff tied to the initiatives. These are monitored continuously for adjustments as needed to provide the best possibility for student success.

Basic Mindset.34 It is the primary role of the school leader to consistently measure progress to outcomes and adjust as necessary

The principal is constantly measuring student progress using the agreed upon standards and outcomes. This process includes the adjusting of support and resources.

PART III – CONSTRUCTED RESPONSES – DESCRIPTION

The state mandated 268 Principal TExES exam will include the normal selected responses such as, the entry-level principal is given a scenario and the candidate must select from choices A through D. It could also include a choice of multiple correct answers such as "both A and C" for the answer. The entry-level principal needs to have background knowledge of the information provided in the EPPs preparation courses to help answer these questions. He/She must have assimilated the information regarding knowledge, skills, and mindsets, to be successful.

Additionally, included in the exam will be four questions called Constructed Response questions that will require the entry-level principal to answer in a much more detailed response. The entry-level principal must be able to address the instructional challenges teachers are faced with as they strive to help students achieve mastery. The entry-level principal should be prepared to deconstruct the barriers to a given scenario. By using a series of steps, you will be asked to identify the one or two highest leverage points in the scenario. You want to identify the points that will make the greatest gains in improving the instructional delivery of the teacher and eventually, improve student achievement.

The entry-level principal will be given a scenario that will most likely include some background information, a description of the current situation and a video to review. In addition, some supporting data will be given to the entry-level principal to read, assimilate, decipher, and decide upon a plan of action from that point. There may be some lower level leverage points as distractors for the candidate. It is important the candidate recognize what are the more important issues, highest leverage points, those issues or concerns to be corrected, and which could make the biggest gain in improving the instructional concerns of the scenario.

Additionally, the readers who rate your responses are not looking for perfection. They are looking for justification of your responses based on the steps below. The more you can make a case for your selection and justify it through professional terminology and good judgement, the greater chance you have of being successful on this portion of the exam.

The steps for deconstructing the scenario and reconstructing solutions should include:

1. **Diagnosis** – The entry-level principal must be able to read and analyze the scenario to determine what the highest leverage point is for improving instruction. At this point the entry-level principal is basically becoming an educational physician in attempting to diagnose what the "symptoms" are before moving on to the next step. In other words, "What are the one or two red flags or high priorities that need to be addressed?"

2. **Prioritize and Set Goals** – In step one, there may be many issues, but as an educational physician, the entry-level principal is going to identify the highest leverage point of concern and attack that one first. This is a form of prioritizing what needs to be given the attention by the entry-level principal in helping the teacher to correct the instructional concern.

    Now, that the entry-level principal has identified the one or two highest leverage points, what should the candidate do? The answer is to set goals. It is especially important to set concrete, measurable goals for the teacher to achieve. The more clear and concise these goals are, the better the chance for success on the principal candidate's part as well as for the teacher.

    There should be no more than one or two goals identified for improvement. Having more than that can be overwhelming for a teacher and overly time consuming for both of you. For instance, after a medical checkup, the doctor comes in and says, "You need to lose 20 pounds." There is your goal. It is not 5 pounds. It is not 10 pounds. It is 20 pounds.

    This is the same way with identifying the highest leverage points for the Constructed Responses. No need to be verbose; just state the goal(s) in as clear and concise language as you can.

3. **Plan** – This is the point where the entry-level principal works with the teacher to identify <u>specific</u> strategies that would help the teacher to achieve the one or two goals set forth in step 2. Remember to focus on the specific goal outlined in step two. For instance, in keeping with the medical analogy in the goal of losing 20 pounds, the doctor would say something like, "Limit your total calorie intake to no

more than 1800 calories a day, no sugars whatsoever, walk three times a week, drink plenty of fluids, and stay away from any carbonated drinks, including diet drinks."

As an educational physician, the entry-level principal is going to work with the teacher to prescribe a regimen, some specific actions, that will assist the teacher to get from where the entry-level principal identified the problem, point A, to point B, reaching a successful solution.

4. **Implement/Monitor/Adjust** – This is where the real work begins for the principal candidate. The candidate must identify how the plan will be implemented; identify the steps that will be used to achieve the goal using the plan identified in step 3 above, then explain how the plan will be monitored for success with possible adjustment points along the way.

In keeping with our medical analogy of weight loss, the doctor would say, "You will walk three times a week for thirty minutes, keep a log of the days and times you walked, you will write out what you ate for each meal and keep a log of that as well. You will write down at the end of the day, the amount of fluids you drank in ounces and you will keep a journal of the times you did not stay on the diet and why."

This step is the DOING part of the Constructed Response. It is important for the principal candidate, and the entry-level principal, to closely monitor this part of the process. This might even include the teacher practicing the delivery of the instruction with the suggested changes and working on them until both the teacher and the principal feel mastery has been achieved.

It would also include the process of observing the real-time presentations in the classroom for verification of performance and improvement. As with any plan, adjustments will always be in order, based on the classroom experience, perspectives, perceptions, and results.

CHAPTER 15
BREAKING DOWN THE CONSTRUCTED RESPONSE INTO MANAGEABLE STEPS

This is not an exercise to pass the 268 TExES Principal Exam. It is a process designed to encourage **all principals** to demonstrate their ability to be learning leaders. It is a process of change whereby teachers understand and have developed a mindset that when a principal completes walk-through observations or evaluations, it is for improving the instructional delivery and student achievement. This requires a change in the mindset of the principal and the teachers. In addition, that mindset change begins with the principal.

DIAGNOSE

Do not minimize any of the steps of this process. Certainly, this first step of diagnosing is important because it sets the stage and direction for the rest of the steps that follow. Therefore, when you take your exam or walk into a classroom for a brief observation, it is important to have internalized what skills, topics, indicators, and behaviors to look for to determine if there may be any leverage points. Here are a few of the high points an entry-level principal may look for in the classroom or an entry-level principal may be sensitive to in observing a teacher in action:

- Is the teacher prepared to teach the class with the resources available and ready to use them?
- Do the students understand the objective of the lesson and what they are expected to learn?
- Was the objective clearly defined?
- Is the lesson aligned to the agreed upon standards?
- Are the students engaged in the lesson?
- Are there clear examples of how to demonstrate mastery for the students?
- Is the teacher checking for continuous understanding?
- Is the teacher utilizing proximity with the students during the lesson?
- Is the teacher staying on topic?

- Is the teacher monitoring and adjusting her instructional delivery based on the real-time performance of students in the classroom?
- Are any students demonstrating off task behavior and if so, why?
- Is the teacher ensuring that all students are being called upon during the lesson?
- Do students have an opportunity to demonstrate mastery with guided practice?
- Does the teacher give multiple illustrations of what mastery looks like?
- Does the teacher reinforce positive student performance?
- Does the teacher redirect negative student or off-task behavior?
- Is the teacher evaluating student mastery on an independent level?
- Does the teacher provide enough wait time for students to process information and give a response to questions?
- Are the directions given by the teacher clear and age appropriate for the students?
- Are there any non-verbal concerns being expressed by either the teacher or the students?
- If re-teaching is necessary, is the information presented in a different way to help students to process the information more effectively?
- Does the teacher give students multiple opportunities to demonstrate mastery?
- Is the teacher using technology in a way that assists students in learning the instructional material?
- Are the students using technology efficiently and effectively?
- Is the teacher differentiating instruction as needed?
- Are the resources and manipulatives being used in a manner understood by the students?
- Are the assessments aligned with the teaching?
- Does student performance support successful teaching?
- Does the teacher summarize the learning?
- Are there appropriate reinforcement strategies being implemented?
- Does the teacher utilize an appropriate exit ticket to help assess the teaching process?

- How is the teacher using the information from the exit ticket to readjust the teaching process?

After the entry-level principal has had time to review the data, he/she must then identify the highest leverage point that would provide the greatest amount of gain in the shortest period of time, if corrected. This typically centers on the instructional delivery process and is something that can be measured. Once this is completed, you are now ready to move to the next step.

PRIORITIZE AND SET GOALS

This process requires some direct reflection by the principal candidate. The entry-level principal needs to focus on the items of concern and narrow the selection down to one or two areas for improvement. The question to ask is, "What leverage point, if improved, would make the greatest positive impact in improving student achievement?"
The one that would make the greatest impact on student achievement is considered the highest leverage point and that is where you will begin your work.

To help with identifying the highest leverage point, you might ask these or similar questions when looking at the critical indicators you have identified:

- Which leverage point most closely connects to your vision?
- How much energy and preparation will need to take place with you and the teacher to achieve the necessary improvement?
- Will any additional resources need to be used to achieve the improvement?
- Can this leverage point be clearly and effectively measured?
- Will both parties commit to improvement of this leverage point?

Now, it is time to include the teacher in the process to begin improving the instruction in the classroom. Although you have done the reflection process and are prepared to meet with the teacher, the process is far from over.

In starting the meeting, it is always good to point out parts of the presentation that went well and reinforce that good professional techniques are being used whenever possible. Allow the teacher to respond by asking where he/she felt the lesson went exceptionally well? This provides a solid foundation and these meetings are not just about constructive criticism, but about improving the instructional process.

Then, move to asking the teacher where he/she thinks there were indicators of when the lesson may not have gone well? Allow time for the teacher to reflect and respond to the question. Support the teacher in the responses given, but continue asking if there are other indicators until the teacher feels he/she has exhausted to possibilities. During this part of the process, begin focusing in on the high leverage points you previously identified for this conference. More times than not, the teacher will mention the critical issue and you will be able to begin your focus on this high leverage point.

The critical part at this point is to generate a viable, measurable goal that can show improvement in a relatively short amount of time. The important piece in this process is that the teacher and the entry-level principal agree upon the highest leverage point. The manner in which the goal is evaluated must be measurable.

It is now time to develop the plan!

PLAN

A good place to begin the plan is to collaborate on what the goal would look like if focusing on the identified leverage point, and the teacher met all expectations of the goal. This is not just a brief description but also an in depth picture of perfection. From there, it becomes possible to work backwards and identify the actions of the teacher, the tools, the instructional strategies, and the resources to improve.

The teacher should be able to describe in detail what meeting the goal would look like in the classroom. The entry-level principal should be asking questions all along to reinforce reaching the goal and to help with redirecting possible distractors that could arise during the teaching session. Encourage the teacher to ask clarifying questions about the actions, steps, and resources to be used in the process.

This next part is very important. Practice! Ask the teacher to practice the process to verify the teacher understands the expectations and the proper implementation of the corrective action with the use of identified resources. The first time the process is practiced, the entry-level principal is the coach in every sense of the word. Stop the practice to make suggestions and recommendations. In fact, this is the time the entry-level principal will communicate specific expectations. That is what coaches do. After this practice run, you and the teacher will collaborate on how it went, what needs to be done differently and how the teacher will execute the changes.

Next, comes the final uninterrupted practice run. The teacher will perform the instructional delivery without interruption. When the presentation is finished, you will reinforce the excellent parts and ask the teacher if there are any parts of the presentation that need to be fine-tuned prior to the actual presentation. Once this has been completed, agree on a date and a time to return to the classroom to observe the presentation.

IMPLEMENT/MONITOR AND ADJUST

This process is not an on-the-hook/off-the-hook process. It is a continuous procedure of improving instruction. It is axiomatic by now that the focus of the principal is one of being the learning leader in charge of improving the delivery of instruction so students benefit from this critical process.

This part of the process involves making an observation at the agreed upon time and completely monitoring the full presentation, based on the agreed upon goals. Once the observation is complete, there should be a full review of the presentation using the same process outlined in the planning stage above. Reinforce the positive improvements made and highlight any unresolved issues. This collaborative process should reinforce the positive aspects of the teacher's presentation.

Once that has been completed, you communicate with the teacher that this is an ongoing process and you, the learning leader principal will keep notes on the process as you monitor the teacher's progress. This should reinforce to the teacher the importance of the teaching/learning process and begin developing a culture of focusing on improving instruction.

PART IV - PERFORMANCE ASSESSMENT FOR SCHOOL LEADERS

The Performance Assessment for School Leaders or better known as PASL tasks, were developed to reinforce the principal's ability to identify, address, and resolve instructional issues in collaboration with other campus staff members. The purpose of these tasks is to provide the entry-level principal with the understanding that the expectation of the local communities and the state leaders is for principals to be instructionally proactive on their campuses. These tasks provide some semblance of the knowledge, skills and mindsets needed to be a change agent for improving instruction. Much of the knowledge, skills and mindsets have been included in this textbook.

It would be a good investment for the principal candidate to download the handbook developed by The Educational Testing Services (2017) for a more in depth look at preparing to master these tasks. This site will provide you with all the necessary components of the tasks for the entry-level principal to successfully master the three tasks.

Task 1 currently focuses on the principal candidate's ability to solve a real life problem in the field. In this task, you will demonstrate your ability to address and resolve a significant problem/challenge in your school that influences instructional practice and student learning. The process of this task includes identifying a problem, researching and developing a plan, implementing the plan, reflecting on the plan and developing a resolution. All of these tasks are action-oriented, meaning you are to physically complete each of the steps of the tasks as stated.

Task 2 focuses on the principal candidate's ability to demonstrate skills in establishing and supporting effective and continuous professional development with the staff, for the purpose of improved instruction and student learning. In this task you will be collaborating with your peers in designing building-level professional staff development, implementing the staff development, analyzing three participants' responses to the staff development, and completing some written reflections on that professional staff development.

Task 3 focuses on the principal candidate's ability to facilitate stakeholders' efforts to build a collaborative team within the school to improve instruction, student achievement, and the school culture. In this task, you will be asked to identify a collaborative team. The team will develop a plan to improve instruction, student learning and the school culture. Then you will complete a reflective activity on the collaborative team and school culture.

Each of the tasks require a submission of an unedited video to allow the trained raters to evaluate the performances and processes submitted. Each of the tasks also include a rubric. These rubrics assist the entry-level principal as to what is expected to achieve mastery of the tasks.

The raters who evaluate the tasks understand the principal candidates are novice leaders at this point and are not looking for perfection or amazing results. In fact, honesty and integrity rule the day. The reflection aspects of each of these tasks will tell the raters a lot about you and your ability to learn and grow as a learning leader. Do your tasks, and do them to the best of your ability, but complete them with honesty and integrity in mind.

CHAPTER 16
CLOSING COMMENTS

This textbook has been an effort of constructing a picture of you, the entry-level principal as the leader of learning for your campus. Each chapter has taken an in-depth look at what that looks and feels like.

Chapter 1 introduced you in how to establish and implement a shared vision and culture of high expectations for all stakeholders. The vision drives the campus toward academic success. The culture of the campus is a high priority to reaching your academic goals. Do not overlook the students. They can be the key to establishing a culture focused on high achievement.

Chapter 2 showed you how to work with stakeholders as key partners to support student learning. Too many of our current campuses underutilize the potential resources that are waiting to be used by an innovative principal who recognizes the value that can be added through engaging constituents.

Chapter 3 explained how to collaboratively develop and implement high-quality instruction. High-quality instruction is the single most important resource for improving student achievement. It is imperative principals find ways to develop and retain teachers who demonstrate high-quality teaching.

Chapter 4 gave you information on how to monitor and assess classroom instruction to promote teacher effectiveness and student achievement. Remember that monitoring and improving classroom instruction is a continuous process. This is another mindset for educators to assimilate.

Chapter 5 showed you specific examples on how to provide feedback, coaching, and professional development to staff through evaluation and supervision, knowing how to reflect on his/her own practice, and striving to grow professionally. Professional growth is an outward expression of the entry-level principal's mindset of being a life-long learner.

Chapter 6 continued the emphasis of high-quality teaching by sharing how to promote high-quality teaching using selection, placement, and retention practices to promote teacher excellence and growth. This process is such an important investment in the longevity of improving student achievement. Time invested on having the correct teacher selection process in place will save time and challenges later on.

Chapter 7 presented ideas of how to develop relationships with internal and external stakeholders, including selecting appropriate communication strategies for particular audiences. Building and maintaining healthy relationships with all stakeholders is essential to your success. These relationships go hand-in-hand with developing excellent communication skills and knowing when to use them.

Chapter 8 focused on improving student outcomes through organizational collaboration, resiliency, and change management. This chapter highlighted collaboration. This is essential for overcoming the challenges of identifying and reaching the goals of the campus. The process requires resiliency and the ability to accept change as a part of the process.

Chapter 9 was another deep dive into how to collaboratively determine goals and implement strategies aligned with the school vision that support teacher effectiveness and positive student outcomes. This chapter reiterated the importance of collaboration and began to combine some characteristics of previous chapters into a process of highlighting improved student outcomes.

Chapter 10 pointed out the importance of how to provide administrative leadership through resource management, policy implementation, and coordination of school operations and programs to ensure a safe learning environment. This chapter emphasized the need for the principal to take care of the structural frame of the campus' needs using appropriate administrative processes to keep everything running smoothly.

Chapter 11 explained how to provide ethical leadership by advocating for children and ensuring student access to effective educators, programs, and services. Demonstrating a standard of high ethical conduct by the principal and all educators is an expectation. Practicing strong ethical behavior at all times allows you to focus on improving student achievement.

Chapters 12-14 focused on basic knowledge, skills and mindsets necessary for the entry-level principal to be prepared when entering a school as the learning leader. This information is indispensable if you hope to improve student achievement.

Chapter 15 broke down the components of the 268 TExES Principal Exam into manageable sections for the entry-level principal. Following these suggestions should help the entry-level principal achieve success on the state exam.

A review of the Performance Assessment for School leaders was also given. These three tasks are developed to provide an opportunity for the entry-level principal to demonstrate his/her ability to solve real-life challenges for today's campus leaders.

The information in this textbook is relevant to any principal who desires to have a positive impact on instruction. The principal domains and competencies are not just for preparation courses to establish hoops the principal candidates are to jump through. They are standards for making a difference in improving instruction for every classroom teacher. This begins with a principal who is dedicated to making a difference.

Every child begins public education with an energetic hope of learning and growing as a learner. Hope has a face. It is your job as an educator and especially as campus learning leader to keep hope alive in every child. You be the difference-maker that fans those flames of hope for every child.

ANSWERS TO SAMPLE CHAPTER QUESTIONS

CHAPTER 1

QUESTION	ANSWER	DESCRIPTION
1	B	Complete a process of personal reflection and systemic thinking on what steps, data, resources, and procedures need to be considered to begin this task.
2	C	Investigate research-based theories that would affect the attainment of the instructional goals as they relate to meeting the vision and mission of her campus.
3	A	She explains her need for their help in thinking creatively for ways to change the culture of the campus since they have been there longer than others have. She needs their help to generate ideas on how to create an interest and excitement in the process.
4	B	Set up meetings using the professional learning communities to engage the staff to describe what success would like in their classrooms based on the vision and mission statement.
5	D	Encourage as many staff members who are willing, to stand up and share any student academic success stories. Follow up by praising the staff member publicly in the meeting for his/her efforts.

CHAPTER 2

QUESTION	ANSWER	DESCRIPTION
1	D	He publicly thanks members of each of the stakeholder groups for their efforts in helping to identify themes and expectations for creating a culture of success for all students.
2	A	Present information to the group on the unique stages of creating group dialogue and how groups react to the stages of forming, norming, storming and conforming, as they appear in general group dynamics.
3	B	Call a ten-minute break to allow for some think time for the group. This will allow her to privately approach the two individuals to seek their input about what concerns they have regarding the proposed draft. This also allows each to give feedback in order to clear up any perceived misunderstandings.
4	C	Convert an extra classroom as a safe haven for parents to come and view the books used in the classrooms and

QUESTION	ANSWER	DESCRIPTION
		other literature that would benefit them in helping their children be successful.
5	D	Respond in a handwritten thank you note to the individual participants who were willing to offer ideas and suggestions that helped move the process to its guiding vision and mission statement.

CHAPTER 3

QUESTION	ANSWER	DESCRIPTION
1	B	Start accumulating all data on students and staff that affects student learning from at least the past three years. Familiarize himself to what the data is beginning to tell him.
2	B	What kind of data do they need to help them identify the two or three measurable instructional goals for the next school year?
3	A	Call the groups together and provide some training on how to write measurable goals by giving some clear examples and touching on the important aspects of goal writing.
4	B	Ask the staff to identify what research-based instructional strategies related to the goals would best serve their students in achieving success.
5	D	Formulate a plan to ask some guided questions to the groups at their next PLC meetings that would stimulate conversations about using instructional strategies in the classroom.

CHAPTER 4

QUESTION	ANSWER	DESCRIPTION
1	D	Guide them to review what the formative assessment is evaluating on this particular learning objective. Encourage them to work backwards to determine the best strategies to allow for student success on the assessment using their current student performance data.
2	C	Use guided questions to lead the teachers to the understanding they are to present the material using the agreed upon research-based instructional strategies.
3	A	Asking them to open their district-provided laptop computers, as she opens hers, and encouraging each of them to search the internet by entering how to teach the objective identified. When the teachers come up with

QUESTION	ANSWER	DESCRIPTION
		ideas, guide them in discussing the best strategies to use for the learning objective.
4	C	Train his teachers on how to use action research to improve student achievement. Encourage his teachers to be instructional risk-takers while communicating the results to the professional learning communities and making improvements to the instructional strategies.
5	A	Create time within the professional learning community meetings to develop teacher capacity to evaluate formative student performance.

CHAPTER 5

QUESTION	ANSWER	DESCRIPTION
1	C	Take some time to complete a personal reflection activity and make some electronic notes on what he could do differently.
2	A	Make a personal visit to the central office and discuss face-to-face with the person identifying applicants, what she and her leadership team are looking for.
3	B	Begin developing an agenda with a list of possible resources that can be used to conduct staff development once the teachers report back to school.
4	D	Asking a few questions about the action research project and encourage the teacher to move forward. Explain he is looking forward to hearing about the results.
5	D	Communicate with the staff his expectations for improving student achievement, how he will utilize walk-through observations, formal observations and feedback to support the process of improving instruction.

CHAPTER 6

QUESTION	ANSWER	DESCRIPTION
1	C	Assign each member of the interview team to review an application, check the references and secondary references, and report to the interview team on the findings.
2	A	Ask the lead teacher on the committee to review the initial questions to make sure they are relevant for this particular interview and to assign questions to each of the members to ask during the interview.
3	B	Review the strengths and weaknesses of the remainder of the staff, to consider reassigning current staff to other

QUESTION	ANSWER	DESCRIPTION
		positions that would provide the greatest opportunity for student mastery.
4	D	Meet with lead teachers of the professional learning communities and determine if they can develop some professional development training that would address the instructional challenge. Assure them she will provide the necessary resources to help address the issues.
5	C	Go to his office, review his notes, and prepare specific questions to ask the teacher that will allow her to respond without feeling threatened when he meets with her after school.

CHAPTER 7

QUESTION	ANSWER	DESCRIPTION
1	D	Call the superintendent and set up a meeting to discuss the proposed campus changes with him/her.
2	C	Set up an individual meeting with each campus employee, to create an opportunity to get to know them and begin building healthy relationships among the staff.
3	A	Thank the person for being willing to ask the question and inform the person that it is an excellent question, Explain this issue has been addressed by the students, staff, central office, and the administration. Explain that every group mentioned has supported keeping the current name and direct the person to visit the school's website for more information on the subject. Then say, "I don't believe I have had the pleasure of meeting you," and extend your hand.
4	C	Bring the campus leadership team together to review the campus strategies for disseminating the important changes.
5	D	She should introduce herself to the parent, explain she was the one who helped create the new discipline consequences and invite the parent into her office to hear the parent's concerns.

CHAPTER 8

QUESTION	ANSWER	DESCRIPTION
1	B	Develop and implement a process that will keep the staff inspired about the changes, which include verifying the plan has been implemented with fidelity.

QUESTION	ANSWER	DESCRIPTION
2	A	Utilize some problem-solving techniques to get a better understanding of what the issue is with the two teachers.
3	D	Suggest to the teachers to talk to the student, to see if she has had anything to eat recently because she is aware the student lives in a high poverty government housing.
4	C	Assemble the teachers together and show them the data from the campus-based assessments that indicate the changes made at the beginning of the year are showing positive results. Remind the staff they completed a systemic process to anticipate this very type of feedback. Encourage them to stay the course and keep up the good work.
5	B	Pull the leadership team in for a full training session on how to conduct a PLC meeting with a focus and consistency of delivering the instruction in a manner consistent with one another. Explain to them that this is not a suggestion, but an expectation for all PLC teams to adhere to the remainder of the school year.

CHAPTER 9

QUESTION	ANSWER	DESCRIPTION
1	D	Begin with the end in mind. Use the data to determine where the two or three highest leverage points are to begin planning staff development.
2	A	Make an executive decision to bring the group back on task for the moment. Make a mental note to pull in the lead teacher for some intentional training on how to conduct a professional learning community using the campus-designed agenda.
3	B	Indicate to the staff that based on the goals established for the year, the current budget will be scrubbed. The budget will be realigned for any excess funds to help with the necessary resources needed to meet the stated goals.
4	C	Ask the staff to meet in their PLC teams to establish specific roles and routines for ensuring the success of implementation of appropriate instructional strategies. Each team will be instructed to be prepared to report to the group.
5	A	Decide to call a meeting of the lead teachers from each of the subject areas to collaborate on the need for more time for reading and math, as well as the need for more

QUESTION	ANSWER	DESCRIPTION
		manipulatives. Ask them to help come up with a schedule and review their budgets for any additional funds for manipulatives.

CHAPTER 10

QUESTION	ANSWER	DESCRIPTION
1	A	Review current discipline management policies for fair and equitable administration of consequences to make plans for a review of the expectations at the next staff meeting.
2	C	Let the parents know it is the responsibility of the school to contact parents about students sent to the office on disciplinary referrals, to inform the parents of the infraction and the consequences. He additionally will give some immediate training for the assistant principal on expectations of communication with parents whenever students are sent to the office on a referral.
3	D	Explain to the teacher we are all here to ensure the students' IEPs are implemented as written and that she will ensure that all Individual Education Programs (IEPs) are being carried out by the teacher and support staff as approved in the ARD.
4	A	Meet separately with the identified teachers. Remind them to accurately take attendance for each class at the designated time. Inform them that student attendance is how districts and campuses are allotted money the following year. It is important to follow those procedures closely.
5	D	Thank the parent for bringing the concern to his attention. Then contact the transportation department and explain the concern. Ask that the department to review the student's transportation home, to find a quicker route to delivering the student home in a reasonable amount of time. Mr. Hadley calls the parent to inform her of what has been done and that the concern will be corrected as quickly as possible.

CHAPTER 11

QUESTION	ANSWER	DESCRIPTION
1	D	Call a meeting of the leadership team to ask them how the team can collaborate to come up with ways to recognize the diversity of the campus. Encourage them to develop a plan to organize a week of diversity

QUESTION	ANSWER	DESCRIPTION
		celebration and pull in some parent representation from each of the ethnic groups.
2	A	Inform the parent the teacher had an unexpected emergency in her family. Suggest that the meeting be postponed until another day when the teacher can be present to give a full report on the student's progress.
3	D	Call the parents into the office. See if there is a way to keep the student at the high school. Clarify with them that since the student is 18 years of age, the Family Education Privacy Act will not allow the school to release records to anyone until the school receives a signed released from the student, who has been called to the office to do so.
4	B	Set up a meeting with the head coach during his conference period. Inform him that he will meet with the coach in his classroom. At that time, bring up the concerns by the parent and ask the coach to clarify. If in fact, the coach is using the instructional conference period for coaching, instruct the coach to stop using the instructional period for coaching responsibilities. Reiterate it is to be used for instructional planning, PLC meetings, and working with students who are requesting additional help.
5	C	Bring the leadership team together to share what she observed. Ask them to begin planning ways that the campus could celebrate with the students, staff and community about the diverse cultural practices demonstrated on the campus.

APPENDIX A
PRINCIPAL DOMAINS

DOMAIN I—SCHOOL CULTURE (School and Community Leadership)

Competency 001: The entry-level principal knows how to establish and implement a shared vision and culture of high expectations for all stakeholders (students, staff, parents, and community).

- K. Creates a positive, collaborative, and collegial campus culture that sets high expectations and facilitates the implementation and achievement of campus initiatives and goals
- L. Uses emerging issues, recent research, knowledge of systems (e.g., school improvement process, strategic planning, etc.), and various types of data (e.g., demographic, perceptive, student learning, and processes) to collaboratively develop a shared campus vision and a plan for implementing the vision
- M. Facilitates the collaborative development of a plan that clearly articulates objectives and strategies for implementing a campus vision
- N. Aligns financial, human, and material resources to support implementation of a campus vision and mission
- O. Establishes procedures to assess and modify implementation plans to promote achievement of the campus vision
- P. Models and promotes the continuous and appropriate development of all stakeholders in the school community, to shape the campus culture
- Q. Establishes and communicates consistent expectations for all stakeholders, providing supportive feedback to promote a positive campus environment
- R. Implements effective strategies to systematically gather input from all campus stakeholders, supporting innovative thinking and an inclusive culture
- S. Creates an atmosphere of safety that encourages the social, emotional, and physical well-being of staff and students
- T. Facilitates the implementation of research-based theories and techniques to promote a campus environment and culture that is conducive to effective teaching and learning and supports organizational health and morale

Competency 002: The entry-level principal knows how to work with stakeholders as key partners to support student learning.

- A. Acknowledges, recognizes, and celebrates the contributions of all stakeholders toward the realization of the campus vision
- B. Implements strategies to ensure the development of collegial relationships and effective collaboration
- C. Uses consensus-building, conflict-management, communication, and information-gathering strategies to involve various stakeholders in planning processes that

enable the collaborative development of a shared campus vision and mission focused on teaching and learning
D. Ensures that parents and other members of the community are an integral part of the campus culture

DOMAIN II—LEADING LEARNING (Instructional Leadership/Teaching and Learning)

Competency 003: The entry-level principal knows how to collaboratively develop and implement high-quality instruction.

A. Prioritizes instruction and student achievement by understanding, sharing, and promoting a clear definition of high-quality instruction based on best practices from recent research
B. Facilitates the use of sound, research-based practice in the development, implementation, coordination, and evaluation of campus curricular, cocurricular, and extracurricular programs to fulfill academic, development, social, and cultural needs
C. Facilitates campus participation in collaborative district planning, implementation, monitoring, and revision of the curriculum to ensure appropriate scope, sequence, content, and alignment
D. Implements a rigorous curriculum that is aligned with state standards, including college and career-readiness standards
E. Facilitates the use and integration of technology, telecommunications, and information systems to enhance learning

Competency 004: The entry-level principal knows how to monitor and assess classroom instruction to promote teacher effectiveness and student achievement.

F. Monitors instruction routinely by visiting classrooms, observing instruction, and attending grade-level, department, or team meetings to provide evidence-based feedback to improve instruction
G. Analyzes the curriculum collaboratively to guide teachers in aligning content across grades and ensures that curricular scopes and sequences meet the particular needs of their diverse student populations (considering sociological, linguistic, cultural, and other factors)
H. Monitors and ensures staff use of multiple forms of student data to inform instruction and intervention decisions that maximizes instructional effectiveness and student achievement
I. Promotes instruction that supports the growth of individual students and student groups, supports equity, and works to reduce the achievement gap

J. Supports staff in developing the capacity and time to collaboratively and individually use classroom formative and summative assessment data to inform effective instructional practices and interventions

DOMAIN III—HUMAN CAPITAL (Human Resource Management)

Competency 005: The entry-level principal knows how to provide feedback, coaching, and professional development to staff through evaluation and supervision, knows how to reflect on his/her own practice, and strives to grow professionally.

G. Communicates expectations to staff and uses multiple data points (e.g., regular observations, walk-throughs, teacher and student data, and other sources) to complete evidence-based evaluations of all staff
H. Coaches and develops teachers by facilitating teacher self-assessment and goal setting, conducting conferences, giving individualized feedback, and supporting individualized professional growth opportunities
I. Collaborates to develop, implement, and revise a comprehensive and ongoing plan for the professional development of campus staff that addresses staff needs based on staff appraisal trends, goals, and student information/data
J. Facilitates a continuum of effective professional development activities that includes appropriate content, process, context, allocation of time, funding, and other needed resources
K. Engages in ongoing and meaningful professional growth activities, reflects on his or her practice, seeks and acts on feedback, and strives to continually improve, learn, and grow
L. Seeks assistance (e.g., mentor, central office) to ensure effective and reflective decision making and works collaboratively with campus and district leadership

Competency 006: The entry-level principal knows how to promote high-quality teaching by using selection, placement, and retention practices to promote teacher excellence and growth.

E. Invests and manages time to prioritize the development, support, and supervision of the staff to maximize student outcomes
F. Facilitates collaborative structures that support professional learning communities in reviewing data, processes, and policies in order to improve teaching and learning in the school
G. Creates leadership opportunities, defines roles, and delegates responsibilities to effective staff and administrators to support campus goal attainment

H. Implements effective, appropriate, and legal strategies for the recruitment, screening, hiring, assignment, induction, development, evaluation, promotion, retention, discipline, and dismissal of campus staff

DOMAIN IV—EXECUTIVE LEADERSHIP (Communication and Organizational Management)

Competency 007: The entry-level principal knows how to develop relationships with internal and external stakeholders, including selecting appropriate communication strategies for particular audiences.

E. Understands how to effectively communicate a message in different ways to meet the needs of various audiences
F. Develops and implements strategies for systematically communicating internally and externally
G. Develops and implements a comprehensive program of community relations that uses strategies that effectively involve and inform multiple constituencies
H. Establishes partnerships with parents, businesses, and other groups in the community to strengthen programs and support campus goals

Competency 008: The entry-level principal knows how to focus on improving student outcomes through organizational collaboration, resiliency, and change management.

F. Demonstrates awareness of social and economic issues that exist within the school and community that affect campus operations and student learning
G. Gathers and organizes information from a variety of sources to facilitate creative thinking, critical thinking, and problem solving to guide effective campus decision making
H. Frames, analyzes, and creatively resolves campus problems using effective problem-solving techniques to make timely, high-quality decisions
I. Develops, implements, and evaluates systems and processes for organizational effectiveness to keep staff inspired and focused on the campus vision
J. Uses effective planning, time management, and organization of work to support attainment of school district and campus goals

DOMAIN V—STRATEGIC OPERATIONS (Alignment and Resource Allocation)

Competency 009: The entry-level principal knows how to collaboratively determine goals and implement strategies aligned with the school vision that support teacher effectiveness and positive student outcomes.

A. Assesses the current needs of the campus, analyzing a wide set of evidence to determine campus objectives, and sets measurable school goals, targets, and strategies that form the school's strategic plans
B. Establishes structures that outline and track the progress using multiple data points and makes adjustments as needed to improve teacher effectiveness and student outcomes
C. Allocates resources effectively (e.g., staff time, master schedule, dollars, and tools), aligning them with school objectives and goals, and works to access additional resources as needed to support learning
D. Implements appropriate management techniques and group processes to define roles, assign functions, delegate authority, and determine accountability for campus goal attainment

Competency 010: The entry-level principal knows how to provide administrative leadership through resource management, policy implementation, and coordination of school operations and programs to ensure a safe learning environment.

I. Implements strategies that enable the physical plant, equipment, and support systems to operate safely, efficiently, and effectively to maintain a conducive learning environment
J. Applies strategies for ensuring the safety of students and personnel and for addressing emergencies and security concerns, including developing and implementing a crisis plan
K. Applies local, state, and federal laws and policies to support sound decisions while considering implications related to all school operations and programs (e.g., student services, food services, health services, and transportation)
L. Collaboratively plans and effectively manages the campus budget within state law and district policies to promote sound financial management in relation to accounts, bidding, purchasing, and grants
M. Uses technology to enhance school management (e.g., attendance systems, teacher grade books, shared drives, and messaging systems)
N. Facilitates the effective coordination of campus curricular, co-curricular, and extracurricular programs in relation to other school district programs to fulfill the academic, developmental, social, and cultural needs of students

O. Collaborates with district staff to ensure the understanding and implementation of district policies and advocates for the needs of students and staff
P. Implements strategies for student discipline and attendance in a manner that ensures student safety, consistency, and equity and that legal requirements are met (e.g., due process, SPED requirements)

DOMAIN VI—ETHICS, EQUITY, AND DIVERSITY

Competency 011: The entry-level principal knows how to provide ethical leadership by advocating for children and ensuring student access to effective educators, programs, and services.

H. Implements policies and procedures that require all campus personnel to comply with the Educators' Code of Ethics (TAC Chapter 247)
I. Models and promotes the highest standard of conduct, ethical principles, and integrity in decision making, actions, and behaviors
J. Advocates for all children by promoting the continuous and appropriate development of all learners in the campus community
K. Implements strategies to ensure that all students have access to effective educators and continuous opportunities to learn
L. Promotes awareness and appreciation of diversity throughout the campus community (e.g., learning differences, multicultural awareness, gender sensitivity, and ethnic appreciation)
M. Facilitates and supports special campus programs that provide all students with quality, flexible instructional programs and services (e.g., health, guidance, and counseling programs) to meet individual student needs
N. Applies legal guidelines (e.g., in relation to students with disabilities, bilingual education, confidentiality, and discrimination) to protect the rights of students and staff and to improve learning opportunities
H. Articulates the importance of education in a free, democratic society

APPENDIX B
EDUCATOR'S CODE OF ETHICS

(1) Professional Ethical Conduct, Practices and Performance.

(A) Standard 1.1. The educator shall not intentionally, knowingly, or recklessly engage in deceptive practices regarding official policies of the school district, educational institution, educator preparation program, the Texas Education Agency, or the State Board for Educator Certification (SBEC) and its certification process.

(B) Standard 1.2. The educator shall not intentionally, knowingly, or recklessly misappropriate, divert, or use monies, personnel, property, or equipment committed to his or her charge for personal gain or advantage.

(C) Standard 1.3. The educator shall not submit fraudulent requests for reimbursement, expenses, or pay.

(D) Standard 1.4. The educator shall not use institutional or professional privileges for personal or partisan advantage.

(E) Standard 1.5. The educator shall neither accept nor offer gratuities, gifts, or favors that impair professional judgment or that are used to obtain special advantage. This standard shall not restrict the acceptance of gifts or tokens offered and accepted openly from students, parents of students, or other persons or organizations in recognition or appreciation of service.

(F) Standard 1.6. The educator shall not falsify records, or direct or coerce others to do so.

(G) Standard 1.7. The educator shall comply with state regulations, written local school board policies, and other state and federal laws.

(H) Standard 1.8. The educator shall apply for, accept, offer, or assign a position or a responsibility on the basis of professional qualifications.

(I) Standard 1.9. The educator shall not make threats of violence against school district employees, school board members, students, or parents of students.

(J) Standard 1.10. The educator shall be of good moral character and be worthy to instruct or supervise the youth of this state.

(K) Standard 1.11. The educator shall not intentionally, knowingly, or recklessly misrepresent his or her employment history, criminal history, and/or disciplinary record when applying for subsequent employment.

(L) Standard 1.12. The educator shall refrain from the illegal use, abuse, or distribution of controlled substances, prescription drugs, and toxic inhalants.

(M) Standard 1.13. The educator shall not be under the influence of alcohol or consume alcoholic beverages on school property or during school activities when students are present.

(2) Ethical Conduct Toward Professional Colleagues.

(A) Standard 2.1. The educator shall not reveal confidential health or personnel information concerning colleagues unless disclosure serves lawful professional purposes or is required by law.

(B) Standard 2.2. The educator shall not harm others by knowingly making false statements about a colleague or the school system.

(C) Standard 2.3. The educator shall adhere to written local school board policies and state and federal laws regarding the hiring, evaluation, and dismissal of personnel.

(D) Standard 2.4. The educator shall not interfere with a colleague's exercise of political, professional, or citizenship rights and responsibilities.

(E) Standard 2.5. The educator shall not discriminate against or coerce a colleague on the basis of race, color, religion, national origin, age, gender, disability, family status, or sexual orientation.

(F) Standard 2.6. The educator shall not use coercive means or promise of special treatment in order to influence professional decisions or colleagues.

(G) Standard 2.7. The educator shall not retaliate against any individual who has filed a complaint with the SBEC or who provides information for a disciplinary investigation or proceeding under this chapter.

(H) Standard 2.8. The educator shall not intentionally or knowingly subject a colleague to sexual harassment.

(3) Ethical Conduct Toward Students.

(A) Standard 3.1. The educator shall not reveal confidential information concerning students unless disclosure serves lawful professional purposes or is required by law.

(B) Standard 3.2. The educator shall not intentionally, knowingly, or recklessly treat a student or minor in a manner that adversely affects or endangers the learning, physical health, mental health, or safety of the student or minor.

(C) Standard 3.3. The educator shall not intentionally, knowingly, or recklessly misrepresent facts regarding a student.

(D) Standard 3.4. The educator shall not exclude a student from participation in a program, deny benefits to a student, or grant an advantage to a student on the basis of race, color, gender, disability, national origin, religion, family status, or sexual orientation.

(E) Standard 3.5. The educator shall not intentionally, knowingly, or recklessly engage in physical mistreatment, neglect, or abuse of a student or minor.

(F) Standard 3.6. The educator shall not solicit or engage in sexual conduct or a romantic relationship with a student or minor.

(G) Standard 3.7. The educator shall not furnish alcohol or illegal/unauthorized drugs to any person under 21 years of age unless the educator is a parent or guardian of that child or knowingly allow any person under 21 years of age unless the educator is a parent or guardian of that child to consume alcohol or illegal/unauthorized drugs in the presence of the educator.

(H) Standard 3.8. The educator shall maintain appropriate professional educator-student relationships and boundaries based on a reasonably prudent educator standard.

(I) Standard 3.9. The educator shall refrain from inappropriate communication with a student or minor, including, but not limited to, electronic communication such as cell phone, text messaging, email, instant messaging, blogging, or other social network communication. Factors that may be considered in assessing whether the communication is inappropriate include, but are not limited to:

(i) the nature, purpose, timing, and amount of the communication;

(ii) the subject matter of the communication;

(iii) whether the communication was made openly, or the educator attempted to conceal the communication;

(iv) whether the communication could be reasonably interpreted as soliciting sexual contact or a romantic relationship;

(v) whether the communication was sexually explicit; and

(vi) whether the communication involved discussion(s) of the physical or sexual attractiveness or the sexual history, activities, preferences, or fantasies of either the educator or the student.

REFERENCES AND RESOURCES

Archer, Anita; Hughes, Charles A. (2001). Explicit instruction: effective and efficient teaching. The Guilford Press. (pgs. 39-41).

Bambrick-Santoyo, Paul. (2012). Leverage leadership: A practical guide to building exceptional schools. Jossey-Bass. (p. 5, 21, 191).

Bolman, L. G., & Deal, T. E. (1997). Reframing organizations: Artistry, choice, and leadership. San Francisco: Jossey-Bass. P. 34, 40, 102-103,163, 216-217.

Bolman, Lee: Deal Terry. (2017). Reframing Organizations: Artistry, Choice and Leadership. Jossey-Bass. (p.16, 20, 43).

Booher-Jennings, J. (2005). Below the bubble: Educational triage and the Texas accountability system. *American Educational Research Journal,* 42(2) (231-268).

Community Tool Box. https://ctb.ku.edu/en

Eaker, Robert; DuFour, Richard; DuFour, Rebecca. (2003). Getting started: reculturing schools to become professional learning communities. Solution Tree. (pg. 19).

Egle, Caron. (2009): A guide to facilitating Adult Learning, Department of Health and Ageing, Australian Government, (pgs. 4-5).

Educational Testing Service. (2017). Performance assessment for school leaders (PASL: candidate and educator handbook. ETS.

DuFour, Richard; DuFour, Rebecca; Eaker, Robert; Many, Thomas (2006). Learning by doing. Solution Tree Press. (pgs. 3-5).

Green, Reginald, (2017). Practicing the art of leadership: A problem-based approach to implementing the professional standards for educational leaders. Pearson. (p.38.).

Greenwald, R.; Hedges, L.; and Laine, R. (1996). The effect of school resources on student achievement. *Review of educational research*, 66, 361-396.

Interactive Practice Exam: Principal as Instructional Leader: http://www.tx.nesinc.com/TestView.aspx?f=HTML_FRAG/TX268_PrepMaterials.html

Lezotte, Lawrence W., Snyder, Kathleen McKee. (2011). What effective schools do: Re-envisioning the correlates. Solution Tree Press. (p.44; pgs. 70-71)

Marshall, Kim. (2013). Rethinking teacher supervision and evaluation: how to work smart, build collaboration, and close the achievement gap. Jossey-Bass. (pg. 1)

Miles, Karen Hawley, Frank, Stephen. (2008). The strategic school: making the most of people, time, and money. Corwin Press. (P.29).

Nassau Guardian, The; (2015). Web address https://thenassauguardian.com/2015/09/10/characteristics-of-bad-teachers

Paterson, Kerry; Grenny, Joseph; McMillan, Ron; Switzler, Al. (2012). Crucial conversation: Tools for talking when stakes are high. McGraw Hill. (pgs. 1-4; 13, 23, 182).

Rivkin, S., Hanushek, E., Kane, J. (2000) *Teachers, schools and academic achievement.* (Working Paper No. 6691). Cambridge, MA: National Bureau of Economic Research.

Rodriquez, L. (2008). Teachers know you can do more – Understanding how school cultures of success affect urban high school students. *Educational Policy,* 22(5), 758-780.

Schneider, Joseph, E.; Hollenczer, Lara L. (2006). The principal's guide to managing communication. Corwin Press. (pg. 146).

Southern New Hampshire University, 2019. Web address https://www.snhu.edu/about-us/newsroom/2017/12/qualities-of-a-good-teacher

Texas Administrative Code of Ethics. 19 TAC §247.2. Code of Ethics and Standard Practices for Texas Educators.

Texas Education Agency (2017). *Principal as instructional leader pillars: domains and competencies with aligned ksm's.*

Texas Education Agency (2019). Principal Competencies and Domains.

Wilmore, Elaine L. (2019). Passing the principal TExES exam as instructional leader. Corwin Press.

INDEX

action plan, 215, 216, 242, 243, 244, 251, 252
Assessments, 12, 13, 70, 125, 141, 153, 272
Attitudes, 22, 175
Behaviors, 22
best practices, 35, 61, 116, 203, 209, 221, 236, 237, 242, 276
climate, 18, 24, 30, 43, 172, 175
coaching, 33, 82, 84, 85, 86, 104, 108, 109, 193, 194, 209, 211, 212, 251, 265, 274, 277
Code of Ethics, 184, 188, 280, 285
collaboration, 24, 26, 29, 32, 37, 47, 50, 55, 58, 62, 64, 80, 138, 139, 140, 144, 145, 146, 147, 148, 157, 158, 159, 161, 162, 173, 174, 207, 209, 211, 224, 234, 236, 263, 266, 275, 278, 285
commitment, 13, 28, 84, 99, 123, 142, 172, 175, 185, 196, 201, 211, 239, 248
communicate, 26, 28, 29, 33, 34, 45, 48, 61, 65, 99, 111, 112, 113, 114, 124, 131, 132, 133, 137, 148, 163, 169, 174, 175, 186, 189, 200, 201, 221, 225, 227, 233, 246, 249, 262, 278
communication, 26, 48, 60, 61, 82, 83, 91, 98, 101, 121, 122, 123, 124, 125, 126, 127, 128, 130, 131, 132, 147, 161, 175, 177, 181, 199, 200, 201, 202, 222, 225, 227, 243, 246, 247, 249, 266, 273, 275, 278, 282, 283, 285
Conflict management, 48, 199
consensus, 43, 48, 50, 51, 58, 59, 64, 115, 138, 199, 275
consensus-building, 48, 275
continuous improvement, 104, 148, 211, 215, 216, 254
Cultural competence, 249
culture, 18, 19, 20, 21, 22, 23, 24, 25, 27, 28, 29, 30, 33, 34, 35, 36, 37, 41, 43, 45, 46, 47, 49, 50, 51, 55, 93, 100, 106, 107, 108, 109, 115, 117, 123, 142, 147, 148, 169, 172, 174, 184, 198, 201, 207, 210, 213, 214, 219, 220, 221, 225, 227, 231, 238, 239, 240, 245, 249, 252, 253, 254, 262, 264, 265, 268, 275, 276
curriculum, 54, 59, 61, 62, 63, 67, 68, 69, 70, 71, 72, 73, 74, 75, 76, 78, 86, 89, 109, 125, 134, 153, 154, 162, 163, 165, 166, 179, 202, 205, 217, 223, 224, 225, 227, 234, 237, 247, 276
discipline management, 168, 169, 173, 174, 175, 176, 177, 179, 180, 212, 273
Diversity, 184, 249

emotional constancy, 240
Equity, 184, 249
ethics, 12, 184, 186
facilitator, 27, 226
feedback, 33, 34, 47, 48, 51, 53, 62, 71, 72, 74, 82, 83, 84, 86, 89, 95, 100, 102, 105, 113, 119, 131, 136, 148, 153, 175, 190, 198, 203, 210, 217, 227, 229, 231, 233, 236, 240, 250, 251, 254, 265, 268, 270, 272, 275, 276, 277
Formal feedback, 84
formative assessments, 69, 70, 76, 79, 203, 215, 224, 225, 238
Frames of Cognition, 9, 11
goals, 9, 20, 22, 29, 30, 31, 32, 33, 34, 35, 37, 45, 48, 55, 59, 60, 64, 65, 66, 85, 86, 90, 99, 100, 101, 102, 104, 107, 108, 112, 113, 115, 116, 122, 126, 133, 134, 139, 144, 149, 150, 151, 153, 155, 156, 157, 158, 159, 161, 162, 163, 164, 165, 166, 178, 180, 205, 206, 209, 210, 212, 214, 215, 216, 217, 218, 230, 231, 234, 236, 237, 238, 239, 241, 242, 243, 244, 247, 252, 254, 256, 262, 266, 268, 269, 272, 275, 277, 278, 279
high leverage, 46, 126, 141, 143, 144, 157, 159, 163, 164, 165, 166, 197, 216, 217, 234, 261
high performing teachers, 141, 206, 232, 247
Highest leverage, 205
high-quality instruction, 12, 53, 55, 56, 57, 58, 59, 60, 61, 64, 265, 276
high-quality teaching, 69, 81, 106, 109, 111, 265, 277
Human Capital, 80, 81, 87
human resource frame, 9
Individual Education Programs, 170, 179, 182, 273
Informal feedback, 82
instructional leader, 3, 8, 11, 12, 16, 19, 26, 27, 28, 53, 55, 57, 59, 60, 73, 82, 83, 95, 98, 99, 109, 285, 286
intentional, 8, 16, 23, 89, 99, 134, 164, 229, 240, 272
knowledge, 8, 12, 23, 31, 36, 44, 49, 56, 67, 68, 69, 80, 85, 91, 92, 94, 106, 140, 147, 156, 185, 190, 196, 197, 198, 199, 200, 201, 204, 211, 223, 226, 227, 230, 251, 252, 255, 263, 275
Leadership courage, 86
Least Restrictive Environment, 170

287

mindsets, 8, 12, 21, 23, 56, 80, 140, 196, 197, 231, 263
mission, 19, 20, 21, 22, 23, 24, 25, 26, 27, 28, 30, 33, 36, 37, 42, 46, 47, 50, 52, 95, 99, 102, 115, 145, 155, 157, 161, 178, 200, 213, 214, 239, 240, 246, 252
multiple learning styles, 211
outcomes, 62, 98, 115, 138, 139, 140, 156, 159, 161, 162, 215, 226, 227, 231, 233, 235, 236, 238, 247, 248, 254, 266, 277, 278, 279
Performance Assessment for School Leaders, 8, 263
political frame, 10, 107
problem-solving techniques, 149, 150, 152, 215, 272, 278
Professional development, 85, 252
professional learning community, 28, 31, 34, 38, 39, 53, 69, 72, 74, 76, 77, 78, 79, 92, 105, 113, 118, 152, 154, 159, 164, 210, 270, 272
quality teacher, 107, 111, 207, 229, 248
reflective questioning, 209, 215, 228, 235, 236, 251
Resiliency, 139
root cause analysis, 214, 215, 236, 241, 242
scaffolded learning, 237
scaffolding, 90, 93, 94, 217, 225, 251
school culture, 18, 19, 22, 41, 246, 254, 264
skills, 8, 12, 15, 21, 23, 29, 54, 56, 73, 86, 89, 91, 98, 100, 101, 108, 112, 122, 125, 140, 153, 156, 159, 166, 196, 197, 201, 204, 207, 208, 213, 223, 227, 233, 237, 251, 252, 255, 258, 263

staff development, 59, 64, 82, 83, 85, 100, 101, 105, 109, 112, 119, 126, 163, 164, 165, 173, 174, 180, 209, 236, 237, 238, 263, 272
stakeholders, 10, 20, 22, 23, 24, 25, 27, 30, 33, 34, 35, 36, 37, 38, 40, 41, 42, 45, 46, 47, 48, 53, 122, 123, 125, 198, 200, 219, 220, 221, 243, 246, 264, 265, 266, 275, 278
structural frame, 9, 55, 89, 208, 228
summative assessment, 69, 76, 277
symbolic frame, 10, 214, 239
systemic thinking, 20, 36, 87, 128, 130, 139, 147, 227, 268
teaching-learning process, 49, 99, 216
TExES Principal Exam, 8, 11, 12, 16, 19, 36, 53, 258
vertical alignment, 225
vision, 19, 20, 21, 22, 23, 24, 26, 27, 28, 29, 30, 31, 32, 33, 34, 35, 36, 37, 38, 41, 42, 43, 44, 45, 46, 47, 48, 49, 50, 51, 52, 53, 64, 89, 95, 99, 102, 104, 108, 115, 150, 155, 156, 157, 158, 161, 163, 178, 198, 199, 200, 201, 213, 214, 217, 219, 220, 222, 239, 240, 246, 248, 252, 260, 265, 266, 268, 269, 275, 276, 278, 279
vision and *mission*, 20, 21, 22, 23, 24, 26, 27, 28, 29, 30, 31, 32, 33, 34, 35, 36, 37, 38, 41, 42, 43, 44, 45, 46, 48, 50, 51, 89, 99, 104, 108, 150, 157, 158, 163, 198, 199, 200, 201, 213, 219, 220, 222, 246, 248, 252, 268, 275, 276
walk-through, 53, 71, 84, 89, 91, 93, 95, 96, 100, 103, 105, 109, 111, 115, 119, 150, 180, 208, 215, 229, 241, 258, 270

Made in United States
Orlando, FL
26 December 2023